MW00586089

'Some writers find it difficult to be boring; Jim Packer was one of them. How many evangelicals do you know who could (or would) write a column titled 'It's wrong to eat people'? Or there's Jim avowing that he is God's plumber and sewage man. I think I read every one of these pieces when they first appeared; I am grateful beyond words that this new format allows me to read them again."

D. A. CARSON
emeritus professor of New Testament,
Trinity Evangelical Divinity School

"There was—and is—no churchman and theologian from whom I have learned more about Christianity than Dr. Packer, who in life exemplified a model of orthodoxy and grace combined with an enviable gift for clarity. While many know him through his books, he also enjoyed influence as a writer of journalistic pieces for *Christianity Today*, where he brought his wit, wisdom, and faith to bear on a variety of issues. At once both a commentary on the times and explications of the faith, these shorter pieces are delightful, devotional gems."

CARL R. TRUEMAN
professor of biblical & religious studies,
Grove City College

'Years ago I bought access to Christianity Today's digital archive simply to harvest the best of J. I. Packer's columns and articles. The painstaking work yielded bushels beyond what I expected—nearly six decades of gold. But if I were a more patient man, I could have just waited for this collection, an indispensable volume for any Packer reader."

TONY REINKE
journalist, and author of
Newton on the Christian Life: To Live Is Christ

"This valuable collection of the late Jim Packer's essays in Christianity Today reveals a man who was often insightful, occasionally whimsical, and always deeply personal. Readers will discover his opinions on a wide range of subjects and quarry this volume for quotes and illustrations they can use in their own ministries. A valuable resource that will keep its author's name alive for the next generation and beyond."

GERALD BRAY
research professor of divinity,
Beeson Divinity School

POINTING

to the

PASTURELANDS

POINTING

to the

PASTURELANDS

—

Reflections on
Evangelicalism,
Doctrine, & Culture

J. I. PACKER

LEXHAM PRESS

Pointing to the Pasturelands: Reflections on Evangelicalism, Doctrine, & Culture
Best of Christianity Today

Print ISBN 9781683595434
Digital ISBN 9781683595441
Library of Congress Control Number 2021940532

Lexham Editorial: Elliot Ritzema, Abigail Stocker, Abigail Salinger
Cover Design: George Siler, Brittany Schrock
Typesetting: Fanny Palacios

CONTENTS

Part 2: Articles

FOREWORD

On the same summer day in 2020, the world lost two historic figures—the civil rights leader John Lewis and the evangelical Anglican theologian J. I. Packer. What immediately came to my mind, for both of them, was the word "trouble." Lewis, of course, had said, "Never, ever, be afraid to make some noise and get in good trouble, necessary trouble." Packer, much less memorably but just as truthfully, had once said, "Like a good pietist I've always wanted peace, and like Richard Baxter I've been involved with trouble, trouble, trouble, all the way." In both cases, the notion of "good trouble" was able to sum up a life.

In Lewis's case, many of us know exactly what is meant by "good trouble." After all, despite the fact that we came to know him as an refined, elderly leader in the halls of Congress, we had all seen the pictures of him as a young man, beaten and bloodied by segregationist police forces attacking him and his fellow protesters as they marched against the Edmund Pettus Bridge. We thought of Lewis in terms of his courage in taking on an unjust and violent Jim Crow system in the American South. For Packer, though, the concept of "trouble" might not seem as readily evident.

After all, most evangelical Christians came to know Packer through his writings about God, the gospel, and the way of spiritual formation. For some, that came because someone handed them a copy of *Knowing God* in a church small-group study. For me, it came through my reading, as a teenage Baptist in Mississippi, of Packer's columns each month in *Christianity Today*. I once talked to a Roman Catholic businessman who knew very little about evangelical Christianity but said he had read several of the Puritans. "How did you come across the Puritans?" I asked. He explained that Packer's work on evangelical-Catholic cooperation had led him backward to many of Packer's interests—including the Puritans he loved. Packer no doubt knew he was trying to introduce John Owen, Richard Sibbes, and others to a new generation of evangelicals, but he probably never imagined that such efforts would cross the Tiber too.

However we were first introduced to Packer, most of us were drawn to him not because he was in "trouble," but because he seemed to us to be the antidote to much of what we saw had gone awry in evangelical Christianity.

When many were angry culture warriors, Packer was winsome and calm. When many were emotionally manipulative, Packer was reasonable. When many were anti-intellectual, Packer took the mind seriously. When many seemed to reduce Christian theology to syllogisms, Packer modeled piety and warmth of heart. When many wanted to downplay the supernatural or the morally rigorous aspects of the Christian faith to gain a hearing with modern culture, Packer pointed us back to the old paths of biblical authority. When many others wanted to keep narrowing evangelicalism down to an ever-smaller remnant of the convinced, Packer sought to remind us that there is one Lord, one faith, one baptism—and that we have no right to seek a kingdom smaller than the one for which Christ died. In each of these, Packer took his readers seriously—and he spoke to us with both authority and tranquility, with both reason and compassion. I suspect most of us believed what seemed to be true to me as a young man reading those *Christianity Today* columns: that if we were ever to meet J. I. Packer, we would find not an evangelical "celebrity" but a Christian who would seem to us almost like a grandfather in the faith, ready to pray with us and to encourage us to keep trusting Jesus.

This doesn't seem like trouble. But looking back over Packer's life, we do indeed see trouble. Liberal Christians dismissed Packer as a "fundamentalist" because of his commitment to biblical inerrancy and the supernatural realities of Christian orthodoxy, while conservative evangelical separatists denounced him for staying within the Anglican Communion. Even within that communion, higher-church Anglicans sometimes saw him as too much of a "Billy Graham" type of evangelical, while lower-church evangelicals sometimes ignored his commitment to the sacraments. Progressives opposed him for his refusal to "evolve" on matters of sexual ethics, while the more narrowly Reformed of his fellow evangelicals acted betrayed when he coauthored and signed the "Evangelicals and Catholics Together" statement. This was all trouble. And, at every point, when Packer believed the integrity of faith or witness was at stake—whether in biblical inerrancy or in avoiding unnecessary schism in his church or any other matter—he was willing to stand and to speak and to write.

The reason we don't think first of his "trouble," though, is precisely for the reason he mentioned. He was a pietist. He loved Jesus, and he loved Jesus's church. He was not, as are so many, a quarrelsome fighter seeking to find a "brand" by the intensity with which he fought his opponents. Instead, Packer truly believed that those who disagreed with him could be persuaded.

And his primary audience was not those seeking the entertainment of controversy, but the One he knew would greet him at the judgment seat—One for whom the kingdom of God consists not in theatrics but in power, One who sees such power won not in an argument but in an empty tomb.

In all of this, Packer showed us what it was like to age and to die—without vindictiveness, revenge, bitterness, or moral collapse. His convictions were clear, but he was not spending his life seeking to police boundaries or to hunt heretics. Perhaps that is why books by authors who never would have spoken to each other would bear endorsement blurbs by J. I. Packer.

His life was one long column of what it means to know God and to grow into Christ, in suffering but always with joy. As you read this collection of essays, you can perceive what it means to be a thoughtful, reasonable, joyful model of evangelical Christianity. Behind all of these words, from various eras of his life, Packer shows us what it means to be in good trouble because he shows us what it means to carry good news.

—Russell Moore
Public Theologian,
Christianity Today

Part 1

—

COLUMNS

Chapter 1

———

SATAN SCORES TWICE

I t is distressing to see an old friend in trouble. It is doubly so when the trouble is of his own making. And since last year, my life has had in it one such source of distress—namely, the doings of a man whom I had regarded as a spiritual ally ever since we were student counselors together at an evangelistic boys' camp.

His name is David Jenkins, and he is the bishop of Durham, in the Church of England. He won his spurs professionally as a brilliant upholder of orthodox faith. He has written books on God, on man, and on Christ, which, despite their hectic and tortuous style, seemed to me to be top-class pieces of Christian exposition.

His recent pronouncements, however, reveal that he now thinks—and wants us all to know that he thinks—that when commending faith in the incarnate and risen Christ, it is best not to get hung up on the actuality of Christ's virgin birth or his bodily resurrection. One should, he thinks, leave open the question of how, physically, Christ entered and left this world. Thus David finds it appropriate to sanction skepticism about what the opening and closing chapters of Matthew's and Luke's Gospels tell us on these points. He himself, he says, is uncertain here.

Naturally, he has been lumped in English Christian minds with the great army of liberals, radicals, and modernists who, denying supernatural explanations, have surrendered belief in the eternal deity of the Lord Jesus and thus reduced him to a historical memory with role-model force, like Socrates or Winston Churchill.

But Bishop Jenkins does not belong in this camp. His books show him to be a trinitarian according to Nicea (one God, three coequal persons), and an incarnationalist according to Chalcedon (one person, two undiminished natures). Yet he still thinks it sensible to promote agnosticism on the virginal conception and the empty tomb. Why?

Assuming that nomination as a bishop did not alter his views, it looks as if he has simply not rethought a widespread assumption of our student days: namely, that by teaching some Christian facts (such as the Virgin Birth) as uncertain and smudging the outlines of your doctrines of God, Creation, sin, Christ, and salvation, you could speed the evangelistic task, for then the gospel would be easier to accept.

What such simplification does, however, is destroy credibility. It turns one's faith more or less into a private oddity shaped by fashion and fancy and salesmen's instincts rather than by facts. No one who thus debones Christianity for public consumption can escape the pincer effect of these two questions: Since you believe so much of the biblical message, why do you not believe more? And since you believe so little of that message, why do you not believe less? The effect of straining at the gnats of virgin birth and empty tomb after swallowing the camels of divine triunity, incarnation, and resurrection is to call in question whether God the Creator is really Lord of all, sovereign in and over the physical world that he made. I am sure David did not mean to do this, but he has done it.

So there is bitter irony in what has happened. Jenkins feels doubts that are a hangover from the bad old days. He thinks, as so many once did, that this skepticism enhances Christianity's intellectual credentials. He fails to see that his own understanding of a pre-existent, all-powerful God makes these doubts unnecessary and unreasonable.

The Church of England, which during the past generation has experienced a significant conservative swing, is outraged, perceiving, as Jenkins does not, that his agnosticism challenges the truth of theism, the status of the catholic creeds, and the authority of the Bible and, in the end, makes the task of evangelism not easier but harder. Bishop Jenkins's credibility is now suspect across the board, and good things he says are unlikely to be taken seriously. Thus Satan scores again, twice over.

Do you wonder that I am distressed?

Chapter 2

'TECS, THRILLERS,
AND WESTERNS

T he cat came out of the bag at a recent CT senior editors' meeting. To avoid scandal, I give no names; but it emerged that for relaxation one of us reads westerns (Louis L'Amour), another goes for espionage thrillers (Frederick Forsyth), and I devour mysteries. ('Tecs I call them.)

I started young, ingesting my first Agatha Christies when I was seven. Since then I have read, among others, all the Sherlock Holmeses, Father Browns, and Peter Wimseys; all the Ellery Queens, Agatha Christies, and Carter Dicksons; all the John Dickson Carrs and Dick Francises except one; all the full-length stories of Hammett, Chandler, James, and Crispin; and all the work of new arrivals Amanda Cross, Antonia Fraser, Simon Brett, and Robert Barnard; not to mention most of Margery Allingham, Austin Freeman, Freeman Wills Crofts, Erle Stanley Gardner, Rex Stout, Ruth Rendell, and Julian Symons.

What have I gained? Fun, to start with. Where else could I have made the acquaintance of characters like Stout's Nero Wolfe (world's heaviest genius and largest ego), Dickson's Sir Henry

Merrivale (the Old Man, but no gentleman), Gardner's Perry Mason (incompetent, irrelevant, and immaterial), Christie's Miss Marple (mesmeric village knit-wit), and the prewar Poirot, who bounced and burbled like Maurice Chevalier?

I have also gained some elementary instruction, learning chemistry from Freeman's Dr. Thorndyke, railway operation from Crofts's Inspector French, basic Christianity from Chesterton's Father Brown, Reformed Judaism from Kemelman's Rabbi Small, post-Vatican II Catholicism from Kienzle's Father Koesler, and up-to-date liberal Methodism from Merrill Smith's Reverend Randollph.

But it is not for general education that I read 'tecs, nor for examples of life and instruction of manners, for which the Thirty-nine Articles say that Anglicans read the Apocrypha. What I enjoy is the poignant perplexity of the puzzle, the sleuth's superior brainwork, and the doing of justice by clearing the innocent and exposing the guilty.

Ought my fellow senior editors and I repent of time wasted in our light reading? Not necessarily. If overloaded academic and literary people never read for relaxation, their brains will break. And 'tecs, thrillers, and westerns, while not great literature, are among the most moral fiction of our time. Goodies and baddies are distinguished, and killers finally get it in the end. Writing that upholds fundamental morality is neither degenerate nor corrupting.

Also, these are stories of a kind that would never have existed without the Christian gospel. Culturally, they are Christian fairy tales, with savior heroes and plots that end in what Tolkien called a *eucatastrophe*—whereby things come right after seeming to go irrevocably wrong. Villains are foiled, people in jeopardy are freed, justice is done, and the ending is happy. The protagonists—detectives, Secret Service agents, noble cowboys and sheriffs, or whatever—are classic Robin Hood figures, champions of the needy, bringers of merited judgment and merciful salvation. The gospel of Christ is the archetype of all such stories. Paganism unleavened by Christianity, on the other hand, was and always will be pessimistic at heart.

Do I urge everyone to read detective and cowboy and spy stories? No. If they do not relax your mind when overheated, you have no reason to touch them. Light reading is not for killing time (that's ungodly), but for refitting the mind to tackle life's heavy tasks (that's the Protestant work ethic, and it's true).

You must find what refreshes you, as your senior editors have found what refreshes them. And if you will not accuse us of being wicked worldlings for our light reading, I will not accuse you for watching all those TV sitcoms and sports programs that so bore me. Fair? Surely—and Christian too.

Chapter 3

A BAD TRIP

All who work for the firm identified on an envelope I once received as "God & Son Inc., Doing Business for 2,000 years with Sinners Like You" receive regular in-service training. A few months ago, God gave me a refresher course on patience. I flunked it.

Patience means living out the belief that God orders everything for the spiritual good of his children. Patience does not just grin and bear things, stoic-like, but accepts them cheerfully as therapeutic workouts planned by a heavenly trainer who is resolved to get you up to full fitness.

Patience, therefore, treats each situation as a new opportunity to honor God in a way that would otherwise not be possible, and acts accordingly. Patience breasts each wave of pressure as it rolls in, rejoicing to prove that God can keep one from losing his or her footing. And patience belongs to the ninefold fruit of the Spirit, which is the sanctifying profile Jesus set for his disciples.

As a Calvinist, I have a strong doctrine of providence; and as a devotional instructor, I often deal with sanctification. So I had taken it for granted that patience was something I was good at.

(You always fancy yourself good at that of which you know the theory.) But look at what happened.

I was committed to being in England after Christmas, but a memorial service for a long-time friend required my presence there just before the holiday. Thus, for the first time ever, I had to be away from home at Christmas. *Self-pity and grumbling.* At Chicago I learned that an unscheduled stop would delay the London flight two-and-a-half hours, so I had to call ahead and change arrangements. *Resentment.* The plane had no ground heating, so at both Chicago and Detroit we boarded into 8 degrees of frost—the same temperature as outside. *Cold contempt—emotionally cold, I mean—and prideful pleasure that it wasn't Britain's or Canada's national airline that was doing this to me.*

Organization in Britain seemed sloppy, and British Rail did badly. *Cynical gloom.* A phone call from Vancouver contained a hurtful personal criticism. *Seething anger, which kept me awake all night.* I flew out of Heathrow full of hard thoughts about my travel agent for not booking me on another airline, where the mileage would have been credited to me under one of the half-dozen bonus schemes to which I belong. *Petty greed.*

Poor performance? Very poor indeed. (Didn't I tell you I flunked the course?)

Two things made my lapses of temper especially disgraceful. First, the trip was marked by all sorts of blessings—a new friendship, old friendships renewed, an evangelistic opening that I had prayed and waited ten years for, and more. Finding that God is with me should have banished all bitterness of the kind that I was indulging. Where should I ever want to be, save in the place of God's appointment?

Second, I know the theory of patience so well. The Murphy's Law aspect of life is set out in detail by my favorite biblical author in Ecclesiastes; and Romans 8:28 has been a key text in my teaching for years. My moods were a series of sins against knowledge, outwardly dissembled, inwardly cherished. *Hypocrisy.* However, the Father and the Son still do business with sinners like me, and as I left Britain, "I mercy sought, and mercy found." "I said, 'I will confess my transgressions to the LORD'; then thou didst forgive the guilt of my sin" (Ps 32:5).[1]

On the way back from England, the film provided by the airline was a movie I had long wanted to see, but the sound channel was not working. Another of the entertainment channels offered Verdi's *La Traviata* complete, but after the first hour it clicked back to the beginning, so that I only heard the first act— three times. Now, at baggage claim in Miami, I find one of my bags kicked in. Suspicion rises to certainty: I am being made to repeat the course I flunked.

Maybe I can do better this time round. *Pride? Self-confidence?* We'll see.

---

[1] Scripture quotations in this article are from the Revised Standard Version.

Chapter 4

—

THE UNSPECTACULAR PACKERS

In England, where I lived until 1979, there are people with names like Cholmondeley (pronounced Chumley), Featherstonehaugh (pronounced Fanshaw), Fiennes (pronounced Finch), and Sidebottom (pronounced, in at least one case known to me, Siddybuttoom).

No such exotic label graces me, however.

Packer is, I guess, a trade name like Carter or Carpenter, telling the world my ancestors filled bags or peddled door to door. It is an uncommon name: Among the half-million personal entries in the Vancouver phone book, there are only 16 Packers. (Packers thus have rarity value, whatever else they may lack.)

My notion of Packers always was that, in addition to being few and far between, we were a quiet, unobtrusive lot, rural in our style and passive in our stances. This, I am sure, was an extrapolation from my immediate forebears. My great-grandfather was a wealthy man who fell on hard times. My grandfather was successively a farmer, miller, and innkeeper—doing poorly at each. And my father was a railroad clerk in charge of another clerk and two typists.

Were Packers always unspectacular? One of us (a money man who built railroads and endowed Lehigh University; no direct relation) got into the *Encyclopedia Britannica*. But since when did one swallow make a summer? On the other hand, no major criminal was ever called Packer. Maybe harmless mediocrity really is the authentic Packer way.

But behold! The mail brought a promotional circular that said: "After months of work, *The Amazing Book of the Packers in Canada* is ready for printing, and *you* are listed in it! ... [W]e have spent a great deal of effort and thousands of dollars. ... I believe this is the only book of its kind in the entire world ... you must order right away ... the book is printed for you alone." In it is a Packer coat of arms 600 years old, with instructions for tracing my family tree. "You will want to have your own copy—use the order form enclosed."

Wow! Amazed thoughts ran off everywhere. I wondered, for instance, if my CT colleagues had ever received such honor.

I wondered, too, if my entry in the *Amazing Book* would be correct, and I found lying behind that query the paranoid egoism of original sin—the quality that prompts you, when your new phone book comes, to look up your own entry to see if it is misprinted.

Then I wondered what Packerish proclivities the circular was meant to appeal to. What, in essence, was its selling line? Was it to some notion of family pride—pride of race, or of place, or even of grace (the worst of the lot)? Or to some feeling like Alex Haley's, that you do not know your identity unless you know your roots? Or simply to the desire to possess a book that is "hand bound with a beautiful burgundy grained finish and ... richly gold embossed" with one's name printed in it? Whatever the point of appeal, ego-boost was clearly the name of the game.

When I saw this, sanity supervened. I remembered John the Baptist, who settled for being a voice in the wilderness, and

George Whitefield, greatest post-apostolic evangelist ever, who said, "Let the name of Whitefield perish, if only Christ is glorified!" I brooded on the words "I have called you by name; you are mine," and on Jesus' directive, "Rejoice that your names are written in heaven." I reflected that while exploring one's lineage need not be sin, to draw one's sense of worth and dignity from his or her place in a human family rather than in God's family of saved sinners could never be right. I reminded myself that pride smolders in me all the time, and that the risk of fanning it into flame is best not taken.

So I shall pass up *The Amazing Book of the Packers* and continue concentrating on the amazing grace of God. The wedding garment will do more for me than the Packer coat of arms. What use, after all, will a coat of arms be to me or anyone else on judgment day? "Let him who boasts, boast of the Lord" (1 Cor. 1:13, RSV).

Chapter 5

———

GREAT GEORGE

This year Christians in Gloucester, England, celebrated one of the city's noblest sons, George Whitefield. Oxford Methodist, Puritan Calvinist, and roving evangelist, Whitefield was for over 30 years the acknowledged spearhead of revival on both sides of the Atlantic. Wesley extolled him after his death for having preached the gospel more widely and fruitfully than anyone since the apostles.

Nineteen eighty-six was the two-hundred-fiftieth anniversary of Whitefield's ordination. Gloucester made much of it, with a commemorative service, lectures, exhibitions, and a specially written play. I was involved. (Why? Because I am a Gloucester boy who went to Whitefield's old school, that's why.)

I reconstructed Whitefield's gospel, an exercise that proved a tonic to my soul. To Vaughan Williams, John Barbirolli was Glorious John; to me, George Whitefield is Great George.

Not everyone understood Whitefield in his own day; not everyone understands him now. Said the program note on the 1986 play: "Whitefield underwent a sudden conversion at Oxford, the exact nature of which it is now impossible to determine."

Impossible? Horse feathers! Whitefield's own narrative explains everything.

In 1944, by God's grace I too underwent a sudden conversion in Oxford, not 50 yards from the site of his; and when soon after I read Tyerman's life of Whitefield I resonated with his conversion story and evangelistic zeal. As Jesus said, those born of the Spirit are a mystery to those who are not; they are, however, no mystery to each other!

With his huge, sweet voice and overwhelming expression of concern for his hearers (honest tears usually marked his pulpit references to hell), Whitefield was and remains in a class by himself among British evangelists. Only the Baptist Charles Spurgeon, who took Whitefield as a role model, ever came close to him.

Both were pastoral Calvinists of genius, marked by tremendous inner intensity, vividness of imagination, freshness of vision, and sublimity of rhetoric. But Spurgeon's tincture of country-boy truculence and his obtrusive melancholy streak put him behind Whitefield. Mesmeric speaker, superior writer, and generally better brain that he was, Spurgeon neither roared nor soared in the pulpit as Whitefield did. As a preacher, Whitefield was supreme.

You could call him a sanctified barnstormer. God gave him actor's gifts as his resource for communicating Christ. Garrick, England's leading player, once said, "I'd give a hundred guineas to be able to say 'Oh!' like Whitefield," and added that Whitefield could move a crowd to tears of joy just by his way of pronouncing "Mesopotamia."

Communication was his life. For many years he spoke in public an average of 50 hours a week. He recorded himself as having preached over 18,000 sermons of one to two hours each. "I love those that thunder out the Word!" he said; and in evangelistic application he thundered it out in a way that not only great churchfuls but open-air crowds of up to 30,000 (Ben Franklin vouched for the number) found convincing and electrifying to the last degree. Yet for more than half his ministry he was asthmatic, and vomited after preaching!

What kept him going? "Christ's laborers must live by miracle," he wrote, and maybe that is the answer.

I look at Whitefield, and love him. He restores my faith in biblical preaching and my hope of church revival. And his dictum, "Let the name of Whitefield perish, if so be that Christ is glorified," does me no end of good. One of life's richest blessings, so I find, is to be kept in sight of Great George.

Tailpiece: Whitefield, who signed his letters "less than least of all," would certainly dislike this article.

Chapter 6

—

ALL THAT JAZZ

Hans Rookmaaker, the late pipepuffing pundit of Amsterdam, colleague of Francis Schaeffer, and "Rooky" to his young Anglo-Saxon admirers, had a lifelong passion for early jazz. I, too, was grabbed in my teens by the glory of this simple, subtle, cheerful, poignant, bright-colored music, and I venerated Jelly Roll Morton, King Oliver, Louis Armstrong, Johnny Dodds, Sidney Bechet, Tommy Ladnier, Bix Beiderbecke, Bubber Miley, Tricky Sam Nanton, and Muggsy Spanier as its top dispensers.

At 18 I was playing jazz, after a fashion (sloppy gas-pipe clarinet modeled on Pee-Wee Russell). To listen to what was going on in the band around me and help make it happen was as exhilarating an experience as I have ever had.

But when I was converted I could not see, nor could anyone tell me, how this or any other form of secular music or art could be pursued with a Christian motivation. So I gave up jazz, sold my clarinet and records, and let folk around me think I shared their view that what I called New Orleans and they called Dixieland had a devilish influence on its devotees. It came to me as a test of loyalty to my Savior to renounce what I enjoyed so much, and from that standpoint, giving up jazz no doubt did me good.

Yet when Rookmaaker came to faith, he did no such thing. And now my heart says of him, wise man!

In my twenties the pietistic Manicheism (not called that, of course) in which I had been nurtured began to dissolve into an authentic biblical humanism, such as Calvinistic Holland had been able to give Rookmaaker. By my thirties, I had begun to mutter what Rookmaaker was ready to shout from the house-tops—namely, that by Christian standards of judgment, early jazz was among the twentieth century's most valuable cultural products.

Academically, Rookmaaker was an authority on this music (he wrote record sleeves, and a book on the subject, locked up, alas, in Dutch). It was a delightful experience to hear a tape of his and to realize that he and I, the amateur in aesthetics once "sent" by Jelly Roll Morton, were at one in this field.

Please remember now, that the jazz I speak of is the march-dance-lament music that was born in New Orleans among blacks and creoles at the turn of this century, became the rage in the twenties, went underground in the thirties, and was finally negated in the forties when new ways of playing and a new harmonic language, expressing a changed mentality, altered jazz radically. Modern jazz—cool, cerebral, and often protesting, trading in unresolved dissonances over an enigmatic tonal base and so mirroring life's endless tensions—does not speak to me, and I am not discussing it.

Once, I think I made Rookmaaker's day by introducing him to a student audience as one of the few people who knew the significance of the occasion when Louis Armstrong carried a trumpet into the recording studio instead of his familiar cornet. To the uninitiated, let me say that what this marked was the superseding of early jazz's preference for collective polyphony (into which the mellower cornet blends well) by solo display on more brilliant instruments. Armstrong crossed that watershed, and almost everyone followed. But early jazz was essentially fellowship music, group music rather than individualistic display music; that was one Christian value built into it.

There were other "built-in" values, too. Classic jazz, as this amalgam of dance music, rag music, military music, and folk music is deservedly called, bubbles with joy in living. Though sometimes sad, it is never savage or bitter. It is happy music. Tuneful and rhythmical, free but controlled, sprinkling "blue" notes in the melody line over solid major-key harmonies and deploying three-line polyphony that recalls Bach—it energizes you by relaxing you, and its simple climaxes leave you content and refreshed.

So those old records minister to me. (I do not play the clarinet nowadays.) And I hope I do not outrage anyone by letting this be known. After all, there might be refreshment here for you as well.

Chapter 7

AN ACCIDENTAL AUTHOR

This little pig went to market, this little pig stayed home ...
and this little pig went to India, where he was greeted with a
request from a student magazine for an article that would encourage India's budding Christian writers.

Why, I wonder, did they pick on me? I suppose they must see
me as a senior writer who has made the grade, and so can serve
as a role model for the young. Are they wrong? Not entirely. My
books have gone into ten languages and sold over a million-and-
a-half copies. And they have helped all sorts of readers, old and
young, male and female, academic and unlettered, Calvinist and
Arminian, Christian and pagan. (I know this from the flow of testimonies that the mailman has brought me over the years.) It
amazes me that God should use my material so constantly in this
way, but in his mercy he does, so that my writing has become the
central item in my ministry. I ought, therefore, not to refuse to
strut my stuff as a model for tomorrow's wordsmiths, however
much my (British? elitist? modest? spiritual? lazy? hypocritical?)
instincts urge me to do just that.

But am I a good role model as a Christian writer? I doubt it.
Certainly, I have been putting things in print for 30 years, and my

bibliography has 200 entries. Certainly, I try to give the world a book a year, and shall continue trying as long as my brains hold out. And certainly, I feel myself under constraint in this: Woe is me if I do not write the gospel! But even allowing for the way my mind highlights all that seems odd, I cannot but think myself a very odd writer indeed.

To start with, I can't do fiction, or poetry, or travelogues, or honest autobiography. (I could do dishonest autobiography, but who wants that?) I can write only about ideas and issues of mind and heart before the Lord. My range is absurdly narrow.

Moreover, I am untutored; I never read a book or took a course on writing in my life. One of Iris Murdoch's novels is called *An Accidental Man*; well, I am an accidental writer. I got into it by being obliging, writing what I was asked to write for no better reason than that I was asked to write it. One day I was asked to write up a talk I had given, and like Topsy, the script "just growed" into a full-length book that sold 20,000 copies in its first year. Behold! I had become an established author. By now, I suppose, I should count myself a professional, having published so much. But to myself I remain an amateur who scribbles till he likes his flow and wording, then mails the result to the publisher (usually late), and moves on to the next thing so hastily that within 24 hours he forgets what he has written. What sort of a role model is a man like that?

Wait a minute, though; that is not a complete statement. (Give yourself a kick in the pants, Packer.) I have to remember that God made me a communicator. No one ever had to teach me how to make myself clear, nor tell me that good communication is half rational analysis and half pictorial and dramatic imagination, as in Isaiah and Ecclesiastes and Jesus and Paul and Luther and C. S. Lewis. No one ever had to admonish me to start by deciding who my ideal reader was, and to write for him throughout. Thus

I began with certain natural advantages, which some would-be authors clearly lack.

What I find that I know about writing boils down to this: There are four rules. First, have something clear to say. Second, keep it simple. Third, make it flow. Fourth, be willing to redraft as often as is necessary to meet these requirements.

Writing is both an art and a craft, and you learn it by doing it. To see things you want to say, and to have ideas about how to say them, is how it starts: then you have to find the sound of your own voice talking on paper, and you can only do that by reading your initial drafts and making improvements. It is as simple—and as difficult—as that. "The Teacher searched to find just the right words," says Ecclesiastes (12:10 [NIV84]), and in this he was the model for all writers anywhere in any age.

Okay, CT, that's enough for you. I must get on with my article for India.

Chapter 8

DECADENCE À LA MODE

"Chocolate chocolate cake," said the dessert menu; "layers of fudge and decadence. A *must* for chocolate lovers!"

Decadence? Surely that word belongs in the world of sociology, morality, philosophy, theology, and history, rather than of cake and fudge. Yes, it does—but I can see why the menu writer brought it in. He wants us to know that the taste of this chocolate chocolate cake will set us ecstatically indulging with no thought of long-term consequences (the thickening shadow, the bulging belly, clothes that no longer fit, shortness of breath, etc.). Irresponsibility about consequences is certainly a mark of decadence.

Also, he is encouraging those whom we may call choc-nuts to see their self-indulgence as right and proper, on the ground that sweetness, however sinful, should never be passed up. Putting pleasure first, and identifying happily with Oscar Wilde's "I can resist anything but temptation" is another mark of decadence. Yes, the word fits.

What we have here is in fact the *Playboy* philosophy applied to the taste buds. Gluttony, like lust, was once recognized as a deadly sin—that is, one that kills the soul. Here, however, it is made to seem chic, and the hint is dropped that truly spunky souls will always settle for pleasure seeking because they will see it as the only wise way. Smart guys regard self-indulgence as a *must*; hail, hedonism! Any energy left over from worshiping the two great gods power and profit (status and success, if you prefer) should go into the service of pleasure, a third god hardly less great. I used to point to the Jacuzzi as the supreme symbol of our hedonistic mindset, but this come-on for chocolate chocolate cake would have done just as well.

Decadence means going morally and spiritually downhill. The modern West is very decadent, as we all know, and its decadence threatens the church, as worldly ways always do. "The place for the ship is in the sea," said D. L. Moody, speaking of church and world, "but God help the ship if the sea gets into it."

Here in Vancouver, B.C., where everybody who is anybody sails a boat, some friends recently proved the literal truth of Moody's dictum; their boat sank in rough water, and they scarcely escaped with their lives. Today, great segments of North American Christianity seem to be desperately waterlogged by worldliness, particularly over pleasure seeking. Am I wrong?

Comparing today's evangelicals with those of yesterday and of the New Testament (a habit without which we are unlikely to see what we are looking at when we gaze around us), I note a widespread passion for biblical orthodoxy that comes close to that of the best Fathers and Reformers and Puritans, and of Spurgeon and Warfield among my heroes; but with it, alas, goes a widespread lack of moral strength that reminds me of the later Middle Ages and of Anglicanism before Wesley—which is bad news. George Gallup's comment, that though American evangelical numbers grow, evangelical community impact remains minuscule and does not increase, confirms my perception: Decadence—weakening worldliness, spiritual AIDS—has infected us, and is pulling us disastrously down.

Though we negate secular humanist doctrine, we live by its value system and suffer its symptoms: Man-centeredness as a way of life, with God there to care for me; preoccupation with wealth, luxury, success, and lots of happy sex as means to my fulfillment; unconcern about self-denial, self-control, truthfulness, and modesty; high tolerance of moral lapses, with readiness to make excuses for ourselves and others in the name of charity; indifference to demands for personal and church discipline; prizing ability above character, and ducking out of personal responsibilities—is any of that Christian? The truth is that we have met the secular humanist enemy, and ethically, it is us. Shame on us? Yes, every time.

By now, no doubt, you are wondering whether I had any of the chocolate chocolate cake. No, I am not a chocoholic; if I have dessert I look for apple pie with ice cream or cinnamon sauce or both.

Why did you want to know?

———

Chapter 9

WHAT LEWIS WAS
AND WASN'T

A mericans, hearing that I am an Oxford man, often ask me if I knew C. S. Lewis, and their faces fall when I say no. American interest in Lewis, who died 25 years ago never having visited America, staggers me. Writing about him is a growth industry (and some of Lewis's own books still sell by the thousands); he is the star of the Wade Collection at Wheaton College (Ill.); Christian institutions mount courses on him; and Washington, DC, has an academic unit called the C. S. Lewis Institute. Yet do North Americans see clearly the Lewis on whom they gaze? I wonder.

When I say I did not know him, I mean I had no personal link with him. (Nor did most of his pupils; they found him an awesome academic who hid his sensitive heart behind a debater's façade of urbane, loud-voiced pugnacity. "I'm a butcher, a rough and brutal man," he told one of them.) I heard him speak once, on the medievalism of the Anglican theologian Richard Hooker. He was supposed to be the best lecturer in Oxford, and on that showing it could have been true, though in the Oxford of my day the compliment meant less than you might think.

I have been a Lewis reader for 45 years. As an unbeliever, I enjoyed *Screwtape Letters* and *Mere Christianity* more for their manner than for their matter, for Lewis's writing style made him seem both a fellow schoolboy and a wise old uncle simultaneously, and that was fascinating. His subsequent Christian essays, which I read after conversion, seemed less schoolboyish and more grandfatherly; but maybe the change was more in me than in him. His supreme achievement, for my money, is the stark and stunning *Pilgrim's Regress*, his first apologetic book, which I reread for pleasure as often, I guess, as I do Bunyan's allegory that inspired it.

Lewis's fiction thrills me less, due to its lapses from the admirably adult to the archly adolescent, and from the childlike to the childish. His no-nonsense, midtwentieth-century way with words served a late-Victorian imagination streaked with sentimentality, and the results were uneven. *Perelandra* (Eden replayed, with a different outcome) and Aslan in the Narnia books are surely Lewis's best fictional achievements. *Till We Have Faces* is more perfect as art but less powerful as vision, while *That Hideous Strength*, despite its fine title, is (to my mind, anyway) hideously bad.

His brand of Christianity was conservative Anglicanism with "catholic" (non-Roman!) leanings; hence his nonpenal view of the Atonement, his nonmention of justification, his belief in purgatory, his praying for the dead, and his regular confession to his priest. His conversion was a return to a boyhood faith lost two decades before.

Like other Oxbridge dons, he was something of a high-minded eccentric. The quixotic chivalry with which he housed the mother of a dead friend for 30 years and then married a Jewish Christian divorcée on what appeared to be her deathbed, plus (going from the near sublime to the near ridiculous) his resolute refusal to read newspapers, equally show this.

Like other Ulstermen, he loved verbal battles in which he could challenge the conventional and upset apple carts. This is as clear in his professional writing as literary critic and historian of ideas as in his joyous reassertion of old original Christianity against its detractors.

He loved beer, too, though he was never drunk.

A standard-issue evangelical? Hardly. But he was a Christian thinker and communicator without peer on three themes: the reasonableness and humanity of Christian faith; the moral demands of discipleship; and heaven as *home*, the place of all value and all contentment. The vivid way in which Lewis, who was something of a homeless child all his life, projects this vision in *The Voyage of the Dawn Treader*, *The Last Battle* (last page), and *The Great Divorce* verifies utterly the fundamental formula of communication: that reason plus imagination, tuned together, equals power. The wisdom and greatness of Lewis may—indeed, must—be measured by moments like these.

Thank you, Mr. Lewis, for being you. I wouldn't have missed you for the world.

Chapter 10

———

IT'S WRONG TO EAT PEOPLE

Once upon a time I announced in this column that the Packer clan, though unspectacular, had at least proved harmless. "No major criminal," I wrote, "was ever called Packer." Maybe I was getting a bit above myself when I said that, for I have had to eat my words. A letter from Vienna, Austria, cut me down to size.

"One of the most famous criminals of Colorado—nay, American—history bears your name," I read.

"Alferd E. Packer is the only man in American history to be tried and convicted of cannibalism. He was a mountain guide who took three men into the Rockies for dinner (literally)."

Well, chase my Aunt Fanny round the gasworks, as British vaudevillians used to say.

"Why," continued the letter, "you probably didn't know that there is an 'Alferd E. Packer Memorial Dining Hall' on the Colorado University Denver campus!"

No, sir, I didn't; and frankly, it is not something I would have expected.

"Hope this enlightening tidbit brightens your next family gathering." Thank you friend, for your kind thought.

It is indeed wrong to eat people, whether literally or metaphorically. In Scripture, "eating up" people is a picture of ruining them, not physically killing them, for personal gain. God chillingly portrays this as cannibalism on the part of leading citizens "who tear the skin from my people and the flesh from their bones; who eat my people's flesh, strip off their skin and break their bones in pieces; who chop them up like meat for the pan, like flesh for the pot" (Mic. 3:2–3). The direct reference is to brutal economic exploitation. But people can be eaten up in other ways, too.

A brilliant man I know regularly eats people in debate. He practices overkill, destroying not only arguments, by logic; but opponents, by ridicule. That is bad. As we should hate the sin yet love the sinner, so we should love the errorist, however little we like his views (even trying to allure that person out of those views). Zeal for truth on other fundamental matters will seem hollow and carnal if we are not equally zealous to love our neighbor even when he errs, as Christ requires us to do.

Other ways of eating people include character assassination (watch your gossip); the big squeeze, whereby you pull strings to push out someone whose place you want to take, or whose power you want to grab; and the vendetta, in which you work to destroy someone who has displeased you, or whom you feel to be a threat. (Have you ever been the object of a vendetta? I have; it is no fun.)

Are these ways of eating people found among Bible-believing Christians, in faithful, gospel-preaching churches? Are there pastors and ex-pastors whose ministries have been ruined through being eaten—eaten alive, they would say—by members of their congregations who behaved in one or other of these ways? I think you know the answer. Does such behavior adorn the gospel and honor the Savior? I think you know the answer to that question, too.

One of the most revolting things I ever saw was one of our children's hamsters eating its young. Abortion, whereby a mother-to-be uses medical personnel as her agents to "eat up" the small person of whom she gets rid, is the human equivalent. The immorality of the Supreme Court decision of 1973 that gave American women the right to do this particular wrong has often been pointed out. The Supreme Court of Canada has just declared that our fledgling constitution gives Canadian women the same immoral right. To me, as a new Canadian, this also is revolting.

Certainly, neighbor love requires us to care for women in trouble, and as all Christians know—pastors, in particular—some pregnancy troubles are truly horrific. But a pregnant woman constitutes two neighbors to be loved, not just one, and it is not neighbor love to help one eat up the other. Even when the law scandalously allows it, eating people remains wrong.

When will North America see this? O Lord, how long?

Chapter 11

———

NOTHING FAILS
LIKE SUCCESS

When I was young, British, and pagan, I thought the sky was the limit and nothing I wanted to do was beyond me. My dreams ranged from being a star cricketer to a top comedian, with much bizarre stuff in-between. Since I am a perfectionist who hates to do anything badly, my dreams were always of spectacular success in every undertaking, and every failure hurt because it punctured my conceit.

When I became a Christian at university, I had the simplistic zeal you expect of a convert; so when I read Charles Finney, I loved him (I still do), and absorbed uncritically his boundless optimism as to what God can do if only his people are willing. When Paul's letter to the Romans, followed by the Puritans, got into my heart, I began to see it was not as simple as that; for years, however, I went on thinking that spectacular success in one's work for God was the right thing to pray for, and the only sure sign that one was serving the Lord as one should.

When I came to North America, I found that most churches, pastors, seminaries, colleges, and parachurch agencies and agents were in the grip of this secular passion for successful expansion in a way I had not met in England. Church-growth theorists, evangelists, pastors, missionaries, and others all spoke as if: (1) numerical increase is what matters most, (2) numerical increase must come if our techniques and procedures are right, (3) numerical increase validates ministries as nothing else does, and (4) numerical increase must be everyone's main goal.

Four unhappy features marked the situation. First, big and growing churches were viewed as far more significant than others. Second, parachurch specialists (evangelists, college and seminary teachers with platform skills, medicine men with traveling seminars, convention-circuit riders, top people in youth movements, full-time authors and such) were venerated, while hard-working pastors were treated as near-nonentities.

Third, lively laymen and clergy were constantly being creamed off, or creaming themselves off, from the churches to run parachurch ministries, in which quicker results could be expected and where accountability was less stringent. And fourth, many ministers of not-so-bouncy temperament were returning to secular employment in disillusionment and bitterness, having concluded that the pastoral life is a game not worth playing.

It is not that I do not value parachurch ministries. Amid the complex cultural pluralism of our age, local churches cannot stockpile all the skills needed to minister to all types in any effective way. But these supplementary forces with specialized abilities must be seen as giving to the churches, so strengthening them, rather than taking from the churches and, in effect, impoverishing them.

Nor is it that I am against churches growing numerically. I recognize that a megachurch with powerful preaching and an adequate infrastructure for pastoral care has its place; and when I see church growth that is qualitative as well as quantitative, I am thrilled. But when numerical growth is idolized, so that churches and their clergy get rated failure for not achieving enough of it, my heart sinks.

You will understand, then, why I got excited a few weeks ago when there came my way a new book titled *Liberating Ministry from the Success Syndrome.* The authors, Kent and Barbara Hughes, pastor and pastor's wife in Wheaton, Illinois, tell how the quest for numerical success nearly broke them, and how they learned that faithfulness, godliness, and loving service are the divine measure of real success in ministry. What they say out of their own experience is exactly what needed to be said; thank God they said it!

So I shall use my column this time round to recommend that every pastor first read the Hugheses' book privately, and then go over it with his lay leaders. Doing this will not be less than a milestone, and might well be a watershed. "How good is a timely word!" (Prov 15:23). The sickness of worshiping growth more than God is rampant; here, however, is a cure.

Chapter 12

———

JOHN'S HOLY SICKNESS

I have been thinking a lot recently about John.

A cheerful, genial little Welshman who could have become a professional cricketer (ballplayer to you), John chose instead to be a clergyman in the Church of England. He served small congregations for a quarter of a century before a brace of massive coronaries took him to glory.

A few of us thought of him as one of the best Reformed pastors in the business, but he was not well known. Balaam, the Faustian prophet who found himself unable to curse Israel even though he had sold his soul in order to do so, said, pathetically enough (for his sin had already ensured that in his case this could not be), "Let me die the death of the righteous, and may my end be like theirs!" (Num 23:10).[1] Though the world and the church hardly noticed John, I think of him every time I meet Balaam's words.

He was a revival convert, brought to faith in his early teens when the Holy Spirit moved powerfully through his high school. I only found this out a decade after his death, but I should have

---

[1] Scripture quotations in this article are from the New International Version (1984).

deduced it from the start. I have never seen revival, but I have known enough revival converts to perceive that they are in a class by themselves. In revival, God comes close; the light of his holiness shines into the depths of memory and desire, highlighting the ugliness of one's sins and making the burden of them intolerable. The conscience-cleansing blood of Christ becomes precious as never before, and the revival convert remains supremely sensitive to sin, both in himself and in others. Certainly, this was so with John all the years I knew him.

Our first conversation (in seminary) lasted about three hours. Its theme throughout (don't laugh; it may sound funny, but it wasn't) was the mortification of sin, a subject that had come up over the meal table. ("Mortification!" he said. "Let's have a talk.") Our shared awareness that salvation is neither in sin nor for sin, but from sin, was a factor that made us friends for life.

John's pastoral preaching gained notice everywhere (not always friendly notice, be it said) because of the amount of pulpit time and analytical care he invested in detecting and exposing sin. That did not discourage him; he knew that invalids often dislike the taste of their medicine. In his later years, God used him to bring to chastity a number of practicing homosexuals, referred to him by other pastors and physicians who could do nothing with them.

I asked him the secret of his effectiveness. "They have got to see that it's sin," he told me; "I hold them to that." I could see that there was more to it; had John not been a relaxed man's man who walked with the strugglers in disciplined accountability relationships marked by warmth of pastoral friendship, I do not suppose he would have had this success. But insisting on the sinfulness of the sin was the hinge on which his entire therapy turned.

In the pulpit he explored tirelessly the realities of the life of faith, as God's way of deliverance from the misery brought by disobedience and unbelief. He saw all our lapses, beginning with Eve's in Eden, as springing from thoughtlessness that lets blind impulse take over, and insisted that under God the cure for sins and the road to righteousness starts with right thinking. As a biblical expositor he hammered away at this, modeling and enforcing it in message after message. Those who wanted a quick fix spiritually lost patience and left, but others found the diet nourishing and became increasingly human and wise in Christ.

John loved life and had not expected to die as early as he did, but during his ten days in the hospital before the second coronary struck he was a very peaceful patient. "I've done all I could, and I'm ready to go," he said. He went, unnoticed by anyone, during a moment when the nurse's back was turned. I think that is how he would have wished it; no self-advertisement, and no fuss. For the Puritans, making a good end was the proper climax of discipleship. If you and I make as good an end as John, we shall do well. I hope we shall.

Chapter 13

———

HYPE AND HUMAN HUMBUG

I was asked to write an extended blurb to promote a teaching
aid that a friend had produced. I said I would. I was then told
that to save me time a draft blurb would be prepared, based on
things I had said in my books. All I would have to do was sign it.

The draft duly arrived, and behold! it began by making me tell
a personal story that never happened, and went on to make me
declare a personal debt to material I have never yet encountered.
As advertising, it was no doubt a well-calculated come-on, but as
literature (well, what else can I call it?) it was fiction dressed up
as fact. Could you have signed such a thing? I couldn't.

What to do? Rather than penalize my friend for the crass-
ness of his entourage, I wrote a truthful blurb, and since I was
able to adapt some parts of the original draft, I dare say some of
my time really was saved. But just as mint candies, called hum-
bugs in England, leave an aftertaste in the mouth, so this brush
with human humbug, in the Dickensian sense of that word, left
an aftertaste in my mind—and it was not a pleasant, warm glow,
either.

Here was one evangelical devising false statements for
another evangelical in the interests of a third evangelical, his boss.

The justification offered would no doubt be that these statements, whether true or not, would encourage the use of good Christian teaching material, and that was all that mattered. That would be a way of saying that these statements fall in the category of what Plato called "the useful lie," a type of statement that managers make in order to manipulate people into doing what seems good for them (and, of course, for their masters, too). To see the end as justifying the means, or, as old-time Jesuit casuists put it, to treat a lawful intention as legitimizing whatever is done to fulfill it, is typically modern. But it is not right.

Surely the means to any end has a moral quality of its own. Surely I am not respecting God's image in my neighbor if I conspire to bamboozle him. Surely advertising a product by making false statements to people who expect me to tell the truth would be a case, even if small-scale, of doing evil that good might come—a way of acting that God condemns. Surely the Devil is the father of white lies as well as of black ones. Surely the old dictum that those who tell white lies soon become colorblind is true.

Said Samuel Johnson, that eighteenth-century man-mountain of Christian common sense: "Accustom your children constantly to this: if a thing happened at one window and they say, when relating it, that it happened at another, do not let it pass, but instantly check them; you do not know where deviation from truth will end." The contemporary willingness of Christians to trade in hype and untruths suggests that some of us were not brought up on this wise principle of meticulous respect for the facts.

Evangelical Christians have become sensitive over the past few years about the sanctity of life. Thank God we have! But is it not high time we developed an equally sensitive conscience about the sanctity of truth?

Have you ever wondered why, following a solemn call to patience under pressure and before an equally solemn call to sustained prayerfulness, James inserts: *"Above all*, my brothers, do not swear. ... Let your 'Yes' be yes, and your 'No,' no, or you will be condemned" (James 5:12)?[1] People swear, we know, in order to commend falsehoods as true, as when Peter swore that he did not know Jesus. James only echoes Jesus (Matt. 5:34–37) in requiring plain, honest truth at all times, and no doubt his reason for making the point here is that he knows how those under pressure can be tempted to affirm untruths in order to get out from under.

But why *"above all"?* Why does James treat total truthfulness as so very important? Because, I think, he knows that nothing corrupts character so quickly or so deeply as habits of deception and untruth. I too know that; don't you? There is no Christ-like consistency, no deep-level discipleship, without a passion for truth everywhere. I suggest we need to consider our ways.

---

[1] Scripture quotations in this article are from the New International Version (1984).

Chapter 14

MISTAKING ROME
FOR HEAVEN

W hy would any Protestant ever become a Roman Catholic? I first wondered about that more than 40 years ago when an undergraduate friend "Poped" (as English slang used to put it). The question recurred recently as I read Malcolm Muggeridge's gentle, wise, and transparently honest account of his passage from boyhood fascination with the New Testament to reception into the Roman Catholic communion at 79. A trickle of other Christians whom I have known over the years have gone the same way. Why?

All but two of the people I am thinking of were Episcopalians. Is there something about Episcopalianism that makes it a slippery slope Romewards? As an Episcopalian myself, able to speak from inside, so to speak, I do not think so. I have solid reasons for being an Episcopalian and not being a Roman Catholic, and they grow more solid with the years.

I am a reformed and reforming Episcopalian of an old-fashioned sort, which puts me out of step with many current trends. I believe in the infallibility of the Bible as an inerrant and theologically self-interpreting body of divine teaching. I find no biblical warrant for the idea that the church is empowered to interpret the Bible infallibly, making it an article of faith that what the church says, God says. I find the official papacy and Vatican bureaucracy to be grotesque, antibiblical institutions, however true it may be that this or that pope is a good man. And the "irreformable" definitions of transubstantiation, the Mass sacrifice, and the immaculate conception and assumption of Mary strike me as biblically very wrong.

For these reasons I refuse Roman Catholicism. So do liberal and "high" Anglicans; but not all their reasons are mine any more than all mine are theirs.

Is it, however, *reasons*, in the ordinary sense of that word, that turn Protestants into Roman Catholics? I doubt it. Muggeridge, who affirms the Incarnation while holding, mystifyingly, that Christian truth is artistic rather than historical, says straight out that he can no more offer an intellectual explanation of conversion (he means conversion not just to Christ, but also to Catholicism) than he can explain "why one falls in love with someone whom one marries. It's a very similar thing." I guess he is right. Individuals feel that Roman Catholicism fits them, that it is where they belong, and so they move in.

Three things, I think, draw these Protestants to Rome. They are looking for an institutional focus of authority, or for reality (consistency and courage, as distinct from compromise and cowardice) in Christian commitment, or for maturity and poise, as distinct from ham-fisted play acting, in practicing the faith. They believe they see these qualities in Rome rather than in the Protestantism they know, and they make their move accordingly.

Nor is it just that the grass on the other side of the fence always looks greener. Many modern Protestants (including Episcopalians, in case you wondered) really do wobble with a zany wildness, while Rome stays fairly steady. Protestants' conceited man-centeredness can make one feel they are playing a game called religion rather than serving God, whereas Rome is serious and sincere. Protestant amateurism in preaching, prayer, and pastoral dealing contrasts unhappily with Rome's cool professionalism and discipline.

I have sometimes wondered if the systematic dilution and killing of real religion in the liberal churches is not a Screwtape-type plot to drive all zealous souls into Rome's arms.

But it rarely works like that. Commoner is the move into Bible-believing, gospel-preaching, law-keeping, conservative Protestant communities, into which a steady stream of Roman Catholics flows, too. Traffic between Protestantism and Rome is not all one way. And I observe that what makes Roman Catholics into Protestants is always convictions about God's revealed truth. So now I ask: Is it healthier for a change of church allegiance to be motivated by a feeling of at-home-ness, or by a conviction of truth? Over to you.

Chapter 15

THE PRAYBOY CLUB

I never went near a Playboy Club till I went to Lausanne II in Manila. I thought they had all been closed down because they had proved unprofitable. But our "land package," as it was landed us at the hotel Playboy Club remains alive and kicking, and when we checked in, the desk clerk handed me complimentary passes to it. My strong-minded wife grabbed, tore up, and handed back the passes in silence. Good for her! Left to myself, I suppose I would have taken the passes, just because they were given me (I'm a wimp, I fear, that way), and trashed them privately; but Kit's gesture was the appropriate one.

The management got us into the Playboy Club after all, by the simple expedient of serving our meals there. Someone must have said something, because after the first meal the bunny girl at reception vanished, and after two days the eating place itself was changed. Yet throughout the Congress, the German contingent held their morning prayer meeting in the Playboy Club, and one of them said gleefully that they were turning it into the Prayboy Club for the duration. I thought of Cornwall's Billy Bray, who told a gang of yobbos that if they carried out their threat to nail him up in a beer barrel, he would shout "Glory to God!" through the bung-hole. I wish I had more of that victory-side spirit.

My vividest memory of the hotel, however, is of standing in a crowd with Kit, wearing an identification wristband and a blue label round my neck bearing my name, waiting to be numbered off to walk out of the foyer to the bus that would take us to the Convention Center. We were not heading for a gulag or concentration camp, but it felt like it.

We were actually in what England's *Church Times*, reporting the congress, headlined as "Murder and Mayhem in Manila." Murder? Yes. A union official had been killed on the premises, and the day after his funeral the staff went on strike. Glass was broken, there were punch-ups, the police fired shots, and thereafter we were picketed. The land-package people negotiated continued service for Lausanne folk, but we had to travel in couriered groups. We prayed. Did that make a difference? Well, none of us suffered violence, and surely that was part at least of God's answer.

Our wristbands and labels were to get us through the tight security at the Convention Center, where an eye-catching notice told us to leave all our weapons at the door. Manila was full of weapons, carried by armed security guards, police, soldiers, and probably others; it is a wildish city, and we were advised not to walk out at night. Like Calcutta, Manila has a vast poverty problem, with thousands of people living off the huge municipal garbage dump. And it is the pedophile capital of the world, where children are sold into prostitution at a horrifically early age.

But Manila was not all horrors. Recent years have seen spectacular evangelical church growth there, largely Pentecostal in style; and alongside Lausanne II ran the "parallel congress," a Filipino venture, as large as Lausanne itself, borrowing Lausanne speakers and concerned with evangelizing the Philippines. I found there an exuberance and expectancy that, frankly, I missed in the bland, laid-back, production-number sessions of Lausanne itself. Pentecostal electricity? Call it that if you like; I am not bothered about the label. But, oh boy, wasn't it refreshing!

And then on Sunday, halfway through, the Roman Catholic Church, which claims 85 percent of Filipinos and was not, I suppose, willing to be upstaged, held an all-day Bible rally attended by tens of thousands, featuring testimonies to conversion (not called that, of course; renewal after postbaptismal lapsing is the Roman concept), and raising funds to buy Bibles for the destitute. Kit and I saw some of it on television. Who would have expected such a thing? Surely the Holy Spirit, as well as Satan, is busy in Manila.

So back we came to cool-cat, brittle, affluent, self-indulgent, unchurched Vancouver, full of thoughts, and none the worse for our adventure.

Chapter 16

———

KLAUS BOCKMUEHL'S
RICH LEGACY

C hristians come in all shapes and sizes, and it is fascinating to see how God works in us to make us both more like each other and more different from each other than we were before.

As we draw closer to Christ, and he draws us closer to himself, our mind-sets, value systems, character qualities, behavior patterns, perceptions, and reactions become increasingly like his. Thus we converge on each other, fulfilling Paul's dictum that mature Christians should take the same view of things.

But knowledge that one is loved makes for the blossoming of individuality, and so every believer who basks in the love of Christ develops an increasingly distinctive flavor (what other word works?).

All this runs through my mind as I think of Klaus Bockmuehl, honored friend and beloved colleague at Regent College, once a CT columnist, later a section editor for CT's *The Best in Theology*. Klaus died last June at 58 after a long and draining fight with cancer. Resourceful medical treatment gave him more months of life than were expected, enabling him to finish a last book that he wanted the world to have, and to speak from his wheelchair at Regent's degree ceremony a month before he died, manifesting the triumph of a poised spirit over a ruined body in a way that those present will not forget. I found myself very close to Klaus in outlook while feeling quite different from him in human flavor, and the combination of these two facts made our friendship a delight to me.

Klaus was very much his own man in Christ. Into his making went German genes and work habits; Reformation faith, focused on forgiveness; the visionary pietism of Frank Buchman's Moral Re-Armament; the rough-and-tumble of the London School of Economics; theological salt and pepper from Barth and Moltmann; a sweetly solid marriage; and long-term martyrdom to migraines. With his formidable learning and fastidious skill in speech went a childlike simplicity and straightforwardness that made him fascinating to know, and the intensity of his devotion to Jesus could be stunning in its impact. Students found, sometimes to their surprise, that his intellectual rigor was wedded to compassionate care. In faith-full fortitude he was a model to many—and to me.

Here are two gems from the dying professor's last address.

I have come to think that among the "multitude of God's mercies" (Ps 106:7) which I have received, my recent illness was to teach me this lesson. ... In the past, if someone had called me a workaholic, I would secretly have responded: "Of course, what else?" A workaholic in the kingdom of God, that was a title of honor! I saw my Christian and human dignity, my self-confidence, and reason for self-respect in being a "worker" in God's vineyard. ... Let us beware of the seductive glory of Christian workaholism, of the moments when we tell ourselves secretly how wonderful it feels to be exhausted in the work of the Lord. ... No, it is far better to do a few inconspicuous things but to do them under God's instruction. ... Listening to the voice of God comes first and must precede all action.

From a practicing Christian one may expect radiation of light and warmth, giving to others both orientation and an experience of shelter. Those who listen to God promote healing instead of creating new problems. They truly become spiritual *resource people*, constant sources of inspiration instead of a constant source of irritation in their surroundings. This is not a matter of human endeavor and achievement. It comes from listening; it is the outcome of communion with Christ."

Thus Klaus, being dead, yet speaks, setting before us the most basic truths about the spiritual life—that being must precede doing, listening must precede acting, receiving must precede any attempt to give. This, I believe, is wisdom that religious people in North America today need desperately to take to heart. I know that I do, and I guess that you who read this column are in the same boat with me. The only recognition Klaus ever wanted was that people should take seriously what he had to say. So—what about it? Shall we start?

Chapter 17

—

WHY I LIKE MY PIE
IN THE SKY

Ever since I read Richard Baxter's sprawling, rhapsodic classic, *The Saints' Everlasting Rest*, 40 years ago, I have thought that today's Christians ought to be much more heavenly minded than we are. Baxter showed me how the hope of heaven should spur us to resolute effort in our discipleship ("run in such a way as to get the prize," 1 Cor. 9:24) and also bring us joy, since heaven is our real home. When persons suffering loss of memory cannot recall where their earthly home is, we pity them; but Christians who forget that heaven is their true home, and never think positively about heaven at all, are much more to be pitied. Yet this, it seems, is how most of us proceed most of the time.

Are we surprised when we find that televangelists and others lack motivation for holy living, and that moral standards and sensitivities among Bible-believers are fast eroding? The situation calls for grief, but not surprise: Our failure to focus our minds on our heavenly home explains it all. Of the prospect of being one day with Jesus, and like Jesus, John wrote: "Everyone who has this hope in him purifies himself, even as he is pure" (1 John 3:3).

The hope of a holy heaven, to be enjoyed in company with our holy Savior, is a potent motive to holiness now. Small wonder, however, if persons whose hearts are not full of this hope fail here.

After Baxter had shared with me—across the 300-year gap that separated us—his own infectious excitement about heaven, I wondered if I was the only person alive who felt this way. Today, however, I can name four others at least who, in my lifetime, have shown that they too feel this excitement.

When I passed from reading C. S. Lewis as an apologist, at which he was good, to reading him as a teacher of spirituality, at which he was better, I found that he was most brilliant and moving when he drew on the resources of his sanctified imagination to portray heaven's glory (something he often did), and that could hardly have been so had heaven not grabbed his heart.

A Step Further, by quadriplegic Joni Eareckson Tada, pioneer of ministry to the disabled, with its final mouthdrawing of her wheelchair empty and labeled "For Sale," poignantly marks her out as a child of this happy hope.

Peter Kreeft's two books, *Heaven: The Heart's Deepest Longing* and *Everything You Ever Wanted to Know about Heaven but Never Dreamed of Asking* (who said brevity is the soul of wit?), reveal him also as a member of my club. And John Gilmore's recent *Probing Heaven: Key Questions on the Hereafter* (466 pp.!) shows him to be another.

But why are there so few Christians these days who can honestly affirm that they have anchored their hearts in heaven and are continually excited about it? Worldliness, alas, is the cause. Secular materialism, preoccupied with the present, and Marxist mockery of "pie-in-the-sky-when-you-die," combine to make Christians feel embarrassed about their hope of glory, as if having it is somehow bad manners; so they do not talk about it, and soon they stop thinking about it. Rarely in today's Christianity does excitement about heaven break through. When did you last hear a sermon on the subject?

Yet, speaking pastorally now, aging Christians like me need to hear a lot about heaven; for knowing what you have to look forward to, and actually looking forward to it, keeps you alive inside, whatever the state of your body, so that you may fairly be described as so many years *young* rather than *old*. Junior Christians, too, need to hear about heaven, lest the world, in J. B. Phillips's phrase, "squeeze [them] into its own mould," as it has done to so many churchpeople of my generation, who see this world as home and leaving it as the supreme tragedy.

If the prospect of being with Jesus Christ, closer than ever before—all frustration, weakness, and pain having been left behind—does not thrill us constantly, our Christianity is dreadfully substandard. If we really loved our Lord, would not this guaranteed hope be a source of eager delight? And is not loving the Lord the heart of real Christianity? Think about it!

See you in heaven, I hope.

Chapter 18

HUMOR IS A FUNNY THING

"I t need not be humorous." These grave words, in a memo to CT's Senior Editors about their column, were triggered, I fear, by some pieces of Packer in which I had not managed to stifle my sense that this fallen world is as full of absurdities as it is of tragedies. CT is, of course, serious reading for serious people, and I can well understand the erstwhile fear (the memo was written three years ago) that too many jokes would spoil the broth.

Yet what a difference quality giggles make to life! I am drafting this column as I fly home from a heavy teaching conference in which the mapping of spiritual life and death was punctuated with "tons of fun."

(During the conference, for example, the director said that while there, he had met a man who had been a husband all his life. The dean, stringing along, or maybe falling for it, said he would like to meet such a man. "Stand up, Mr. Husband!" cried the director; up got the man with the improbable name; and we whooped, clapped, and hooted for a full half-minute. Abbott and Costello couldn't have done it better.)

Do good gags dispel seriousness? Not always. Labored humor does make preachers seem frivolous, and it kills serious sermons as effectively as does portentous dullness. Yet every spontaneous giggle yields another five minutes of empathetic listening, and every preacher will agree that is a precious boon.

Humor was one of the ways C. H. Spurgeon kept 6,000 listening for 40 minutes twice a Sunday. A lady called him unspiritual for saying so many funny things in the pulpit; he told her she wouldn't think so if she knew how many funny things he thought of in the pulpit and didn't say. Humor is a bad master, yet a good servant.

Humor is a strange thing. One may say of it what Augustine said of time: when I am not being questioned about it I know what it is perfectly well, but when I am asked to define it I can't.

Humor is elusive. It can be grim or jolly, giggly or grotesque, verbal or visual, friendly or ferocious. As ragtime is a way of playing things, so humor is a way of saying things—one that focuses on the deflating of false dignity (the banana-skin) or on the discovery of shrewdness within stupidity (the wisecrack) or on oddity within order (the fantastic idea). The only constant factor seems to be surprise, a kick in either your own pants or those of the guy you are laughing at. The moment of mental relaxation and refreshment that each quality giggle brings is, however, a precious gift from God: be grateful!

Jesus was the most shatteringly serious preacher ever, and was never a comic or a clown. Yet he, God incarnate and perfect man, displayed a strong sense of the ridiculous, which he used to make his teaching stick.

Take, for instance, the camel—the spitting, pitching, rocking, rolling ship of the desert, classically described as a horse designed by a committee. Jesus used the camel twice, unforgettably, to describe the most grotesque folly. He pictures the

Pharisees, meticulously majoring in minors while missing all that matters, as filtering their wine to get out a struggling gnat, then failing to notice that a camel has fallen in too, and swigging that camel as part of the cup that cheers.

Then he invites us to imagine a camel trying to thread itself by pushing its way through the eye of a needle. Imagine it, and then realize that it is harder for a rich man wedded to his wealth to enter the kingdom of God than for that jerking, shoving camel to make headway. We cannot help grinning—nor can we help remembering.

Had we no sense of humor we should have no sense of proportion (humor being an awareness of disproportion). And without a sense of proportion our sinful hearts, tempted as they always are to play God, would take themselves far too seriously.

Surely, when Jesus called us to be childlike, he was remembering that children know how to laugh without ceasing to be serious. Unsmiling seriousness is really no virtue—not even when one is writing for CT!

Chapter 19

———

FAN MAIL TO CALVIN

D ear John,
 This is a fan letter, naked and unashamed, one that I have long wanted to write, even though for obvious reasons I cannot mail it to you. But public acknowledgment of one's debts is good for the soul, and when one is a teacher of theology it is good for the church, too. I don't know why, but Christians I meet seem to think that theologians who teach spring fully formed from the womb and work in isolation from one another—hence the "I am of Calvin" / "I am of Finney" / "I am of Pannenberg," which Paul would surely have nailed as pure Corinthianism. I hope that by declaring my debt I can reduce the possibility of the world or church ever being bothered by "I am of Packer" people.

 I wish people grasped that theologians, like other Christians, learn with the saints in the multigenerational fellowship that is the church, where mentors, pastors, and peers help us to see things we hadn't seen before. Augustine had Ambrose, and you had Augustine, Luther, and Bucer, and I had Owen, Warfield, and you. We get to where we are by standing on others' shoulders and benefiting from their brainwork. You were clear on that—much clearer than some of the hero-worshipers who have written books about you! No true theologian works as a one-man band.

One thing you helped me see is where theologians really fit in. The church lives through the potency of preaching—the mystery of God's Spirit applying God's word to God's people through God's spokesman. So the primary function of theologians is to ensure, so far as human beings can, that the Bible is explained right and applied properly. I think I only give the film version of your thought when I tell people that theologians are the church's plumbers, water engineers, and sewage-disposal agents—backroom boys whose crucial though unspectacular job is to secure for the pulpits a flow of pure and unpolluted Bible truth. You, of course, had a larger role; you were a preaching pastor, and you educated other preaching pastors in the academy. How you managed to get through it all, especially in those grisly last years when you were dying by inches, I shall never know. But it is for your clear grasp of the theologian's task that I admire you now.

Another thing I learned from you was the true nature and ideal shape of what we nowadays call systematic theology. Your *Institutes* is a marvelous tapestry of evangelical wisdom that modeled for me the apostolic way of tying together the many strands of revealed truth about God's grace to a sinful world. You put the sovereignty of God, the mediation of Christ, and the ministration of the Spirit right at the center; you set up the life of faith and praise as the goal; and you did not write a speculative sentence from start to finish of your 700,000 words! I would like you to know that I have had the *Institutes* by me for 40 years, that I keep finding fresh wisdom in its pages to a degree that is positively uncanny, and that I am very grateful.

The way you dealt with predestination, in particular, strikes me as an all-time brilliancy. Like Paul in Romans, you separated it from the doctrine of providence and postponed it till you had spelled out the gospel, with its *bona-fide,* whosoever-will promises; then you brought in the truth of election and reprobation, just as in Romans 8 and 9, not to frighten anyone, but to give believers reassurance, hope, and strength. It's a beautifully biblical and powerfully pastoral treatment.

The irony is, as I expect you know, that in the last century the idea spread that all serious theologians arrange everything round a single focal thought, and yours was predestination, so they lost sight of your biblical breadth and balance and pictured you as a speculative monomaniac who pulled Scripture out of shape to make it fit a scheme of your own devising. That's still your public image, and biblicists like you are still called Calvinists in a way that implies they have lost their biblical footing. Such is life! I expect you're glad to be out of it.

With deepest respect and gratitude,

J. I. Packer

Chapter 20

———

HOW WILL I BE
REMEMBERED?

"How would you like to be remembered?" he asked me. "I mean, what would you like to be remembered as?" "Good question," said I, playing for time (for I had not asked myself the question, and I don't in any case carry snap answers to searching questions on the tip of my tongue); "how do you want to be remembered yourself?"

"As an encourager," he said. (I am sure he will be: Barnabas should have been his middle name.) "But now, what about you?"

"As a voice," I found myself telling him, "a voice that called people back to old paths of truth and wisdom."

"Hum," he said—or it might have been *huh*, or *humph*, or even *ugh*—"I think everybody ought to face that question, don't you?"

"Yes," I said, still wondering what he thought about my answer. He never told me, and maybe by now he has forgotten it. I haven't forgotten it, however, and I have frequently wondered whether I ought to have said anything that sounds in retrospect so grandiose. But I still don't think I could have said anything truer. If you asked me the same question today, honesty would require the same answer.

I was offsetting myself from two things that I have seen happen during the 47 years that I have been a Christian and a Christian watcher. Both are bound up with the emergence of the interdenominational animal called "the evangelical church." Once, denominational identities were primary, interdenominational links were subsidiary, and parachurch ministries were small and few, none venturing to claim to be the church's cutting edge. All this has been reversed in the current mindset that is the essence of "the evangelical church." I do not suggest that this development is unhealthy—after all, it is a much-blessed, worldwide phenomenon. There are, however, two defects in it that I would like to be remembered for having called in question.

Defect one is *the personality cult*. Through travel, books, and the media, individuals become international household words, and then they are elevated to virtual infallibility. On issue after issue people reason thus: "Billy Graham / Martyn Lloyd-Jones / John Wimber / John Stott / Chuck Swindoll / Elisabeth Elliot / R. C. Sproul / (write in here your own preferred authority) says it; I believe it; that settles it." This is a lapse from the Protestant appeal to Scripture into a more-than-papal traditionalism with which I would rather not be linked; I hope to be remembered as a "voice" (like John the Baptist, crying in the wilderness) encouraging people to think, rather than as a personality whose felt status and charisma stopped them thinking. (I am sure, incidentally, that all the victims of the personality cult I have mentioned feel the same, though they cannot do much about it.)

Defect two is *the short memory*. Denominational identity encourages believers to remember at least the denomination's history, but belonging to "the evangelical church" of the late twentieth century seems to lead people to forget all Christian history, and live by moving from one "latest thing" to another. I, too, use my mind on some of these "latest things," but what I live on is what I have learned from yesterday's giants—Augustine, Bernard, Luther, Calvin, the Puritans, Whitefield, Wesley, Edwards, Spurgeon, Ryle—and these lessons constitute the "old paths of truth and wisdom" with which I try to acquaint "the evangelical church." That is why my grandiose-sounding words came out as they did.

My friend's question made me refocus on what I am here for. Discussions of biblical inerrancy, secular humanism, abortion, signs and wonders, women's ordination, prophecy, and Christian healing have to be maintained, but they tend to be barren fields for the soul. I should like to be remembered as one who pointed to the pasturelands.

"I think everyone ought to face that question," said my friend as we moved in to dinner. "I wish you'd write about it in CT."

So I did. How would you like to be remembered?

Chapter 21

SURPRISED BY GRAPHICS

L eft brain for logic and linear thinking; right brain for creative brooding, empathy, free association, dramatic vision,
and the many modes of fantasy, all of which we ordinarily lump
together under the name of imagination. That is what I hear brain
theorists telling me nowadays about our mental makeup, and I
am grateful. This knowledge helps me remember things that as
a communicator I dare not forget.

The first is that good communication involves both sides of
the brain, in both the communicator and (to use the technical
term) the receptor.

Of course! This is why C. S. Lewis, John Bunyan, Charles
Williams, and above all, the Lord Jesus, were such powerful
communicators. They were whole-brained people, who linked
affirmations (teaching, exposition, argument) with images (pictures, analogies, stories) in such a way that each gave vividness,
credibility, and depth to the view of reality projected by the other.
Awesome yet accessible Aslan, the Christ figure in Lewis's Narnia,
illustrates Jesus; the one-by-one crossing of Jordan in *Pilgrim's
Progress* illustrates dying; Chloe's submission to the will of the
stone in *Many Dimensions* illuminates godliness; Jesus' stories

of the lost son and the workers in the vineyard illuminate grace. These display not just great truths, but great power in communication; they are unforgettably vivid and remain unbelievably moving.

Here is a lesson that we who seek to communicate must be learning. As the products of imagination without thought are weird, so the products of thought without imagination will be dull. But no one need be either weird or dull. We can all avoid both sorts of nose-dive if we try.

Trying involves both thinking what we are going to say and imaging how our way of saying it will strike the receptor. Dorothy L. Sayers, a whole-brain communicator herself, had fun with the minor poet who solemnly wrote of how a "flashing torrent, leaping in the air, / Left the astounded river's bottom bare." She would have enjoyed the card that United Airlines once set before me, saying that if I could not read it I should tell a flight attendant immediately. No communicator need lapse into booboos like those.

The second thing is that the impact of truth will be diminished if we clothe it in inappropriate imaginings.

This was brought home to me recently when I read the CT feature, "Heaven and Hell: Who Will Go Where and Why." One graphic that went with Leon Morris's weighty piece on hell was a Gustave Doré illustration, etched for Dante's *Inferno*, showing Dante under Vergil's tutelage with an oh-my-goodness look on his face, contemplating the kicking feet of folk who had been inserted head-first and upside-down into burning pits. (I should explain that senior editors do not choose the graphics, and can be as surprised by them as you are.) Perhaps the picture helped other readers to take hell seriously (as I do, and want everyone else to), but it did not help me; it just jolted me and left me thinking, "I don't believe it."

What do I not believe? That the essence of hell is grotesque bodily discomfort. That idea, I conceive, ultimately misses the deeper point of the lurid word-pictures drawn by Dante, and Jesus, and the New Testament writers. The essence of hell is surely an inner misery of helpless remorse, with recognition that in assigning one to an eternity of self-absorbed unwillingness to receive and respond to divine goodness—the unwillingness that in life one was always cultivating—God is being totally just and has done what is entirely right. Self-hatred and God-hatred will feed each other in hell forever. Dante's imaginings are not speculations, but didactic images designed to help us see the sinfulness of different types and degrees of sin (that is what his *Inferno* is really all about), and Doré's literalism was a hindrance rather than a help to me for zeroing in on Dante's point.

Left brain, right brain—think true thoughts, present them in words and pictures that fit—what a taxing business communication is! Pray for speakers, writers, and editors, including those of CT.

Chapter 22

———

GOD'S PLUMBER AND
SEWAGE MAN

Since I am paid to teach theology, I get typed as a professional theologian. If asked what that is, I describe theologians as the church's plumbers and sewage men, securing a flow of pure truth and eliminating theological effluent. That is my ideal, but it is not the whole story.

Professional theologians are curious creatures, in more than one sense.

First, curiosity drives them. They have a consuming interest in conceptualizing God and working out what is or might be true about him. Sometimes they ask questions that cannot be answered, form notions that cannot be justified, and follow fancies that contradict facts; some brilliant theologians are embarrassing nuisances, suckers rather than seers, whose ideas undermine the faith they claim to teach. Yet interpreting and celebrating God is necessary work: that it is not always done wisely or well does not mean it should be given up, only that we need to have it done better. At one level all Christians, pastors and people alike, are theologians—that is, people who venture to think and say things about God. The professional's job is to help us do it right, and so at our level to be good theologians and not bad ones.

So we should applaud theologians' curiosity. Medieval teachers lambasted the idle curiosity of the merely clever, and rightly so: such curiosity can ruin souls. But when curiosity is wanting to find out all you can about the works and ways of your heavenly Father, so as to enlarge your appreciation of him, it is as natural to the born-again believer as a growing child's interest in what his father does for a living. Rather than censure professionals for showing such curiosity, we should slap our own wrists for not having more of it.

But theologians are curious creatures in another sense. They live the academic life. They teach in universities, or in theological centers that function like universities, and like technicians in every other branch of learning they form professional societies, talk professional jargon, publish books and journals addressed to each other, and advance their own thinking by reaction to each other. So they look and sound less like a down-to-earth Christian task force than a mandarins' club. It is no wonder that those outside the circle are not always sure what to make of them.

Then, too, much present-day theology reflects failure both of nerve and of method. Instead of reaffirming and vindicating the Christian heritage against all forms of unbelief and alternative belief, theologians too often and too respectfully follow the fashions of secular skepticism, seeking only to devise a theology for tomorrow that can roll with the punches that the world throws at the faith today. The agenda sounds enlightened (well, naturally; it is Enlightenment-spawned), but it leads its practitioners to marginalize themselves by endless concedings and relativizings of revealed truth. Thus they muddy the waters of witness and matter less and less for real Christian life. Finally the saints lose patience and write off their theologians as curiosities in the sense of freaks.

This, however, is not the wisest reaction. Theologians take their own work seriously (what else would you expect?), and they are an active lot. They instruct today's and tomorrow's clergy; they pontificate to synods and conferences; they lobby leaders; they take up causes and challenge systems—in short, they make waves. Without knowledge of what they have been up to, we shall never understand why our churches are as they are.

One role of CT, which is a features-news-and-thought journal anchored in the historic faith, is to keep you posted, one way and another, on the theological front. I suppose I should see myself as a kind of point man for this purpose.

But most of all, I want to be a plumber and sewage man, as I said when I started, and most of all, I want CT always to be showing how head and heart should be joining in mature discipleship today. Head-without-heart journals and heart-without-head journals make for misshapen and underdeveloped Christians. It is important that we should find and follow the better way.

Chapter 23

BUNGEE-JUMPING, ANYONE?

Near Peoria, where I was to preach, I stood for two hours in sweltering heat opposite the Big Hook, with hound dog Elvis roaring at me continuously. (Who would have thought a little loudspeaker could make so much noise?) I was waiting to see my pastor friend go into free fall at the end of a bungee cord. England's last hangman reckoned to do each job in 11 seconds flat, and John's descent from the bungee cage (jerk-jerk-jerk-*grounded*) took hardly longer. He said it was worth every cent of the $60. I warned him that some columnist's thoughts had struck me while waiting, and he could expect to meet himself soon in CT. He wasn't worried; so here goes.

First thought: How different God makes us! John had looked forward to his jump for weeks; I would pay $60 any day not to have to do it. One Big Hook for me, however, is the 16 hours of Wagner's *Ring* cycle, which some of my friends would gladly pay $60 not to have to listen to. Taste in what actually refreshes the spiritual system varies greatly from Christian to Christian, and folk wisdom says that tastes, being purely personal, should not be argued about. Not everyone gets re-created by the same things.

The fact is that God the Creator likes variety: so dispositional differences are there from birth, and they continue after new birth. Not only do those born again become more like each other in character through getting closer to their common Master, they also become more individual in taste. Maturing in Christ makes you more yourself than you were before. Therefore, just as I will not have anyone despising Wagner's music (oh, sure, he was a nasty man, but that is not the point here), so I must take care not to sneer at bungee-jumping or Elvis or electronic music or Coke or anything else I don't like that gives good people pleasure.

Second thought: How grand a gift pleasure is! Calvin in the *Institutes* caned Augustine for lacking a biblical appreciation of life's pleasures, and the older I get the gladder I grow that Calvin did this. While one must eschew sinful pleasures because of the sin involved, the asceticism that condemns pleasure as such is phony. To scoop out time for activities that are for you re-creative pleasures (music, hobby reading, good conversation, fine food, tennis, trips away, evenings with your spouse, or whatever) is a proper and needful use of Christian liberty; without it, however far you go in Christian expertise and expression, you shrink as a person. We were not made, nor are we redeemed, to live without leisure. All work and no play makes Jack a dull boy, even if he is a sound evangelical.

Also, God intends our pleasures to act as a reminder of heaven, particularly our very intense pleasures (like mine as I flop in a hot tub, and John's at his bungee jump, and that familiar ache of longing that C. S. Lewis called Sweet Desire). Lewis says somewhere that the raptures of earthly lovers will be as milk and water compared with our future enjoyment of God, and he has to be right. Life's pulse-quickening pleasures remind us that heaven's delights are for real and are our proper goal.

Third thought: How exhilarating it is to push yourself in a good cause! This, I know, is dangerous doctrine; such pushing easily becomes an ego-tripping performance that expresses pure satanic pride masquerading as a sense of duty. John, however, was exhilarated as he went for his bungee jump (he called it a "controlled risk"); so was the paraplegic lifted from his wheelchair into the bungee harness (we gave him a big hand as he swooped and dangled, and surely he deserved it); and this exhilaration expressed not pride, but zeal. Zeal for anything makes you push yourself in pursuit of it, and there is exhilaration in rising to challenges. That is as true of Christian life and service as it is of bungee-jumping.

Watching the zeal of the bungee-jumpers, I found myself wishing I saw more such zeal among Christian people. Now and then it appears, but most of us choose to be conventional, play safe, and plod. That, however, is hardly the spirit of New Testament Christianity—is it?

Chapter 24

PACKER THE
PICKETED PARIAH

ome years ago theologian Carl Henry, no less, was picketed at
a meeting by fellow believers who disliked what he had said
on a public-policy question. I wondered then how it would feel
to be thus treated: now I know.

The college where I teach has just been picketed for an afternoon for something I wrote in CT. Two beefy protesters stood at
the door buttonholing students and passers-by. The big words
on their placards were "Packer," "hijacker," and "ecumenism." I
was not close enough to read the rest. But certainly I was being
trashed.

Both the protesters had previously phoned me, so I knew what
the trouble was. I wrote in CT of some Roman Catholics being
spiritually alive, without saying (1) official Roman teaching about
Mary and the Mass is idolatrous, so that (2) apparent spiritual
life among its adherents has to be hypocritical and unreal. The
Protestant mafia was damning me for these omissions.

To set the record straight: I have in the past written that the
doctrines of the Mass (transubstantiation and sacrifice) and the

practice of Mariolatry, with the Mariological ideas that support it, are not acceptable. These non-scriptural teachings involve a real if unintended obscuring of the true glory of Christ the Savior. On (1) above, therefore, trashers and trashed were substantially agreed, though they express themselves differently. But I have also written that the God of grace does not refuse to bless biblical truths about Christ to sinners who, in what Roman theology calls invincible ignorance, flank them with mistakes. So, as I offend Roman Catholics by thinking them invincibly ignorant (which is, of course, what they think of me), I now offend some Protestants by thinking of Roman Catholics who love the Lord Jesus as real Christians. Maybe I should be surprised that I do not receive more hate mail.

Home I went, then, with my new identity: Packer the picketed pariah. How did I feel? Not exactly good, but not so bad as you might suppose. You will have noticed, as I have, that differences of natural temperament and childhood experience combine to produce in people very different reactions to negative criticism. Some, who have egos like eggshells, find all criticism crushing; others, whose egos are like cannonballs, get exhilarated by the notoriety that criticism brings ("I don't mind what they say about me as long as they spell my name right").

I felt a rush of somewhat childish fury when the pickets barged into my office to tell me what they planned to do, interrupting an academic conference after being asked to wait till I was free; I felt some embarrassment for the college, and a short, cold squeeze on the soul at the thought of having someone declare me worthless; but otherwise I felt very little. A better man might have felt sadder for the protesters than I did.

The episode sparked two thoughts.

First: There are good and bad ways of fulfilling the ministry of criticism among Christians. This ministry is important, for all we who seek truth and wisdom take up from time to time with wrong ideas and need correction. But discussion and debate ordinarily achieve more than gestures of denunciation. To think of sustained denunciation as the essence of faithful witness, and of the mindset that will not see any good in what is not totally good as a Christian virtue, is very wrong. Denouncing error has its place, but since it easily appears arrogant and generates much unfruitful unhappiness, anyone who feels drawn to it should take a lot of advice before yielding to the urge.

Second: Answering criticism that seems ill-informed and irresponsible is not always a duty. John Wimber and his colleagues are doing this again after years of ignoring such criticism: is their new policy as wise as was the old one? Self-defense easily becomes self-exaltation. It is 40 years since I ran across Augustine's prayer, "Lord, deliver me from the lust of vindicating myself." It sticks in my heart still, and I am glad it does. I should certainly be a worse person were it not there.

Chapter 25

———

THE WHALE AND
THE ELEPHANT

*Tweedledum and Tweedledee / resolved to have a battle; / for
Tweedledum said Tweedledee / had spoiled his nice new rattle.*

T his nursery rhyme scores nursery behavior; but adults can
behave that way, too.

Karl Barth and Emil Brunner, the two Swiss giants of neo-
orthodoxy, maintained a Tweedledum-Tweedledee toward each
other for 30 years following their row over whether granting
the validity of natural theology undermined the view they had
developed together. When finally they met again, near the end
of their lives, their conversation dragged, and Barth said he and
Brunner were like the whale and the elephant: two biggies, neither of whom could conceive how the other could exist.

In my youth, England's two most outstanding evangelicals
were Martyn Lloyd-Jones, stellar preacher in central London, and
Frederick Fyvie Bruce, head of biblical studies in the University of
Sheffield, first, and then at Manchester. They were great and good

men, and it was a privilege to know them. They too, however, had something of a whale-and-elephant, Tweedledum-Tweedledee relationship. Both were Celts (one Welsh, one Scottish), and both were Calvinists of sorts, so you might have expected them to behave like blood brothers. But "the Doctor," theological preacher extraordinary, was a Luther, a tireless exponent of God's grace in Christ justifying sinners through faith and renewing them by the Spirit, while "F. F.," historian and man of letters, was an Erasmus, an impeccable scholar committed to the advancement of learning and to the study of Scripture within that frame. They were not on the same wavelength and could not work together at all well.

Each of them was, rightly, sure of the importance of what he was doing. Almost single-handed, Bruce was becoming midwife to a revival of evangelical biblical scholarship; almost single-handed, Lloyd-Jones was pioneering a renewal of experiential exposition in the power of the Spirit. Both projects were necessary: God's church needs both believing scholarship and powerful preaching. But to Lloyd-Jones, Bruce seemed not to be serious about theological truth, while to Bruce, Lloyd-Jones's antithetical definiteness seemed to set restrictions on academic endeavor. Certainly Lloyd-Jones, though a magnificent preacher of the Word of God, was not a scholar in Bruce's sense, and Bruce, though a superb commentator on Scripture, was not a preacher in Lloyd-Jones's sense.

One can see why they found it hard to tune in to each other. But it was a pity they did, since both were such precious gifts to the modern church. I appreciated them both and wish they could have appreciated each other more.

I have heard admirers of each disparage the other as if loyalty to their hero required this of them, and the experience has left me distressed. Such negativism is childish and carnal. The way to view other Christians—preachers, pastors, academics, colleagues, parents, spouses, children, or whoever—is to focus on what by God's grace they are and have, rather than to dwell constantly on what they are not and do not have. Christian elephants and whales may mystify each other, but the rest of us can and should rejoice in the reality of both. God likes variety; cloning is not his way. In the order both of creation and of redemption, different people receive from him different abilities, and with them, different personal priorities. We should enlarge our minds and stretch our sympathies to a positive valuation of every gift and mode of wisdom that our Lord has put in his church, and we should tell ourselves firmly that narrowing our focus here, even when it is zeal for our ministry that leads us to do so, is not a virtue, but a weakness tending to become a vice.

Among the apostles, Paul, the Jerusalem-trained rabbi, and John, the Galilean fisherman, were surely the archetypal whale and elephant, for the spiritual stature of both was enormous while their culture, cast of mind, and emphases in exposition were very different. If they were required to appreciate and affirm each other, no latter-day whale or elephant has any right to criticize (say) women for not being more like men, or Britons for not being more like Americans, or academics for not being more like preachers and vice versa, or Calvinists for not being more like charismatics—need I go on? May the grace of mutual appreciation grow and flourish in today's church.

Chapter 26

———

FEAR OF LOOKING
FORWARD

S
ir Fred Catherwood is older than I am, which makes him fairly elderly, but he is still hard at work. Knighted for public service years ago, he recently ended a spell as a vice president of the European Parliament in order to lead Britain's Evangelical Alliance in a new urban initiative. In September's *Evangelicals Now*, he writes about his venture under the jolting title "Before It's Too Late."

"British society has gone badly wrong," he begins. "You don't just have to look at the terrible statistics. People have started to look back to the good old days—not so long ago—when the streets were safe, everyone had a job, most people had a home, children stayed at school, the family stayed together and we all looked forward to better times." I can testify that there were indeed such days: the years of stubborn national endeavor that followed the Second World War.

"We look back today," he continues, "because we dare not look forward. We live in a violent, greedy, rootless, cynical and hopeless society and we don't know what's to become of it all." When

I revisit Britain as a Brit on family and other business, I meet apprehensive apathy everywhere. I wish Sir Fred was wrong, but I know he's right.

The decline, he tells us, has two causes, both of them signs of how Britain has slipped its historic Christian moorings. The first is greed—"the logical result of the belief that there is no life after death. We grab what we can while we can however we can and then hold on to it hard."

The second cause is moral confusion, the pragmatic amorality of a society in which it is "politically correct" to deny that there are universal moral absolutes. "The powerful use their power and the weak go to the wall, not just the poor, but the weak-willed, and especially all the children, who depend on the age-old disciplines and loving care of the family." Too true.

"As we stop believing in the dignity of man and woman made in the image of God, violence has risen dramatically." Should that surprise?

"Can government turn the tide? I doubt it. ... Around the Cabinet table, ministers will admit that people are deeply anxious because the social pillars of society have been shaken. All down the centuries governments have had moral guidelines to tell them how to shape the social structures. Now ... they do not know what to do."

While politicians confess bafflement and secular caregivers feel beaten, Christians must hear God's call to practice neighbor-love where they are "by helping those whose lives have been wrecked by materialism and the disintegration of stable family life." So the Evangelical Alliance is forming City Action Networks, in which local churches pool resources, human and material, to help the casualties of a self-centered and hard-hearted society— the lonely, the hurting, the homeless, and the untrained. Each church will do what it does best, pass other problems to churches and organizations that have the skill and promises to handle them, and receive from others cases requiring their own expertise.

When each urban network is in place there will be a public launch, so that local politicians, civic leaders, and media are made aware of what is being done. This will identify the collaborating evangelical churches "as part of the community, not an exclusive private club, ... but good neighbors who ... are there to help."

Britain's problems are not exclusive to Britain; North America and Australasia are more or less in the same boat. There are places in North America where leaders of churches regularly meet to pray and strategize for the serving and winning of their communities, and maybe City Action Networks already exist in some of these. But I write to express my belief that Sir Fred's version of the idea, simple, realistic, demanding, and fruitful as it is, should be acted on in all population centers everywhere— before it's too late.

Chapter 27

WHEN PRAYER
DOESN'T "WORK"

M y pagan friend, hospitalized, prayed for healing and is
now well again. My Christian friend, hospitalized, prayed
for healing, but it never came. What sense can I make of that?
Statistics suggest that any form of prayer by anybody, Christian
or not, helps patients recover. Does that make any sort of sense?
Let us see.

Just as an awareness of the divine is natural to human beings
through general revelation, so also is the instinct for petition-
ary prayer in time of need. Everywhere in every era when crises
come, children and adults of any faith or no faith find their minds
forming the cry, "*Please* let *this* (specified) happen, and not *that*
(specified again)." The dictum that there are no atheists in the
trenches bears witness to this. The naturalness of prayer under
pressure is a fact of life.

So it is no wonder when patients who have asked whatever
God they pray to to watch over and heal them, and who are trusting God to do it, relax inwardly in a way that, being natural, is actually therapeutic. And since the true God is in truth very kind and

generous, it is no wonder if those who thus reach out in his direction, ungodly though their beliefs and lives may be in all sorts of ways, find that as they pray their health improves. Nor will it be wrong to read any statistics that substantiate this as witness to God's everyday mercies.

Christian prayer, however, has a more solid base. Christians know the God of creation and providence as their covenant Lord, the God of saving grace, and they pray accordingly. Christian prayer is Trinitarian, addressing the Father through the Son and the Father and the Son through the Holy Spirit. Christians base their approach to the divine throne on their acceptance through the Son's atoning death and their adoption as the Father's children and heirs. They claim the Father's promise to hear and answer their prayers, but their bottom line is always "thy will (not mine) be done," and they know that if through ignorance and lack of wisdom they ask for something that is not really good for them, God in love will answer by giving them something that is really better. So, for example, when Paul prayed to be rid of his thorn in the flesh, God answered by strengthening him to carry on while the thorn remained.

Petitions for healing, or anything else, therefore, are not magic spells, nor do they have their effect by putting God under pressure and twisting his arm, whatever health-and-wealth, bring-down-revival, win-the-world teachers may say to the contrary. Non-Christians' prayers for healing may surprise us by leading to healing; Christians' prayers for healing may surprise us by not being answered that way. There are always surprises with God. But for God's children, "Ask, and you will receive" is always true, and what they receive when they ask is always God's best for them long-term, even when it is a short-term disappointment. Some things in life are certain, and that is one of them.

Part 2

——

ARTICLES

Chapter 28

———

FUNDAMENTALISM:
THE BRITISH SCENE

T hirty years ago, it was generally thought that conservative
    evangelicalism in Britain was a spent force. But this is no
longer so. The editor of the 1955 edition of *Crockford's Clerical
Directory*, in his traditional prefatory survey of Anglican affairs,
noted that "Evangelicalism has had a great revival in recent years,
particularly among young people," and went on to refer with
some regret to "the growth of Fundamentalism in the universities and theological colleges." All the Protestant denominations
have been more or less affected in this way. The Inter-Varsity
Fellowship and other interdenominational evangelical youth
movements have grown rapidly in numerical strength since 1945.
Billy Graham's work, too, has made its own contribution towards
putting evangelicalism back on the map.

   For the first time in many decades, a point is being reached
at which it becomes possible for evangelicals to think in terms of
a planned strategy of theological advance. Liberalism seems to
have shot its bolt, and Anglo-Catholicism to have lost its way; and
with the impetus of both these theological pacemakers slackening,

indigenous British theology is at present not far from the doldrums. The situation calls evangelicals to throw off the defensive and isolationist mentality, which has inevitably been built up during the lean years of endless rearguard actions, and to make a constructive re-entry into the field of theological debate.

In a challenging series of articles in *Christianity Today* (June–July, 1957, since published in fuller form under the title *Evangelical Responsibility in Contemporary Theology*), the Editor called for a serious reconsideration of the Fundamentalist-Modernist controversy. Such an appeal is at least as relevant to the British situation as to that in America; particularly in view of the fusillade of sniping comment—sometimes patronizing, sometimes pompous, sometimes hysterical—that has been sustained during the past two years against "fundamentalism." (The word is placed in quotation marks because, though it is the term which critics habitually use, the majority of British conservatives have never espoused it, do not like it, and prefer, with Dr. Carl F. H. Henry, to call themselves evangelicals, on the ground that this term is more scriptural, meaningful, and less encrusted with unhelpful associations.)

Before 1914

The closing decades of the nineteenth century saw liberal ideas seeping steadily into British Protestant thought. Rationalistic criticism and humanistic theology flourished in the pantheizing atmosphere which a dominant philosophical idealism had generated. Young Robertson Smith stuck out his neck over the Graf-Wellhausen hypothesis and as a result was removed from his chair at Aberdeen for heresy in 1881; but his teacher, A. B. Davidson, a more prudent man, continued quietly propagating "higher criticism" in Edinburgh without let or hindrance. C. H. Spurgeon waged the Down Grade Controversy during 1887 in hope of rallying his fellow nonconformists to the historic Evangelical faith, on which he feared they were losing their grip. But the controversy revealed that the damage was already done, and the majority of Free Church ministers had ceased to be with him.

In the Church of England, the theological running was mostly made by liberal Anglo-Catholics, with Charles Gore at their head. Evangelicals in all the denominations found themselves outnumbered and bypassed. Lacking champions of the calibre of Warfield and Machen, they tended simply to withdraw from the theological battlefield, comforting themselves with the thought that liberalism must sooner or later discover its own inadequacy and burn out, after which there would surely be a return to the old paths. Meanwhile, they would dig in where they were, conserving the traditional evangelical positions, and stay put. They were not in a position to know, as we do, how demoralizing and enervating is the Maginot line mentality. It is not surprising to find that the literature produced by evangelicals during the generation after 1914 was almost all poor, and the impact made on the life of the churches was negligible.

Between the Wars

The fundamentalist crusade of the twenties in America had no British counterpart, although Machen's *What Is Faith?* aroused some discussion when it appeared in a British edition in 1925. Generally, the attention of evangelicals during these years was taken up with missions, conventions and adventist speculations. The most vigorous protagonists for evangelicalism were the conservative leaders in the Church of England. A group of these produced a symposium, *Evangelicalism*, which was intended as a manifesto; but it was a disappointing volume which bore no comparison with the comparable Anglo-Catholic book, *Essays Catholic and Critical*, which appeared in 1926.

During the twenties, the self-styled "liberal evangelical" party within the Church of England announced its arrival with two volumes of essays, *Liberal Evangelicalism* and *The Inner Life.* This group took the position that evangelicalism is essentially an ethos—one stressing the experience of conversion and personal fellowship with God—and that this ethos be wedded to liberal theology, not merely without loss, but with positive profit. It should be pointed out that, if one takes the word "evangelicalism" in its historic sense, as denoting loyalty to the doctrines of the Reformation creeds on a basis of biblical authority, "liberal evangelicalism" is simply a contradiction in terms. The proper name for this standpoint would be "pietistic liberalism," or something of that nature. On the whole, however, this group has made little significant contribution to current theology, and none to the debate between authentic evangelicalism and its opponents.

The Present Position

British evangelicalism is now regaining strength, theologically and numerically. The opening in Cambridge of the Inter-Varsity Fellowship's own residential library and research center, Tyndale House, and the growing band of scholars who work in association with this movement, are encouraging signs of the times. The evangelical resurgence has forced itself on the notice of the rest of the church and evoked a good deal of comment, as we observed earlier.

The most serious critical discussion appearing so far is *Fundamentalism and the Church of God*, by an Anglo-Catholic, Gabriel Hebert (1957). Dr. Hebert professes to deal specifically with "conservative evangelicals in the Church of England and other churches, and with the Inter-Varsity Fellowship" (p. 10). What he writes makes clear that in his view it is among Anglicans and the I.V.F. that the main strength of the movement lies. His book, however, though conscientiously charitable and sober, disappoints; he misses the major issues at stake altogether, and this I have tried to show in my own *'Fundamentalism' and the Word of God* (I.V.F., 1958). Here, however, all that is possible is a brief commentary on the main criticisms which he and others have made.

The Doctrinal Debate

The chief complaint relates to the evangelical view of Scripture. Hebert describes this as belief in the factual inerrancy of biblical assertions, from which, he supposes, evangelicals infer that exegesis should be as literalistic as possible; that is to say, that every narrative should be treated as having the character and style of a modern prose newspaper-report. He is, of course, right to insist that a hermeneutical canon which arbitrarily imposes on Scripture a modern norm, rather than seeking to appreciate the narrative methods of Scripture for what they are, is theologically indefensible. But he is wrong in thinking that British evangelicals espouse any such canon. No one disputes that the Bible itself must be allowed to fix the criteria of the inerrancy to which it lays claim. Hebert here attacks a man of straw.

Moreover, Hebert's account of the evangelical view is incomplete, and reflects a defective critical standpoint. Evidently he has stopped short at asking how far empirical evangelicalism differs from his own position, and has not considered the further question of what evangelicalism is in terms of itself. Otherwise, he could hardly have failed to notice that what is fundamental to the fundamentalism which he is examining is not one particular hermeneutical principle, but an uncompromising acceptance of the authority of all that Scripture is found to teach—including its witness to its own character and interpretation. The constitutive principle of evangelicalism is the conviction that obedience to Christ means submission to the written Word, as that whereby Christ rules his Church; whence arises the evangelical determination to believe all that Scripture asserts, as being truth revealed by God, and to bring the whole life of the Church into conformity with it.

Some excuse for Hebert's misunderstanding may lie in the fact that during the past decades British evangelicalism has been in serious danger of misunderstanding itself. Evangelicals have thought and spoken as if the essence of evangelicalism was the maintaining of a distinctive exegetical tradition, which was itself above criticism and could be taken as a yardstick for judging the expository work of others. But such optimism, of course, is not warranted. It does not follow that, because one's approach to the Bible is right, one's exegesis therefore will be skillful. It may be that at some points current evangelical interpretation is inferior to that of other schools of thought. It may be that evangelicals merit some censure for their past unwillingness to criticize their own exegesis and to learn from other sources outside their own constituency. (Not that they would in that case be the only guilty parties in Christendom, by any means.) But all this has nothing to do with the question of what evangelicalism is. The most that it can show is that modern evangelicalism has on occasion failed to be true to itself. If the present outburst of criticism helps British evangelicals to see this, and to realize more clearly what kind of a position evangelicalism really is, it will do immense good.

The other doctrinal point of substance that has been raised concerns the atonement. Evangelicals are criticized for adhering to the doctrine of penal substitution. This criticism comes, not from liberals of the older school, which rejected this doctrine on rationalistic grounds while admitting that the Bible taught it, but from representatives of the modern "biblical theology" movement (notably, Hebert, the Archbishop of York, and Professor G. W. H. Lampe), who profess to reject the doctrine on exegetical grounds, doubting whether the Bible teaches it, at any rate in the form in which evangelicals assert it. (Hebert would gloss the penal idea in terms of Aulen's "classic" theory; Professor Lampe and the Archbishop, following Maurice, think that Scripture teaches an atoning death which was representative, but not substitutionary.) The issue here, therefore, is a purely exegetical one; for "Biblical Theology," however inconsistently, does not dispute the binding character of any doctrine taught in Scripture, except the doctrine of the unerring truth and unqualified authority of Scripture itself. To the question, whether we should hold the biblical doctrine of the atonement, Hebert and his fellows would say yes, though to the logically prior question, whether we should hold the biblical doctrine of the trustworthiness and authority of biblical teaching as such, they seem, if not to say (for they avoid the question), at any rate to mean no. It would be tempting to reflect on the oddity of this, if space permitted.

Practical Issues

Critics are generous in praising the evangelistic zeal and personal devotedness of evangelicals, but complain, with some justice, of two prevalent weaknesses in their outlook: one ecclesiastical, the other ethical. Both recognizably derive from the somewhat flabby pietism that spread through the evangelical constituency via the convention movement at the end of the last century. The effect of this pietistic conditioning was to focus concern exclusively on the welfare of the individual soul, and to create indifference both to the state of the churches and to the ordering of society. These tendencies were reinforced by reaction, on the one hand, against liberal control of the denominations, and, on the other, against the "social gospel" which liberalism purveyed as its own alternative to the evangelistic message. In addition, dispensational adventism, widely held during the first half of the century, insisted that the growing apostasy of Protestant Christendom was a sure sign of the imminence of Christ's return, and so tended to destroy all interest in trying to remedy the situation. This type of adventism is now, if not exploded, at least out of fashion, and it is to be hoped that the apathetic pessimism which it fostered is on the way out too.

The first weakness specified may be described as the undenominational mentality. The complaint here is that evangelicals regard inter-denominational organizations as filling the center of the ecclesiastical stage. True, these profess to serve the churches; but, it is said, what they do in fact is to divert the energies of their adherents into non-denominational channels, to such a degree that worship, sacraments and service within the local congregation are crowded into second place. There seems to be some truth in this. The strength and attraction of the inter-denominational movements rest in part on the deep sense of brotherhood and mutual loyalty generated within them (English evangelicalism has happily been free from the rancorous temper and fissiparous tendencies which have disfigured parallel movements elsewhere); but this very warmth of fellowship makes evangelicals understandably reluctant to plunge back into the chillier streams of local church life and work for Christ there.

In the writer's judgment, the reinvigorating of the local church as an aggressive witnessing community is strategic priority number one in the present British situation, and evangelicals will fail miserably if they do not direct their chief efforts to this end. In this connection, large-scale inter-church evangelistic campaigns must be judged a mixed blessing, for, however much immediate good they do, they tend to distract attention and effort away from the long-term priorities.

The second complaint is that evangelicals live in the world as if they were out of the world, showing a sublime insensitiveness to the implications of the Gospel for social, political, economic and cultural life, and shirking the responsibility of bearing a constructive Christian witness in these fields. Here, again, there is truth in the accusation. The antinomian tendencies which always hang around pietism have led in this case to a deplorable ethical shallowness; evangelicals today are not noted for personal integrity, public spirit and passionate love of righteousness in the way that (say) Shaftesbury and Wilberforce were. In this connection, perhaps the healthiest current sign is a widespread reawakening of interest in Puritan theology. This, with its profoundness and passion, its clear-cut delineation of grace and godliness, its broad world-view and consuming concern for the glory of God in all things, is perhaps better adapted than any other part of the evangelical tradition to restore spiritual depth and moral fibre to British evangelicals today.

The present revival of evangelical fortunes is heartening. But it comes at the end of three-quarters of a century of moral, spiritual and intellectual decline, during which evangelical influence in the churches and the country has grown steadily less till now it is very small; and though many non-evangelicals have recently acquired an evangelistic veneer, evangelicalism proper does not seem as yet to have regained any of its lost ground. Rather, its inner resurgence has coincided with the exertion of new pressures, ecclesiastical and ecumenical, designed to squeeze it into an alien mold and thereby terminate its distinctive existence. These pressures seem likely to increase; no doubt some gruelling years lie ahead. Our hope is that the strength of God may be made perfect in the weakness of his servants.

Chapter 29

CHRISTIANITY AND NON-CHRISTIAN RELIGIONS

C hristianity has always been a missionary religion. At the close of his earthly ministry, our Lord commissioned his followers to go and make disciples of all nations (Matt. 28:19), and it is generally admitted today that the Church of later generations has no right to call herself apostolic unless she acknowledges this missionary obligation to be her own. Now, the universal missionary imperative implies an exclusive claim, a claim made by our Lord himself: "I am the way, the truth, and the life: no man cometh unto the Father, but by me" (John 14:6).[1] To deny that men can know the Father apart from Christ is to affirm that non-Christian religion is powerless to bring them to God and effective only to keep them from him.

---

[1] Unless otherwise noted, Scripture quotations in this article are from the King James Version.

Only One Saving Religion

Accordingly, the summons to put faith in Christ must involve a demand for the endorsement of this adverse verdict, and for the avowed renunciation of non-Christian faith as empty and, indeed, demonic falsehood. "Turn from these vanities to the living God" (Acts 14:15)—that was what the Gospel meant for those who worshiped the Greek pantheon at Lystra in Paul's day, and that is what it means for the adherents of non-Christian religions now. The Gospel calls their worship idolatry (1 Thess. 1:9) and their deities demons (1 Cor. 10:20), and asks them to accept this evaluation as part of their repentance and faith.

And this point must be constantly and obtrusively made; for to play down the impotence of non-Christian religion would obscure the glory of Christ as the *only* Saviour of men. "There is none other name under heaven ... whereby we must be saved" (Acts 4:12). If Christless religion can save, the Incarnation and Atonement were superfluous. Only, therefore, as the Church insists that Christless religion, of whatever shape or form, is soteriologically bankrupt can it avoid seeming to countenance the suspicion that for some people, at any rate, our Lord's death was really needless.

What of Other Religions?

It is beyond dispute that this is the biblical position, but naturally it raises questions. How does the Gospel evaluate the religions which it seeks to displace? How, in view of its condemnation of them, does it account for the moral and intellectual achievements of their piety and theology? And how does it propose to set about commending Christ to the sincere and convinced adherents of the religions it denounces, without giving an impression of ignorance, intolerance, patronage, or conceit?

These questions press more acutely today than at any time since the Reformation, and there are three reasons for this. In the first place, a century's intensive study of comparative religion has made available more knowledge than the Church ever had before about the non-Christian faiths of the world, and in particular of the intellectual and mystical strength of the highest forms of Eastern religion. This makes it necessary at least to qualify the sweeping dismissal of these faiths as ugly superstitions which to earlier missionary thinkers, who knew only the seamy side of Eastern popular piety, seemed almost axiomatic. Fair dealing is a Christian duty, and everybody of opinion has a right to be assessed by its best representatives as well as its worst. (How would historic Christianity fare if measured solely by popular piety down the ages?)

In the second place, the great Asian faiths are reviving and gaining ground partly, no doubt, through the impetus given them by upsurging nationalism. It is no longer possible naively to assume, as our evangelical grandfathers often did, that these religions must soon wither and die as the Gospel advances. As we meet them today, they are not moribund, but confident, aggressive, and forward-looking, critical of Christian ideas and convinced of their own superiority. How are we to speak to their present condition?

In the third place, Christian evangelism has been accused, and to some extent convicted, by Eastern spokesmen in particular of having in the past formed part of a larger cultural, and sometimes imperialistic, program of "Westernization." These thinkers now tend to dismiss Christianity as a distinctively Western faith and its exclusive claim as one more case of Western cultural arrogance, and to insist that the present aspirations of the East are compatible only with indigenous Eastern forms of religion. There seems no doubt that Protestant missionary policy during the last hundred years really has invited this tragic misunderstanding. Too often it did in fact proceed on the unquestioned assumption that to export the outward forms of Western civilization was part of the missionary's task, and that indigenous churches should be given no more than colonial status in relation to the mother church from which the missionaries had come. It is not surprising that such a policy has been both misunderstood and resented. The Protestant missionary enterprise needs urgently to learn to explain itself to the new nations in a way that makes clear it is *not* part of a cunning plan for exporting the British or American way of life, but is something quite different. This necessitates a reappraisal on our part of non-Christian religions which will be, if not less critical in conclusions, more sympathetic, respectful, and theologically discriminating in method than was the case in earlier days. Christian missionary enterprise inevitably gives offense to those of other faiths simply by existing; but the Church must watch to see that the offense given is always that of the Cross and never of fancied cultural snobbery and imperialism of the missionaries.

It seems that the need for a deepening of accuracy and respect in the evangelistic dialogue with other religions is more pressing than evangelical Christians generally realize. This, perhaps, is because evangelical missionary effort during the past fifty years has been channeled largely through small inter-(or un-) denominational societies which have concentrated on pioneer and village work, whereas it is in the towns that resentment and suspicion of the missionary movement are strongest. But it is very desirable that evangelicals should appreciate the situation and labor to give the necessary lead. They are uniquely qualified to do this, having been preserved from the confusion about the relation of Christianity to other religions which has clouded the greater part of Protestant thinking since the heyday of liberalism fifty years ago. Though liberalism is now generally disavowed, its ideas still have influence; and its ideas on this particular subject are the reverse of helpful, as we shall now see.

Liberal Bias Lingers

The liberal philosophy (you could not call it a theology) of religion was built on two connected principles, both of which have a pedigree going back to the philosophical idealism of Hegel and the religious romanticism of Schleiermacher. The first principle was that the essence of religion is the same everywhere: that religion is a genus wherein each particular religion is a more or less highly developed species. This idea was usually linked with the reading of man's religious history as a record of ascent from animistic magical rites through ritualistic polytheism to the heights of ethical monotheism—a specious speculative schematization, the evolutionary shape of which gave it a vogue much greater than the evidence for it warrants. (In fact, the evidence for primitive monotheism, and for cyclic degeneration as the real pattern of mankind's religious history, seems a good deal stronger. Romans 1:18–32 cannot now be dismissed as scientifically groundless fantasy.)

The second principle, following from the first, was that creeds and dogmas are no more than the epiphenomena of moral and mystical experience, attempts to express religious intuitions verbally in order to induce similar experiences in others. Theological differences between religions, or within a single religion, therefore, can have no ultimate significance. All religion grows out of an intuition, more or less pure and deep, of the same infinite. All religions are climbing the same mountain to the seat of the same transcendent Being. The most that can be said of their differences is that they are going up by different routes, some of which appear less direct and may not reach quite to the top.

If these ideas are accepted, the only question that can be asked when two religions meet is: Which of these is the higher and more perfect specimen of its kind? And this question is to be answered by comparing, not their doctrines, but their piety and the characteristic religious experiences which their piety enshrines. For religions are not the sort of things that are true or false, nor are their doctrines more than their by-products. Nor, indeed, has any existing form of religion more than a relative validity; the best religion yet may still be superseded by a worthier. Accordingly, the only possible justification for Christian missions is that Christians, whose piety and ethics represent the highest in religion that has emerged to date, are bound by the rule of charity to share their possessions with men of other faiths, not in order to displace those faiths, but to enrich them and (doubtless) to be enriched by them. And from this pooling of religious experience a still higher form of religion may well be developed. This position was expounded at the academic level by Troeltsch and on the popular level in such a document as the American laymen's inquiry, *Rethinking Missions* (1931), which Hendrik Kraemer has described as "devoid of real theological sense ... a total distortion of the Christian message," involving "a suicide of missions and an annulment of the Christian faith" (*Religion and the Christian Faith*, 1956, p. 224). (This is just what J. Gresham Machen said when the report came out, but with less acceptance than Kraemer's words command today.)

A Change for the Better

Since 1931, however, the theological atmosphere has changed for the better. The liberal philosophy of religions has been demolished by the broadsides of such writers as Barth, Brunner, and Kraemer himself, and attention is being given once again to the theology of religions found in the Bible.

What is this theology? It can be summed up in the following antithesis: Christianity is a religion of revelation received; all other faiths are religions of revelation denied. This we must briefly explain.

Christianity is a religion of revelation received. It is a religion of faith in a special revelation, given through specific historical events, of salvation for sinners. The object of Christian faith is the Creator's disclosure of himself as triune Savior of his guilty creatures through the mediation of Jesus Christ, the Father's Word and Son. This is a disclosure authoritatively reported and interpreted in the God-inspired pages of Holy Scripture. Faith is trust in the Christ of history who is the Christ of the Bible. The revelation which the Gospel declares and faith receives is God's gracious answer to the question of human sin. Its purpose is to restore guilty rebels to fellowship with their Maker. Faith in Christ is no less God's gift than is the Christ of faith; the faith which receives Christ is created in fallen men by the sovereign work of the Spirit, restoring spiritual sight to their blind minds. Thus true Christian faith is an adoring acknowledgment of the omnipotent mercy of God both in providing a perfect Saviour for hopeless, helpless sinners and in drawing them to him.

Non-Christian religions, however, *are religions of revelation denied.* They are religions which spring from the suppression and distortion of a general revelation given through man's knowledge of God's world concerning the being and law of the Creator. The *locus classicus* on this is Romans 1:18–32; 2:12–15. Paul tells us that "the invisible things" of God—his deity and creative power—are not merely discernible but actually discerned ("God manifested" them; they "are clearly seen," 1:19 f., ERV) by mankind; and this discernment brings knowledge of the obligation of worship and thanksgiving (vv. 20 f.), the duties of the moral law (2:14 f.), God's wrath against ungodliness (1:18), and death as the penalty of sin (1:32). General revelation is adapted only to the needs of man in innocence and answers only the question: What does God require of his rational creatures? It speaks of wrath against sin but not of mercy for sinners. Hence it can bring nothing but disquiet to fallen man. But man prefers not to face it, labors to falsify it, and willfully perverts its truth into the lie of idolatry (1:25) by habitual lawlessness (1:18). Man is a worshiping being who has refused in his pride to worship his Maker; so he turns the light of divine revelation into the darkness of man-made religion, and enslaves himself to unworthy deities of his own devising, made in his own image or that of creatures inferior to himself (1:23). This is the biblical etiology of nonbiblical religion, from the crudest to the most refined.

Flashes of Common Grace

Yet common grace prevents the truth from being utterly suppressed. Flashes of light break through which we should watch for and gratefully recognize (as did Paul at Athens when he quoted Aratus, Acts 17:28), and no part of general revelation is universally obscured. Despite all attempts to smother them, these truths keep seeping through the back of man's mind, creating uneasiness and prompting fresh efforts to blanket the obtrusive light. Hence we may expect to find in all non-Christian religions certain characteristic recurring tensions, never really resolved. These are a restless sense of the hostility of the powers of the universe; an undefined feeling of guilt, and all sorts of merit-making techniques designed to get rid of it; a dread of death, and a consuming anxiety to feel that one has conquered it; forms of worship aimed at once to placate, bribe, and control the gods, and to make them keep their distance except when wanted; an alarming readiness to call moral evil good, and good evil, in the name of religion; an ambivalent attitude of mind which seems both to seek God and to seek to evade him in the same act.

Therefore, in our evangelistic dialogue with non-Christian religions, our task must be to present the biblical revelation of God in Christ not as supplementing them but as explaining their existence, exposing their errors, and judging their inadequacy. We shall measure them exclusively by what they say, or omit to say, about God and man's relation to him. We shall labor to show the real problem of religion to which the Gospel gives the answer, namely, how a sinner may get right with his Maker. We shall diligently look for the hints and fragments of truth which these religions contain, and appeal to them (set in their proper theological perspective) as pointers to the true knowledge of God. And we shall do all this under a sense of compulsion (for Christ has sent us), in love (for non-Christians are our fellow-creatures, and without Christ they cannot be saved), and with all humility (for we are sinners ourselves, and there is nothing, no part of our message, not even our faith, which we have not received). So, with help from on high, we shall both honor God and bear testimony of him before men.

Chapter 30

—

CHARISMATIC RENEWAL: POINTING TO A PERSON AND A POWER

Charismatics strive to realize the ideals of totality in worship, ministry, communication, and community.

One of the top ten questions among evangelicals today is whether one is for or against the charismatic movement. It is a bad, polarizing, party-minded, Corinthian sort of question; I usually parry it by saying I am for the Holy Spirit. But why is it asked so often and so anxiously? Perhaps it is because some evangelicals feel threatened by charismatics, having perceived (they would say) several errors. I wish to report these, modify them, and then zero in on a number of significant insights non-charismatics can profitably gain from charismatics.

First, a word of introduction. The charismatic movement has its Roman Catholic, Eastern Orthodox, and liberal Protestant components, and focuses on celebrating the ministry of the Holy

Spirit. The evangelical movement plays a minority role in most older Protestant bodies, and focuses on a longing to see God's revealed truth reform and renew Christendom. These two movements, charismatic and evangelical, are overlapping circles; many evangelicals define themselves as charismatics; many charismatics define themselves as evangelicals.

Charismatic theology may look loose and naive beside evangelical formulations, sharp-honed as these are by nearly five centuries of controversy. But the two constituencies are plainly at one on such supposedly evangelical distinctives as personal conversion to Christ, lives changed by the Spirit's power, learning about God from God through Scripture, bold expectant prayer, small group mutual ministry, and a love for swinging singing.

Most of what is distinctive in charismatic theology comes from older Pentecostalism, which sprang at the start of this century from the yet older Wesleyan tradition. Though charismatic Christianity treats experience rather than truth as primary and embraces people with many nonevangelical beliefs, it remains evangelicalism's half-sister; this may explain why evangelical reactions to charismatic renewal seem sometimes to smack of sibling rivalry.

Commonly Voiced Concerns

Why do some evangelicals say they feel threatened? They mention the following:

1. *Irrationality in glossolalia.* Charismatics see their tongues as God-given prayer language, perhaps angelic. But to those who would only ever address God intelligibly, and who know from professional linguistic scholars (who are unanimous on this) that glossolalia has no language-character at all, it can seem shockingly silly, self-deceived, and irreverent. Granted, earlier diagnoses of glossolalia as a neurotic, psychotic, hypnotic, or

schizophrenic symptom are not tenable; on the contrary, the evidence reveals glossolalia in most cases both psychologically and spiritually health-giving, so far as man can judge. Yet many still find the thought of making nonsense-noises to God deeply disturbing, and are unnerved by people who are exuberantly sure that this is what God wants them to do.

2. *Elitism in attitudes.* Charismatics see their kind of communal spirituality as God's current renewal formula, and themselves as his trailblazers in this. Hence, they naturally talk big about the significance of their movement, and easily leave impressions of naive and aggressive arrogance as if they thought only charismatics matter, and none really count for God who do not join their ranks. The old Oxford Group had a similar self-image, and left similar impressions.

3. *Judgmentalism in theology.* Protestant charismatics (Catholics less so) tend to theologize their experience as man-centered in terms of recovering primitive standards of Christian experience through seeking and finding what was always available but what earlier generations lacked faith to claim, namely, Spirit-baptism and sign-gifts (tongues; interpretation; miracles; healing; and as charismatics believe, prophecy also). This Arminian "restorationism," the equivalent in spirituality to Anabaptist ecclesiology, implies that noncharismatics are substandard Christians, and that the only reason why any lack charismatic experience is that either through ignorance or unwillingness they have not sought it. Such beliefs, however gently and charitably stated, are inescapably threatening.

4. *Disruptiveness in ministry.* The charismatic movement often invades churches in the form of a reaction (sometimes justified) against formalism, intellectualism, and institutionalism, in favor of a free-wheeling experientialism. Such a swing of the pendulum is bound both to win converts and produce division;

frustration-fed reactions always do. Many churches have split because charismatics have either hived off or, in effect, have driven others out—in both cases with an apparently good conscience. Other churches contain charismatic cliques who keep a low profile but constantly scheme to move things their way. Pastors in particular naturally feel threatened.

Evaluating These Concerns

Judgmentalism evokes judgmentalism; many Christians, evangelicals and others, have written off the charismatic movement entirely as a delusive and perhaps demonic distraction. But inasmuch as it produces conversions, teaches people to love Christ, the Bible, and their neighbors, and frees them up for worship and witness, demonic delusion cannot be the whole story. A more discerning estimate is required.

Charismatic "restorationism" (a restoring of first-century experiences) is certainly doubtful. There is no way to establish the disciples' Spirit-baptism at Pentecost as a normative experience for all later believers. Indeed, quite apart from the fact that as an experience we know very little about it, its dispensational uniqueness rules that out. Nine o'clock on Pentecost morning was the singular, unrepeatable moment when the promised Spirit first began his new covenant ministry of communicating communion with the glorified Christ. Since that moment all Christians have enjoyed this ministry from conversion on (Acts 2:38–39: Rom. 8:9–11: 1 Cor. 12:12–13). Because the disciples became believers before Pentecost, their experience had to be "two-stage" in a way no later Christian's can ever be.

Moreover, though the subsequent experience of those who testify to having received Spirit-baptism may be far richer than it was before, it does not seem significantly to differ from that of devoted people who have not known this "second blessing."

Contrary claims at this point simply force the question: Who is kidding whom?

Nor is there any way to make good the claim that the sign-gifts that authenticated the apostles (Rom. 15:19; 2 Cor. 12:12; Heb. 2:3f.) are now restored. The nature of those gifts is in many respects uncertain, and must remain so. We cannot be sure that charismatic phenomena fully correspond to them. For instance, charismatics commend private glossolalic prayer, but New Testament tongues are signs for use in public; charismatics who claim healing gifts have a spottier success record than did Christ and the apostles; and so on.

Yet one can doubt restorationism (which in any case is not approved doctrine among Roman Catholic and German Protestant charismatics) and still rejoice in the real enrichment that charismatics have found in seeking the Lord. Their call to expectant faith in the God who still on occasion heals supernaturally and does wonders can be gratefully heard, and their challenge to seek radical personal renewal can be humbly received without accepting all their theology. We should be glad that our God does not hide his face from those who seek him—neither from charismatics nor noncharismatics—until their theology is correct. Where would any of us be if he did? And we should not refuse to learn lessons from charismatics while contesting some of their opinions.

In passing, I urge that a better way to theologize what is called or miscalled Spirit-baptism is as an intensifying of the Spirit's constant witness to our adoption and inheritance (Rom. 8:15–17), a deepening of the communion with Father and Son of which Christ spoke (John 14:21–23), an increase of what Paul prayed the Ephesians might enjoy (Eph. 3:15–19), and a renewing of that unspeakable joy in Christ (1 Peter 1:8) of which the Puritan John Owen wrote: "There is no account to be given, but that the Spirit worketh it when and how he will; he secretly infuseth and distills it into the soul, filling it with gladness, exultations, and sometimes with unspeakable raptures of mind."

Vivid awareness of the divine love seems always to be the essence of the experience, whatever its adjuncts, as it has been also of countless comparable experiences. These have included sealing with the Spirit among the Puritans, entire sanctification among the Wesleyans, the noncharismatic Spirit-baptism of Finney, Moody, and Torrey, the Keswick experience of consecration and filling with the Spirit, the mystics' "second conversion," and other meetings with God to which no such brand name has been given. I propose the same theological account of God's work in all such experiences as being biblically viable and fitting the facts.

Charismatic Contributions

Despite some unhappy theology, the charismatic movement overall bears marks of genuine spiritual renewal, and though it or sections of it may have lessons to learn in doctrine, it has its own lessons to teach concerning practice.

Doubtless they are not unique, and could be learned elsewhere. But when God has brought new life to so many along charismatic channels, it would be perverse conceit on the part of noncharismatics to be unwilling to look and learn.

The charismatic movement, like the evangelical movement, is a fairly self-sufficent, transdenominational, international network, with its own established behavior patterns, literary resources, and leadership. How far to identify with all this, or with what one's local charismatic community is doing, is something that each individual must decide for himself. But it seems to me Christians can learn more about the meaning of ideals to which lip service is too easily given.

First Ideal: Total Worship

The charismatic conviction is that worshiping God should be a personal realizing of fellowship with the Father and the Son through the Spirit, and therewith—indeed, thereby—a realizing of spiritual oneness with the rest of God's assembled family. Liturgical structures therefore must be loose enough to allow for spontaneous contributions and ad libs, and relaxed, informal, and slow-moving enough to let all bask in the feeling of togetherness with God and with each other. In pace, in cultivated warmth, and in its way of highlighting points by repetition, charismatic worship is to historic liturgy as Wagner and Bruckner are to Mozart and Haydn: romantic, that is, in the sense of directly expressing attitudes and feelings rather than classical, focusing on excellence of form. The aim is total involvement of each worshiper, leading to total openness to God at the deepest level of one's being. To achieve this, charismatics insist, time must be taken; their worship meetings thus may be two or three hours long.

What does this say about the brisk, stylized 60-minute canter—clergy, and choir pulling along a passive congregation—which is the worship diet of so many Christians on so many Lord's Days? All would no doubt protest that total worship was their aim, too—but are all as realistic and perceptive as charismatics in seeing what this involves? Charismatic practice, however childish and zany it may seem on the surface, convicts the restrained, formal behavior in church that passes for reverence of not being the most vivid, lively, and potent way of communicating the reality of God. Let all consider how "atmospheric communication" can best be effected.

Second Ideal: Total Ministry

It was Paul and Peter who first affirmed that every Christian has a gift or gifts for use in the church (Rom. 12:4–6; 1 Cor. 12:4–7; Eph. 4:7,

11, 16; 1 Peter 4:10.). Thus, the charismatics insist (making a point that is distinct from their hazardous claim that sign-gifts are back) that every-member ministry, achieved by discerning and harnessing each Christian's ordinary gifts, should be standard practice in the body of Christ. Congregational behavior patterns must be flexible and decentralized enough to permit this.

There's the rub! Every-member ministry is an ecumenical shibboleth as well as a charismatic slogan these days, and few hesitate to mouth it. But are all as practical as charismatics in devising new structures and reshaping old ones so as to make it happen? No. In many churches the complaint is heard that the talents of gifted people lie unused, and obvious needs in personal and neighborhood ministry go unmet because the pastor insists on being a one-man band and will not treat his flock as a ministering team. Some members of the team do some things better than he. Yet charismatics as a body are past this blockage point in a way that radically challenges all who are not.

Third Ideal: Total Communication

Charismatic singing (both from books and "in the Spirit"), clapping, arm-raising and hand-stretching, the glossolalia ritual of lead-passing from one followed by interpretation from another, delivery of prophecies from God to the group, loose and improvisatory preaching and corporate dialogue with the preacher by interjection and response, are features that impress different people differently; but none, can fault the purpose it serves: to make all that God's people do together deepen, and share sense of God's presence and power and openness to his leading at all points. When this is achieved in any measure, you have what Walter J. Hollenweger calls "atmospheric communication," an established revival phenomenon.

Without advocating the practices mentioned or any technique of "working up" meetings (for manufactured excitement never communicates God), I urge that the charismatic purpose is right.

Fourth Ideal: Total Community

Community or fellowship, which means having Christ in common and sharing what we have from him, is a quality of Christian relationships that charismatics seek to maximize. Their distinction is that they share well, giving both themselves and their substance generously, sometimes recklessly, to help others. In their prayer groups, their discipling relationships, and their experiments in communal living, the strength of their desire to serve in love, whether wisely expressed or not, puts others to shame, while the vividness of their vision of each church—the whole church, as a great extended family, is magnificent.

Again, the question that arises is not whether all should imitate the particular things they do, but whether their example does not expose half-heartedness in others who say they want community but settle for locked-up lives and never squander themselves in love. If it does, what steps will those others now take in the matter?

We have seen that some Protestants are hostile to the charismatic movement because they disagree with some strands of its teaching, or because they feel it threatens them. Others, we know, patronize it as involving illusions that some people need which, therefore, should not be resisted, only ignored. These responses seem inadequate. The movement is forcing all Christendom to ask what it means to be a Christian, and to be Spirit-filled. It is bringing into recognizably evangelical experience people whose ears were closed to evangelical witness as such. As "egghead" radical theology invites the church into the wilderness of a new

Unitarianism, is it not (dare I say) just like God to have raised up against it not a new Calvin or Owen, but a scratch movement that proclaims the deity and potency of the Son and the Spirit—not by great theological acumen or accuracy, but by the evidence of renewed lives and lifestyle? A movement which by its very existence reminds both the world and the church that Christianity in essence is not words but a Person and a power? Surely we see divine strategy here.

But whether or not I am right to think this is how Christians of tomorrow will see the charismatic renewal of today, I am sure we shall all do well to try and learn the lessons spelled out here.

Chapter 31

WALKING TO EMMAUS WITH
THE GREAT PHYSICIAN

*The perplexity of God-given hopes seemingly wrecked by God-
ordained circumstances is a reality for many Christians.*

O n Friday afternoon they took him down from the cross, as
dead as a man can be. On Sunday afternoon he walked most
of the seven miles from Jerusalem to Emmaus with two of his
disciples. He had broken through the death barrier, and was alive
and well once more on planet Earth. For 40 days before with-
drawing to the glory where now he lives and reigns he appeared
to those who had been his followers and friends. Why? Because
he loved them, and wanted them to have the joy of seeing him
alive; because he had to explain to them his saving achievement and their role as witnesses to him; and, last but not least,
because some of them were in emotional and spiritual distress,
and needed the therapy that was uniquely his. All this is reflected
in the Emmaus Road story (Luke 24:13–35).

Who were the patients to whom the Great Physician minis-tered there? One was Cleopas (v. 18). The other, not named by Luke, lived with Cleopas, and it is natural to guess (though not possible to prove) that it was Mary, wife of "Clopas" (John 19:25) and mother of James (Mark 15:14), who was at the cross when Jesus died. (In that case, Cleopas was Alphaeus, James's father.) I shall assume that it was husband and wife trudging home that day. They went slowly; most people do on a long walk, and they were sharing perplexity and pain at Jesus' death. Their spirits were very low. They thought they had lost their beloved Master for-ever; they felt that the bottom had fallen out of their world. They were in the shock of a bereavement experience, and hurting badly.

Now picture the scene. Up from behind comes a stranger, walking faster, and falls into step beside them. Naturally they stop discussing their private misery, and there is silence. When we know that grief is written all over our faces we avoid look-ing at other people because we do not want anyone to look at us, and I imagine this couple swiveling their heads and never facing their traveling companion at all. Certainly, "their eyes were kept from recognizing him" (v. 16),[1] so that had anyone asked them, "Is Jesus with you?" the reply would have been. "Don't be silly, he's dead, we've lost him, we hoped he was the one to redeem Israel but clearly he wasn't; we shan't see him again—and noth-ing makes sense any more."

Stop! look! listen! Here is a perfect instance of a kind of spir-itual perplexity which (I dare to affirm) every child of God expe-riences sooner or later. Be warned: it can be appallingly painful, and if you are not prepared to meet it, it can embitter you, maim you emotionally, and to a great extent destroy you—which, be it

---

[1] Unless otherwise noted, Scripture quotations in this article are from the Revised Standard Version.

said, is Satan's goal in it, every time. What happens is that you find yourself feeling that God plays cat and mouse with you. Having lifted you up by giving you hope, he now throws you down by destroying it. What he gave you to lean on he suddenly takes away, and down you go. Your feelings say that he is playing games with you: that he must be a heartless, malicious ogre after all. So you feel broken in pieces, and no wonder.

Examples are easy to find. Here is a Christian worker, maybe a lay person, maybe a minister, who takes on a task (pastoring a church, leading a class, starting a new work, or whatever) confident that God has called, and who expects therefore to see blessing and fruit. But all that comes is disappointment and frustration. Things go wrong, people act perversely, opposition grows, one is let down by one's colleagues, the field of ministry becomes a disaster area. Or, here are a couple who marry in the Lord to serve him together, who dedicate their home, wealth, and in due course children to him, and yet find nothing but trouble—health trouble, money trouble, trouble with relatives and in-laws, and maybe (the bitterest thing of all), trouble with their own offspring. What hurts Christian parents more than seeing the children whom they tried to raise for God say no to Christianity? But do not say that these things never happen to truly faithful folk; you know perfectly well they do. And when they do, the pain is increased by the feeling that God has turned against you, and is actively destroying the hopes that he himself once gave you.

Some 30 years ago a clergyman's daughter was attracted to a young man. She was a Christian; he was not. She did as Christian girls should do at such times: she held back and prayed. He was converted, and they married. Soon the man, who was quite a prosperous farmer, felt called to sell out and train for the pastorate. Hardly had his ministry begun, however, when he died painfully of cancer, leaving his widow with a small son and no money. Today she has a ministry to individuals which, without that experience, she never would have had; yet over and over she has had to fight feelings which say: "God played games with me; he gave me hopes and dashed them; he's cruel; he's vile." I expect she will be fighting that battle till she dies. These things happen, and they hurt.

See it in Scripture. Teen-ager Joseph, youngest in the family, is given dreams of being head of the clan. Furious, his brothers sell him into slavery to make sure it never happens. Joseph is doing well in Egypt as right-hand man of a leading soldier-politician. The lady of the house, perhaps feeling neglected by her husband as wives of soldiers and politicians sometimes do, wants to take Joseph to bed with her. Joseph says no, and this put-down from a mere slave turns the lady's lust to hate (never a hard transition) so that she lies about him, and suddenly he finds himself languishing in prison, discredited and forgotten. There he stays for some years, a model convict we are told, but with no prospects and with nothing to think about save the dreams of greatness that God once gave him. "Until what [God] had said came to pass, the word of the LORD tested him" (Ps. 105:19). "Tested him"—yes, and how! Can we doubt that Joseph in prison had constantly to fight the feeling that the God who gave him hopes was now hard at work destroying them? Can we suppose that he found it easy to trust God and stay calm and sweet?

The heartbreaking perplexity of God-given hopes apparently wrecked by God-ordained circumstances is a reality for many Christians today, and will be the experience of more tomorrow—just as it was for Joseph, and for the Emmaus disciples. Back to their story, now, to watch the Great Physician at work with them.

Good physicians show their quality first by skill in diagnosis. They do not just palliate symptoms, but go to the root of the trouble and deal with that. What did Jesus see as the root cause of this couple's distress? His dealing with them shows that his diagnosis was of *unbelief*, caused by two things.

First, they were *too upset*—too upset, that is, to think straight. It was beyond them to put two and two together. They had slid down the slippery slope from disappointment to distress, through distress to despair, and through despair into what we call depression, that commonest of twentieth-century diseases, for which one in every four North Americans has to be treated medically at some point in life. If you have ever experienced depression, or sought to help its victims, you will know that folk in depression are marvelously resourceful in finding reasons for not taking comfort, encouragement, or hope from anything you say to them. They know you mean well, but they defy your efforts; they twist everything into further reasons why they should be gloomy and hopeless ("it's all right for you, but it's different for me," and so on). They are resolved to hear everything as bad news. That is exactly what we find here in Cleopas's narrative concerning the empty tomb. (It has to be Cleopas at this point; Mary would not be talking to a strange man, and the story is told in a very male manner.)

"It is now the third day since this happened," says Cleopas. "Moreover, some women of our company amazed us. They were at the tomb early in the morning and did not find his body; and they came back saying that they had even seen a vision of angels, who said that he was alive. Some of those who were with us went to the tomb, and [surprise! surprise!] found it just as the women had said; but him they did not see" (vv. 22–24). (Implication: there's nothing in this wild talk of him being alive; someone must have desecrated the tomb and stolen the body, so as to deny it decent burial.) Thus Cleopas announces the empty tomb as more bad news.

Yet over and over before his passion Jesus had foretold not only his death but his rising on the third day (Luke 9:22; 18:33; Matt. 16:21; 17:23; 20:19). Straight thinking about the empty tomb, in the light of these predictions, would have made their hearts leap. "He said he would rise; now the tomb's empty; he's done it, he's done it, he's done it!" But both were too upset to think straight.

This was due to the root cause of their unbelief, which Jesus also diagnosed, namely the fact that they were *too ignorant*—too ignorant, that is, of Scripture. "O foolish ones"—Jesus' tone is compassionate, not contemptuous: "O you dear silly souls" would get the nuance—"and slow of heart to believe all that the prophets have spoken! Was it not necessary that the Christ should suffer these things and enter into his glory?" (vv. 25–26). Jesus spent maybe two hours showing them from Scripture (memorized) that it was in fact necessary. That shows how he saw their fundamental need.

As ignorance of Scripture was the basic trouble on the Emmaus Road, so it often is with us. Christians who do not know their Bible get needlessly perplexed and hurt because they do not know how to make scriptural sense of what happens to them. These two disciples could not make sense of Jesus' cross. Many do not know the Bible well enough to make sense of their own cross. The result is a degree of bewilderment and consequent distress that might have been avoided.

Diagnosing them thus, Jesus did three things to heal this couple's souls. First, he did what all counselors must do: he *asked questions*, got them to talk, established a relationship, and so made them receptive to what he had to say. His opening gambit ("Tell me, what were you talking about?" v. 17) drew from Cleopas only rudeness ("Don't tell me you don't know!" v. 18). Hurting folk often act that way, externalizing their misery by biting your head off. But Jesus was unruffled; he knew what was going on inside Cleopas, and persisted with his question ("Do I know? You tell me, anyway; let me hear it from your own lips"). Had they declined to share their trouble, Jesus could not have helped them. But when they poured out their hearts to him, healing began.

Then, second, Jesus *explained Scripture*—"opened" it, to use their word (v. 32)—as it bore on their perplexity and pain. He showed them that what had been puzzling them, the death of the one they thought would redeem them in the sense of ending the Roman occupation, had actually been prophesied centuries before as God's way of redeeming in the sense of ending the burden and bondage of sin. He must have gone over Isaiah 53, where the servant who dies for sins in verses 1–9 appears alive, triumphant, and reigning in verses 10–12; he produced many passages which pictured God's Messiah traveling to the crown via the cross, and kept them in a state of dawning comprehension and mounting excitement (their hearts "burned," v. 32) till they reached home. Thus healing proceeded.

The principle here is that the most healing thing in the world to a troubled soul is to find that the heartbreak which produces feelings of isolation, hopelessness, and hatred of all cheerful cackle is actually dealt with in the Bible, and in a way that shows it making sense after all in terms of a loving, divine purpose. And you can be quite certain that the Bible, God's handbook for living, has something to say about every life problem involving God's ways that we shall ever meet. So if you are hurting because of what you feel God has done to you, and you do not find Scripture speaking to your condition, it is not that the Bible now fails you but only that, like these disciples, you do not know it well enough. Ask wiser Christians to open Scripture to you in relation to your pain, and I guarantee that you will find that to be so. (To borrow a phrase from Ellery Queen—challenge to the reader!)

Finally, Jesus *revealed his presence*. "Stay with us," they had said to him on reaching Emmaus. (What a blessing for them that they were given to hospitality! What they would have missed had they not been!) At the table they asked him to give thanks, and as he did so and gave them bread "their eyes were opened and they recognized him" (v. 31). Whether recognition was triggered by seeing nail prints in his hands, or by remembering the identical voice and action at the feeding of the five thousand or four thousand, as some have wondered, we do not know; nor does it matter. Now, as then, Jesus' ways of making his presence known are mysteries of divine illumination about which you can rarely say more than that as something was said, seen, read, or remembered—it happened. So it was here; and thus healing was completed.

To be sure, the moment they recognized him he vanished. Yet plainly they knew that he was with them still. Otherwise, would they have risen from the table in their weariness and hurried back to Jerusalem through the night to share their news? Sensible Palestinians did not walk lonely country roads at night, fearing thugs and muggers (that was why Cleopas and Mary urged the stranger to stay with them in the first place). But it is evident that they counted on their Lord's protecting presence as they went about his business. "Stay with us," they had said, and inwardly they knew he was doing just that. Thus their broken hearts were mended, and their sorrow replaced by joy.

Jesus Christ, our risen Lord, is the same today as yesterday, and it belongs to true Easter faith to take to our own hurts the healing of the Emmaus Road. How? First, by telling Jesus our trouble, as he invites us to do each day. He remains a good listener, with what the hymn calls "a fellow-feeling for our pains"; and only as we lay aside prayerless resentment and self-pity and open our hearts to him will we know his help. Second, by letting him minister to us from Scripture, relating that which gives us pain to God's purpose of saving love: this will regularly mean looking to the Lord's human agents in ministry, as well as private Bible study. Third, by asking him to assure us that as we go through what feels like fire and floods he goes with us, and will stay with us till the road ends. That prayer he will always answer.

"We do not have a high priest who is unable to sympathize with our weaknesses, but we have one who has been tempted in every way, just as we are—yet was without sin. Let us then approach the throne of grace with confidence, so that we may receive mercy and find grace to help us in our time of need" (Heb. 4:15–16, NIV). So wrote an apostolic man long ago to ill-treated, distracted, and depressed believers. The Emmaus Road story urges us to do as he says—and it also shows us how.

———

Chapter 32

POOR HEALTH MAY BE
THE BEST REMEDY

But if you've got a headache, thank God for aspirin.

B ad health—that is, bodily malfunctioning and pain, until lowered efficiency, tending towards death—has been a fact of life since the Fall. Had there been no sin, there would have been no sickness. As it is, however, both are universal, the latter being a penal result of the former. So, at least, implies Scripture. So, too, did yesterday's Christians view the matter, and therefore they did not find bad health and chronic discomforts an obstacle to faith in God's goodness. Rather, they expected illness, and they endured it as they looked forward to the health of heaven.

But today, dazzled by the marvels of modern medicine, the Western world dreams of abolishing ill health entirely, here and now. We have grown health conscious in a way that is itself rather sick, and certainly has no precedent—not even in ancient Sparta.

Why do we diet and jog and do all the other health-raising and health-sustaining things so passionately? Why are we so absorbed in pursuing bodily health? We are chasing a dream, the dream of never having to be ill. We are coming to regard a pain-free, disability-free existence as one of man's natural rights.

It is no wonder, then, that Christians nowadays are so interested in divine healing. As Christians, they long for the touch of God, as direct and powerful as possible, on their lives (and so they should). As modern men, they are preoccupied with physical health, to which they feel they have a right. (How much there is of worldliness in this preoccupation is a question worth asking, but it is not one with which we will deal here.) With these two concerns meeting in Christian minds, it was predictable that today many would arise to claim that all sick believers may find bodily healing through faith, whether through doctors or apart from them. And exactly that has happened. A cynic would say the wish has been father to the thought.

But is that fair? That it was natural for this teaching to emerge in our times does not make it either true or false. It presents itself as a rediscovery of what the church once knew, and never should have forgotten, about the power of faith to channel the power of Christ. It claims to be biblical, and we must take that claim seriously.

To support itself from Scripture, this teaching uses three main arguments.

First, Jesus Christ, who healed so abundantly in the days of his flesh, has not changed. He has not lost his power; whatever he did then he can do now.

Second, salvation in Scripture is a wholistic reality, embracing both soul and body. Thoughts of salvation for the soul only without, or apart from, the body are unbiblical.

Third, blessing is missed where faith is lacking, and where God's gifts are not sought and expected. "You do not have, because you do not ask," says James. "Ask and it will be given you," says Jesus. But, Matthew tells us, in Nazareth, where Jesus was brought up, he could not do many mighty works because of their unbelief.

All of this is true. So, then, does Jesus still heal miraculously? Yes, I think that on occasion he does. I hold no brief for blanket denials of healing miracles today. I believe I have known one such case—not more than one, but equally, not less. There is much contemporary evidence of healing events in faith contexts that have baffled the doctors. B. B. Warfield, whose wife was an invalid throughout their marriage, testily denied that supernatural healing ever occurs today. But I think he was wrong.

What is being claimed, however, is that healing through prayer, plus perhaps the ministrations of someone with a healing gift, is always available for all sick believers, and that if Christian invalids fail to find it, something is thereby shown to be lacking in their faith.

It is here that I gently but firmly demur. This reasoning is wrong—cruelly and destructively wrong—as anyone who has sought miraculous healing on this basis and failed to find it, or who has been called on to pick up the pieces in the lives of others who have had such an experience, knows all too well. To be told that longed-for healing was denied you because of some defect in your faith when you had labored and strained every way you knew to devote yourself to God and to "believe for blessing," is to be pitchforked into distress, despair, and a sense of abandonment by God. That is as bitter a feeling as any this side of hell—particularly if, like most invalids, your sensitivity is already up and your spirits down. Nor does Scripture ever require or permit us to break anyone in pieces with words (Job's phrase: it fits) in this way.

What, then, of those three arguments? Look at them again; there is more to be said about each one.

It is true: Christ's power is still what it was. *However*, we must remember that the healings he performed when he was on earth had a special significance. Besides being works of mercy, they were signs of his messianic identity. This comes out in the message he sent to John the Baptist: "Go and tell John what you hear and see ... blessed is he who takes no offense at me."[1] In other words, let John match up my miracles with what God promised for the day of salvation (see Isa. 35:5ff.). He should be left in no doubt that I am the Messiah, whatever there is about me that he does not yet understand.

Anyone today who asks for miracles as an aid to faith should be referred to this passage (Matt. 11:2–6) and told that if he will not believe in face of the miracles recorded in the Gospels, then he would not believe if he saw a miracle in his own back yard. Jesus' miracles are decisive evidence for all time of who he is and what power he has.

But in that case, supernatural healings in equal abundance to those worked in the days of Jesus' flesh may not be his will today. The question concerns not his power but his purpose. We cannot guarantee that, because he was pleased to heal all the sick brought to him then, he will act in the same way now.

Again it is true: salvation embraces both body and soul. And there is indeed, as some put it, healing for the body in the Atonement. *But*, we must observe that perfect physical health is promised, not for this life, but for heaven, as part of the resurrection glory that awaits us in the day when Christ "will change our lowly body to be like his glorious body, by the power which enables him even to subject all things to himself" (Phil 3:21). Full

---

[1] Scripture quotations in this article are from the Revised Standard Version.

bodily well-being is set forth as a future blessing of salvation rather than a present one. What God has promised, and when he will give it, are separate questions.

Further, it is true that blessing is missed where faith is lacking. *But*, even in New Testament times, among leaders who cannot be accused of lacking faith, healing was never universal. We know from Acts that the apostle Paul was sometimes Christ's agent in miraculous healing, and he was himself once miraculously healed of snakebite. Yet he advises Timothy to "use a little wine for the sake of your stomach and your frequent ailments," and informs him that he left Trophimus "ill at Miletus." He also tells the Philippians how their messenger Epaphroditus was so sick that he "nearly died for the work of Christ," and how grieved Paul himself had been at the prospect of losing him. Plainly, had Paul, or anyone else, sought power to heal these cases miraculously, he would have been disappointed.

Moreover, Paul himself lived with "a thorn in the flesh" that went unhealed. In 2 Corinthians 12:7–9, he tells us that in three solemn seasons of prayer he had asked Christ, the Lord and the Healer, to make it go away. But the hoped-for healing did not occur. The passage merits close attention.

"Thorn" pictures a source of pain, and "flesh" locates it in Paul's physical or psychological system, thus ruling out the idea that he might be referring to an awkward colleague. But beyond this, Paul is unspecific, and probably deliberately. Guesses about his thorn range from recurring painful illnesses, such as inflamed eyes (see Gal. 4:13–15), migraine, or malaria, to chronic shameful temptation. The former view seems more natural, but nobody can be sure. All we can say is that it was a distressing disability from which, had Christ so willed, he could have delivered Paul on the spot.

So Paul lived with pain. And the thorn, given him under God's providence, operated as "a messenger of Satan, to harass me," because it tempted him to think hard thoughts about the God who let him suffer, and in resentment to cut back his ministry. How could he be expected to go on traveling, preaching, working day and night, praying, caring, weeping over folk with this pain constantly dragging him down? He had to contend with such "flaming darts of the evil one" all the time, for the thorn remained unhealed.

Some Christians today live with epilepsy, homosexual cravings, ulcers, and cyclical depressions that plunge them into no less deep waters. Indeed, Philip Hughes is surely correct when he writes: "Is there a single servant of Christ who cannot point to some 'thorn in the flesh,' visible or private, physical or psychological, from which he has prayed to be released, but which has been given him by God to keep him humble, and therefore fruitful? ... Paul's 'thorn in the flesh' is, by its very lack of definition, a type of every Christian's 'thorn in the flesh.' "

Paul perceived, however, that the thorn was given him, not for punishment, but for protection. Physical weakness guarded him against spiritual sickness. The worst diseases are those of the spirit; pride, conceit, arrogance, bitterness, self-confidence are far worse, and they damage us far more than any malfunctioning of our bodies. The thorn was a prophylactic against pride, says Paul, "to keep me from being too elated by the abundance of revelations." Seeing that was so, he could accept it as a wise provision on the part of his Lord.

It was not for want of prayer, then, that the thorn went unhealed. Paul tells the Corinthians what came through from Christ as he prayed about it. "He said to me, 'My grace is sufficient for you, for my power is made perfect in weakness.' " It was as if to say, I can use my power better than by making your trouble go. It is better for you, Paul, and for my glory in your life, that I do something else instead: that I show my strength by keeping you going though the thorn remains.

So Paul embraced his continuing disability as a kind of privilege. "I will all the more gladly boast of my weaknesses, that the power of Christ may rest upon me." The Corinthians, in typical Greek fashion, already despised him as a weakling. They did not consider him an elegant speaker or an impressive personality. I am weaker than you thought, says Paul, for I live with my thorn in the flesh. But I have learned to glory in my weakness, "for when I am weak, then I am strong." Now you Corinthians learn to praise God for my weakness, too!

One virtuous commentary doubts whether the thorn can have been illness in view of Paul's "extraordinary stamina" throughout his ministry. How obtuse! Extraordinary stamina was precisely what Paul was promised. Similarly obtuse was the reviewer who described Joni Eareckson's books as a testimony to "human courage." The age of miraculous blessing is not past, thank God, though such blessing does not always take the form of healing. But then, neither did it in Paul's day.

Three conclusions issue from what we have seen.

The first concerns *miraculous healing*. Christ and the apostles only healed miraculously when they were specifically prompted to do so, so that they knew that to attempt to heal was the Father's will. That is why all the attempted healings recorded in the New Testament succeeded. As we noted, miraculous healing for Christians was not universal even then, so there is no warrant for maintaining that it should be so now.

The second conclusion concerns *sanctifying providence*. God uses chronic pain and weakness, along with other sorts of affliction, as his chisel for sculpting our souls. Felt weakness deepens dependence on Christ for strength each day. The weaker we feel, the harder we lean. And the harder we lean, the stronger we grow spiritually, even while our bodies waste away. To live with your complaint uncomplainingly, being kept sweet, patient, and free in heart to love and help others, even though every day you feel less than good, is true sanctification. It is true healing for the spirit. It is a supreme victory of grace in your life.

The third conclusion concerns *behavior when ill.* We should certainly go to the doctor, and use medication, and thank God for both. But equally certainly we should go to the Lord (Doctor Jesus, as some call him) and ask what message of challenge, rebuke, or encouragement he might have for us regarding our sickness. Maybe we shall receive healing in the form in which Paul asked for it. Maybe, however, we shall receive it in the form in which Paul was given it. We have to be open to either.

I thank God that I have known almost 40 years of excellent health, and I feel well as I write this. But it will not always be that way. My body is wearing out; Ecclesiastes 12, if nothing worse, awaits me. May I be given grace to recall, and apply to myself, the things I have written here when my own day of felt weakness comes, whether in the form of pain, paralysis, prostration, or whatever. And may the same blessing be yours in your hour of need, too—"under the Protection," as Charles Williams used to say.

Chapter 33

HOW TO RECOGNIZE A CHRISTIAN CITIZEN

To try to improve society is not worldliness but love. To wash one's hands of society is not love but worldliness.

I t is a paradox of the Christian life that the more profoundly one is concerned about heaven, the more deeply one cares about God's will being done on Earth. The Christians who show most passion to serve others in this world are regularly those with the strongest hold on the other-worldly realities. This has always been true, whether we look at ministers, missionaries, statesmen, reformers, industrialists, physicians, men of wealth and power, or ordinary layfolk.

Service to others, as an expression of love to them, is a Christian priority. But citizenship is a form of service, as most Christians have seen from the start. Despite the Marxist claim that religion anesthetizes one to the needs of Earth, we instead find that, other things being equal, those whose citizenship is in heaven (I echo Paul's phrase in Phil. 3:20) make the best citizens of any state, democratic or totalitarian, Christian or pagan, secular or even atheist.

The Biblical Basis for Public Activism

In the New Testament, civic obligation is emphatically commanded alongside—indeed, as part of—the obligation to serve God. When Jesus answered the question about taxpaying with the words, "Render to Caesar the things that are Caesar's, and to God the things that are God's" (Mark 12:17),[1] this was not a clever evasion of the issue, but a clear acknowledgement that rendering what is due to the existing political regime is part of the Christian calling. When Peter in one breath says, "Fear God. Honor the Emperor" (1 Peter 2:17), he spotlights the same truth; as does Paul when, in the course of his overview of the life of gratitude for grace that is true Christianity, he teaches the Roman Christians to "be subject to the governing authorities" (Rom. 13:1), and tells them that "for the sake of conscience" they should "pay all of them their dues, taxes to whom taxes are due, revenue to whom revenue is due, respect to whom respect is due, honor to whom honor is due" (vv. 6–7).

Paul speaks of each state official as "God's servant for your good" (v. 4). Note that it is pagan Roman officials, from the emperor down, that he has in view! And he further explains that God instituted the state as such to maintain law, order, justice, and "good." "Good" here evidently embraces protection and well-being, and is thus not far removed from the opportunity to pursue happiness, which the American Constitution enshrines.

Hence, although Christians are not to think of themselves as ever at home in this world but rather as sojourning aliens, travelers passing through a foreign land to the place where their

---

[1] Scripture quotations in this article are from the Revised Standard Version.

treasures are stored awaiting their arrival (see 1 Peter 2:11; Matt. 6:19–20), Scripture forbids them to be indifferent to the benefits that flow from good government. Nor, therefore, should they hesitate to play their part in maximizing these benefits for others, as well as for themselves. The upholding of stable government by a law-abiding life, and helping it to fulfill its role by personal participation where this is possible, is as fitting for us today as it was for Joseph, Moses, David, Solomon, Nehemiah, Mordecai, and Daniel (to look no further). We must see it as service of God and neighbor.

As one Christian member of the European Parliament, Sir Frederick Catherwood, trenchantly put it: "To try to improve society is not worldliness but love. To wash your hands of society is not love but worldliness."

Some Misguided Christian Developments

Here, however, we must note three developments in modern Christendom that have set up perplexing cross currents with regard to political duty. Each requires some discussion before we can go any further.

1. *The politicized intentions of some Christian relativists.* When I speak of Christian "relativists," I have in mind certain Protestants who treat biblical teaching not as God's revealed truth but as man's patchy pointer to God's self-disclosure, couched in culturally relative terms that today's Christians are not bound to use and voicing many sentiments that today's Christians are not bound to endorse.

When I speak of "politicized intentions," I mean that their goals reduce the Christian faith from a pilgrim path to heaven into a socio-political scheme for this present world. This scheme is often referred to as establishing God's kingdom on earth by ending society's collective sins—racism, economic and cultural exploitation, class division, denial of human rights—and setting *shalom* (the Hebrew word for communal well-being under God) in its place.

What is wrong here? Not praying for *shalom*, nor working for it as one has opportunity. Neighbor-love in the global village requires every Christian to do this—and to do it on an international as well as a domestic scale. But it is surely disastrous when Christian faith (our grasp of God's revealed purposes among men) and Christian obedience (our efforts to do God's revealed will) are reduced to and identified with human attempts at social improvement. The heart is cut out of the gospel when Christ is thought of as Redeemer and Lord, Liberator and Humanizer only in relation to particular deprivations and abuses in this world. This, however, has become the standard view of liberals and radicals among the Protestant leadership. It is expressed and reinforced by the World Council of Churches. (The "liberation theology" of Roman Catholic Latin America also embodies and feeds these tendencies, but I shall not discuss that now; Protestant North America is my present concern.)

What has happened, putting the matter bluntly, is that clergymen and clericalized laymen in the mainline Protestant bodies have allowed themselves to reinterpret and redefine their basic religious values as political values. Thus they have secularized Christianity under the guise of applying it to life. In doing so, they have turned it more or less into a leftist ideology, in which even revolutionary violence and guerrilla warfare against lawful governments get baptized into Christ. A flow of semi-technical books expressing this viewpoint, the entrenching of it in liberal seminaries, and the verbal dignifying of it as the discipline of "political theology" have made it respectable. Steady propaganda in its favor from Protestant denominational headquarters now leads many laity to equate the Christian citizen's role with pushing this program everywhere.

The basic mistake in all this is that Christianity's transcendent reference point has been lost sight of. Those who revere Bible teaching as divine truth, who see Jesus in New Testament terms as first and foremost our Savior from sin, delivering us from wrath to come, renewing us in righteousness, and opening heaven to us, and who view evangelism as the basic dimension of neighbor-love, ought to oppose social evils just as vigorously as anybody else. To do that is part of the practical Samaritanship to which all Christians are called—that is, the relieving of need and misery every way one can. But it is all to be done in the service of a Christ whose kingdom is not of this world, and who requires mankind to understand this life, with its joys and riches on the one hand and its hardships and sorrows on the other, as a moral and spiritual training ground, a preparatory discipline for eternity. Lose that perspective, however, as the relativists of whom I am speaking have lost it, and the entire enterprise of neighbor-love goes astray.

2. *The pietistic inhibitions of some Christian absolutists.* "Absolutists," as I here use the word, are either those Protestant, Roman Catholic, or Orthodox who believe that God's unchanging truth is given to the church in Scripture, and that only by obeying this truth can one please God. They may be called Christian conservatives, or even conservationists, by reason of their unwillingness to recast or diminish the historic biblical faith. Among Protestant absolutists, many, perhaps most, would prefer to be called evangelicals, since the gospel (the evangel) of Christ is central to their Christianity.

"Pietistic" points to a concern about achieving holiness, avoiding sin, winning souls, practicing fellowship with Christians, and opposing all the forces of anti-Christianity on the personal level.

Pietistic inhibitions take the form of political passivity and unwillingness to be involved in any level of civil government. Some will vote but not run for office, others will not even vote, and all incline to treat political issues as not directly their busi-ness. Their stance as Christian citizens is thus one of withdrawal from, rather than involvement in, the political process.

Why is this? Several factors seem to operate. One is a reaction against the "social gospel" of the more liberal Protestantism such as was described above, from which evangelical pietists want to dissociate themselves as fully as possible. A second is a faulty inference from their eschatology (i.e., their view of the future), which sees the world as getting inevitably and inexorably worse as Christ's coming draws near, and tells us that nothing can be done about it; therefore it does not matter who is in power politically. A third factor, linked with this, is the stress laid on separation from "the world," with its moral defilements, its compromises of principle, and its earthbound, pleasure-seeking, self-serving way of life. Politics, thought of as a murky milieu where principles are constantly being sacrificed in order to catch votes and keep one's end up in the power game, is seen as an eminently "worldly" business, and so off limits for Christians. A fourth factor, potent though imponderable, is an individualism that resolves all social problems into personal problems, feels that civil government is unimportant since it cannot save souls, and so is fundamentally not interested in the political process at all.

But none of this will do. Whatever mistakes the "social gospel" may enshrine, and however true it is that ministry in the church and in evangelism should be our first concern, there remains a social and political task for Christians to tackle.

Even if the Second Coming is near, we need not think that we cannot under God make this world temporarily a little better if we try, and in any case the fear of not succeeding cannot excuse us from trying when God in effect tells us to make the attempt.

Politics is certainly a power game, but it has to be played if social structures are to be improved, and though it belongs to this world it is a sphere of service to God and men that is not intrinsically "worldly" in the proscribed sense. Moreover, political compromise, the basic maneuver, is quite a different thing from the sacrificing of principles, as we shall see.

Finally, the individualism that destroys political concern is a kind of myopia blurring awareness of the benefit that good government brings and the damage that bad government does (think of Adolf Hitler, Pol Pot, and Idi Amin). No. Pietistic passivity cannot be justified, and its present practitioners need to be educated out of it. This is no more valid a stance for the Christian citizen than was the politicized posture that we rejected above.

3. *The political imperialism of some Christian biblicists.* I have in mind the crusading spirit that currently animates certain members of Bible-loving churches and fellowships. They would call themselves "fundamentalist" rather than evangelical, because they feel that the former word implies more of the uncompromising fighting stance.

Here there is no hesitation in announcing objectives and plunging into the hurly-burly of the political world in order to gain them. Problems arise, however, through the temptation to view the democratic power game as the modern equivalent of holy war in the Old Testament, in which God called upon his people to overthrow the heathen and take their kingdom by force. It is because of this temptation that I spoke of "imperialism" in my heading.

In biblical holy war, the heathen had no rights and received no quarter, for God was using his people as his executioners, the human means of inflicting merited judgment. Viewed as a revelation of God's retributive justice (an aspect of his character that shines throughout the whole Bible), holy war made coherent, if awesome, moral sense. But holy war is no part of God's program for the Christian church. Leave retribution to God, says Paul in

Romans 12:19. And it makes no moral or practical sense at all if taken as a model for Christian action in the political cockpit of a modern pluralistic democracy like the United States, India, or Britain.

In a democracy, you cannot govern except as public opinion backs you and retains you in office. Therefore the quest for consensus, and the practice of persuasion with a view to achieving consensus, is all important. Riding roughshod over others as if they did not count will always have a self-defeating boomerang effect. Pressure groups that seek to grab and use power without winning public support for what they aim at will provoke equally high-handed opposition and will typically be short-lived.

Protestants may well rejoice that Roman Catholicism has now given up its long-standing conviction that error has no rights. Should Protestants themselves now flirt with that discredited principle, however, there will very soon be egg on their own faces. And the danger is constantly present. As Paul Henry has pointed out, "righteous zeal" can be very "detrimental to the practice of politics. For 'true believers' of any stripe are always tempted to become hard-core ideologues seeking to impose their truths on society at large." Christian citizens, who ought to have strong beliefs about communal right and wrong, will always need to be careful here.

Why We Support Democracy

Representative democracy as we know it—in which the legislature, the judiciary, and the executive have separate status, the public information services (media) are not under government control, the elected administration always faces an elected opposition, and popular elections on a one-man, one-vote basis recur at regular intervals—is not the only form of government under which Christian citizens have lived and served God. However, there is no doubt that from a Christian standpoint it is a fitter and wiser form than any other.

The Christian recommendation of democracy rests on two insights.

The first is the awareness that government of the people, by the people, for the people, in an open community system that in principle allows anyone to qualify for any office, best expresses in political terms the God-given dignity and worth of each individual.

The second is the perception that, since in this fallen world, as Lord Acton put it, all power corrupts and absolute power corrupts absolutely, the separation of powers and the building of checks and balances into executive structures will limit the dangers of corruption, even if such procedures for restraint will never eliminate them entirely.

These Christian insights mesh with the worldly wisdom that sees that the more citizens can feel they have shared in making the decisions that now shape their lives, the more resolutely they will adhere to them. The pattern of government, therefore, that maximizes public consent will ordinarily be more stable than any other system.

Making Democracy Work

Christian citizens, then, may be expected to show a firm commitment to the principles of democracy, and to see themselves as bound to do all they can to make democracy work. But that means conscientious commitment to the democratic process as the best way of decision making within the body politic.

In democracies that are philosophically and religiously pluralist, like those of the West, the democratic process that achieves consent out of conflict is vitally important. In this fallen world, conflict arising from limited vision and competing interests is an unavoidable part of the political scene. The intensity and integrity of the public struggle whereby a balance is struck between the contending parties then becomes an index of community health and morale.

The name given to the resolution of political conflict through debate is *compromise*. Whatever may be true in the field of ethics, compromise in politics means not the abandonment of principle, but realistic readiness to settle for what one thinks to be less than ideal when it is all that one can get at the moment. The principle that compromise expresses is that half a loaf is better than no bread.

Give-and-take is the heart of political compromise, as compromise is the heart of politics in a democracy. To see this is a sign of political maturity. By contrast, a doctrinaire rigidity that takes up an adversary position towards all who do not wholly endorse one's views and goals implies political immaturity.

Democratic decision making is as public a process as possible, and officials are expected to publish their reasons for action wherever this can be done without jeopardizing the future. But all major political decisions prove to be both complex in themselves and controversial in the community. This is inescapable for at least three reasons.

First, everyone's knowledge of the facts of every case is partial and selective.

Second, values, priorities, and opinions of the relative importance of long- and short-term results will vary. Think, for instance, of the debates that go on about conserving the environment.

Third, calculations of consequences, particularly unintended and undesired consequences, will vary too, and many actions that seem right to some will seem wrong to others because they predict different consequences. Because executive decisions regularly have unwelcome by-products, they become choices between evils—attempts, that is, to choose the least evil and avoid evils that are greater. Think, for example, of the debate about using large-scale nuclear devices in war.

The Christian citizen must accept that in politics no black-and-white answers are available, but God wills simply that all be led by the highest ideals and ripest wisdom that they can discover. The case of Solomon (1 Kings 3) shows that God's gift to rulers takes the form of wisdom to cope creatively with what comes, rather than ready-made solutions to all problems.

What Should the Christian Citizen Do?

The New Testament does not speak about active political partic-ipation, for the very good reason that this was not an option for first-century believers. The Roman Empire was not a democracy, and many if not most Christians were not Roman citizens. They were a small minority from the lower end of the socio-economic spectrum, and were viewed as eccentric deviants from the older eccentricity of Judaism. They had no political influence, nor any prospect of gaining any. (It took a longer period than the 200 years of American independence before Christians secured even political protection; prior to Constantine, their faith was illegal, and they lived everywhere under spasmodic persecution.)

So the only politically significant things they could do were pay their taxes (Matt. 17:24–27; 22:15–21; Romans 13:6–7), pray for their rulers (1 Tim. 2:1–4), and keep the peace (Rom. 12:18; 1 Thess. 5:13–15).

Present-day representative democracy, however, opens the door to a wider range of political possibilities and thereby requires of us more in the way of responsible commitment than circumstances required in New Testament times.

That commitment may be summarized:

1. All should keep informed; otherwise we cannot judge well about issues, vote well for candidates, or pray well for rulers. Political ignorance is never a Christian virtue.

2. All should pray for those in power, as 1 Timothy 2:1–4 directs. The secret efficacy of prayer, as Scripture reveals it, is enormous.

3. All should vote in elections and referendums, whenever expressions of public opinion are called for. We should be led in our voting by issues rather than personalities, and not by single issues viewed in isolation, but by our vision of total community welfare. This is one way, real if small, in which we may exert influence as the world's salt and light (Matt. 5:13–16).

4. Some should seek political influence, by debating, writing, and working within the political party with which they are in nearest agreement. Clergy should not ordinarily do this, since it will be a barrier to the acceptance of their ministry by people who disagree with their politics. It is, however, very desirable that lay people with political interest should be encouraged to see the gaining and exerting of political influence as a field of Christian service, alongside the fields of church life, worship, and witness, with which they are likely at present to be more familiar.

5. Some should accept a political vocation. Who should do this? Those in whom interest, ability, and opportunity coincide, and on whom no rival career has a stronger claim; those with a vision for improving man's lot globally, advancing international peace, replacing unprincipled discrimination with justice, and furthering public decency; those, finally, who are prepared to work hard, with patience, humility, tolerance, and integrity, fleeing fanaticism, riding rebuffs, and putting the public interest before their own. The Bible histories mentioned earlier show that God wants some of his servants as professional politicians, leading and shaping society well, and the discovery that one is

fitted for the role is a *prima facie* summons from God to go ahead and embrace it.

Let none, however, be starry-eyed at this point: The choice is costly. The political path is rough traveling. The goldfish bowl of public life exposes one constantly to pitiless criticism, and to live there requires resilience and involves major self-sacrifice. As Robert D. Linder and Richard V. Pierard have written:

> "The work is often thankless and discouraging, and it sometimes means psychological strain and heartbreak for those involved in it. The problems are difficult, and, no matter what a politician does, invariably someone will be dissatisfied and complain about it. Every person in the community has the right to criticize the acts of any public official, and the critics have the advantage of hindsight, a privilege denied the decision-maker. ... From a personal standpoint, political endeavor places heavy demand upon one's time, family and financial resources. Many friends will automatically assume that an individual is in politics for some ulterior motive, and they will reveal this by the knowing look or sly remark ..."

Politics is a power game, and the envy, hatred, malice, and self-seeking duplicity, which the power game regularly draws out of the sinful human heart, is too familiar to need comment here. No politician of principle can expect an easy passage, certainly not the Christian.

But who ever thought that the fulfilling of any aspect of Christian vocation would be easy? The words with which Sir Frederick Catherwood ends his book *The Christian Citizen* are worth frequent pondering:

We must be humble and not opinionated. We must be prepared to find that we are sometimes quite wrong and be
able to admit it. We serve our fellow-men because of our
love for a Lord who gave his life for us, a debt which, however well we serve, we can never repay. So whatever we
do, we do it from a sense of duty and because it is right.
We do not, like the cults, claim instant satisfaction. We do
not, like the salesmen, guarantee success. The Christian's
time-span is not mortal. One sows and another reaps. One
labors and another enters into his labors. One day with
God is like a thousand years and a thousand years like one
day. The Christian knows the meaning of patience and
endurance. But he also knows the meaning of action.

This is the right formula for Christian politics, just because it is
the right formula for every single part of the Christian life.

Chapter 34

———

WHAT DO YOU MEAN
WHEN YOU SAY "GOD"?

What does it mean to say "God"? Many today would have to answer this question as Augustine did when asked for a definition of time: "When I am not asked I know very well, but when I am asked I do not know at all!"

The doctrine of God is a confused area in Western theology. Each of its three departments—the divine attributes, the Trinity, and God's relation to the world—is disputed territory. This is basically because agreement is lacking as to how the doctrine should be constructed and defended. Different intellectual methods for doing this naturally produce different theological results.

Hybrids often prove unstable, and the Western heritage of theism is a hybrid. It grew out of the apologetic theology of the early centuries, in which much was made of the thought that Greco-Roman philosophy was a providential preparation for the gospel.

This theism, which found its fullest statement when Thomas Aquinas formulated it in Aristotelian terms, was a blend of reasoning from philosophy and the Bible, the former appearing to provide the frame into which the latter has to fit. But that changed with the Kuyperian, Barthian, and neo-Lutheran movements of this century. Each of these, in its own way, drew on Luther's and Calvin's criticisms of natural theology. But they pushed Luther's and Calvin's arguments to the point where it seemed that any appeal to reason to support or confirm scriptural revelation would be out of place. As a result, some aspects of theism in its traditional form have become widely suspect among mainstream theologians.

This means that when facing challenges to theism, Protestant theologians have not always known what to say. They have sometimes been tempted to take up panicky and defeatist slogans like that fathered by the late John Robinson: "Our image of God must go." But that is not the way of wisdom. Certainly some rethinking is called for, but it is minor modification, not abandonment of traditional theism, that we need.

The Anatomy of Theism

It will help us to review the ingredients that make up historic Christian theism. Here is a check list of the usual items, expressed in as simple a way as the thoughts allow.

1. *God is personal and triune.* God is as truly three personal centers in a relationship of mutual love as he is a single personal deity. God is always Three-in-One and One-in-Three, and in all divine acts all three persons are involved. "He" when used of God means "the"—the Father, the Son, and the Holy Spirit

2. *God is self-existent and self-sufficient.* God does not have it in him, either in purpose or in power, to stop existing. He exists necessarily. The answer to the child's question "Who made God?" is that God did not need to be made, since he was always there. He depends on nothing outside himself, but is at every point self-sustaining.

3. *God is simple, perfect, and immutable.* This means he is wholly and totally involved in everything that he is and does, and his nature, goals, plans, and ways of acting do not change, either for the better (for, being perfect, he cannot become better than he is) or for the worse.

4. *God is infinite, without body, all-present, all-knowing, and eternal.* God is not bound by any of the limitations of space or time that apply to us, his creatures, in our present body-anchored existence. Instead, he is always present everywhere, though invisibly and imperceptibly. He is at every moment cognizant of everything that ever was, or now is, or shall be.

5. *God is purposeful and all-powerful.* He has a plan for the history of the universe, and in executing it he governs and controls all created realities. Without violating the nature of things, and without at any stage infringing upon the human free will, God acts in, with, and through his creatures to do everything that he wishes to do exactly as he wishes to do it. By this sovereign, overruling action he achieves his goals.

6. *God is both transcendent over and immanent in his world.* On the one hand he is distinct from the world, does not need it, and exceeds the grasp of any created intelligence that is found in it. Yet on the other hand he permeates the world in sustaining and creative power, shaping and steering it in a way that keeps it on its planned course.

7. *God is impassible.* This means that no one can inflict suffering, pain, or any sort of distress on him. Insofar as God enters into an experience of suffering, it is by empathy for his creatures and according to his own deliberate decision. He is never his creatures' victim. This impassibility has not been taken by the Christian mainstream to mean that God is a stranger to joy and delight. Rather, it has been construed as an assertion of the permanence of God's joy, which no pain clouds.

8. *God is love.* Giving out of good will, for the recipient's benefit, is the abiding quality both of ongoing relationships within the Trinity and of God's relationship with his creatures. This love is qualified by holiness (purity), a further facet of God's character that finds expression in his abhorrence and rejection of moral evil.

9. *God's ways with mankind, as set forth in Scripture, show him to be both awesome and adorable by reason of his truthfulness, faithfulness, grace, mercy, patience, constancy, wisdom, justice, goodness, and generosity.* For these glorious qualities God is eternally worthy of our praise, loyalty, and love. The ultimate purpose of human life is to render to him worship and service, in which both he and we will find joy. This is what we were made for, and are saved for. This is what it means to know God, and to be known by him, and to glorify him.

10. *God uses his gift of language, given to mankind, to tell us things directly in and through the words of his spokesmen—prophets, apostles, the incarnate Son, the writers of Holy Scripture, and those who preach the Bible.* God's messages all come to us as good news of grace. They may contain particular commands, even threats or warnings, but the fact that God addresses us at all is an expression of his good will and an invitation to fellowship. And the central message of Scripture, the hub of the wheel whose spokes are the various truths about God that the Bible teaches, is and always will be God's unmerited gift of salvation, freely offered to us in and by Jesus Christ.

Traditional Theism under Fire

Now, what are the present-day problems with this venerable understanding of God? They come down to its sources and method. The positions themselves, as stated above, are plainly biblical. But the Platonist-Augustinian-Thomist tradition of philosophical theism has persistently held that knowledge of God's reality and of several of the above facts about him can and should be gleaned by rational analysis apart from the Bible's witness. This is where the uncertainty centers.

Karl Barth, in the powerful, Bible-based reassertions of trinitarian theism of his *Church Dogmatics*, spurned the help of this kind of rational theology. (It has traditionally been called natural theology.)

This did more than any other twentieth-century contribution to produce a pendulum swing against attempts to wed theology to philosophy. To be concerned lest philosophy becomes the dominant partner in this marriage is right and proper. Barth, however, wanted to go further, and divorce them—a different agenda altogether.

Barth himself would use philosophical concepts as tools to help investigate biblical teaching. But he would not let these concepts become grids limiting in advance what God is free to say to us through Scripture.

Barth's protest, though justified within limits, threw the doctrine of God into great confusion. It opened the door to a selective reading of the Bible, free of coherent rational control, and operating without regard for any of the traditional fixed points. That is what we face today in many quarters. The pendulum still swings between Thomist and Barthian extremes, and shows no sign of coming to rest.

Karl Barth's Theism

Barth's contribution, though disruptive in the way just described, paves the way for some clarifications of the doctrine of God that we badly need.

Granted, his attack on the basis of natural theology—that is, the recognition that our existence and God's have something in common—was certainly overdone. Granted, too, Barth's denial of general revelation through the created order was a mistake. (His refusal to recognize general revelation, apart from the gospel, in Romans 1:18–32 and 2:9–16, seems little short of perverse.)

Nevertheless, his polemic against the claim of natural theology, to establish for us foundation truths about God as a kind of runway for revelation, now appears as a largely justified attack on nineteenth-century attempts to domesticate God. (Barth's break with liberal theology began around 1915, when prominent German theologians blithely spoke of "using" the Christian faith "for purposes of conducting" World War I.) And Barth's insistence that all our doctrine of God must come from the Bible was healthy and right.

So it will not be enough to dismiss Barth as eccentric and then slump back into traditional postures and parrotings. If Barth with his type of biblicism did not do well enough, we must try with ours to do better. To that end I now venture some comments on the doctrine of God as today's evangelicals have received it.

Three Important Purgings

There are three important respects in which the traditional doctrine needs purging. It needs to be purged of elements of *natural theology*, elements of *mystification*, and elements of *rationalism*. Let me explain.

First, *elements of natural theology* need to be purged. Against Barth, I affirm that general revelation is a fact, and its impact will again and again produce thoughts about God that, so far as they go, are right. (Like those of Epimenides and Aratus that Paul cites in Acts 17:28.) Many are confident that rational apologetics (a form of natural theology) can, under God, trigger and crystallize such thoughts and insights. Unlike Barth, I see no reason to doubt their confidence.

Yet I contend that natural theology needs to be eliminated from our attempts at theological construction. There are five reasons.

First, we do not need natural theology for information. Everything that natural theology, operating upon general revelation, can discern about the Creator and his ways is republished for us in those very Scriptures that refer to the general revelation of these things (see Ps. 19; Acts 14:17, 17:28; Rom. 1:18–32, 2:9–16). And Scripture, which we rightly receive on the grounds that it is God's own word of testimony and law, is a better source of knowledge about God than natural theology can ever be.

Second, we do not strengthen our position by invoking natural theology. On the contrary, claiming that biblical truths rest on philosophical foundations can only give the impression that the biblical message about God's redemption is no more certain than is the prior philosophical assertion of God's reality. And God's reality, on this scenario, must be established by reason—unaided by revelation. Thus revelation becomes distinctly dependent on philosophy.

Third, all expositions of the analogy of being, and all attempts to show the naturalness of theism—all "proofs" for God's existence and goodness, in other words—are logically loose. They state no more than possibilities (for probabilities are only one kind of possibilities) and can all be argued against indefinitely. This will damage the credit of any theology that appears to be building and relying on these arguments.

Fourth, the speculative method for building up a theology is inappropriate. As Louis Berkhof has observed, such a method takes man as its starting point, and works from what it finds in man to what is found in God. "And in so far as it does this," Berkhof writes, "it makes man the measure of God." That, of course, does not "fit in a theology of revelation."

Fifth, there is always a risk the foundations that natural theology lays will prove too narrow to build all the emphases of Scripture upon. Thus, for instance, in Thomas Aquinas's *Summa Theologica*, natural theology purports to establish that there is one God, who is the first cause of everything. But nothing is said about the personal aspects of God's being. This personal dimension is central to the biblical revelation of God, setting it in stark contrast with (for instance) the divine principle in Hindu thought.

Thomas's approach, however, encourages the theologian to downplay the biblical stress on it, to treat God as an impersonal object rather than a personal subject, and to see himself as standing over God to study him rather than under God to obey him.

It seems right to limit our use of natural theology to the realm of supportive apologetics (showing biblical faith to be reasonable), and not to give it any place in our attempts to state what the biblical faith actually is.

Exit Mystification

In retooling traditional theism for today, we need, secondly, to purge *elements of mystification*. By "mystification" I mean the idea that some biblical statements about God mislead as they stand, and ought to be explained away. A problem arises from a recurring tendency in orthodox theism to press the legitimate and necessary distinction between what God is in himself and what Scripture says about his relation to us.

To be specific, sometimes God is said to change his mind and to make new decisions as he reacts to human doings. Orthodox theists have insisted that God did not *really* change his mind, since God is impassible and never a "victim" of his creation. As writes Louis Berkhof, representative of this view, "the change is not in God, but in man and man's relations to God."

But to say that is to say that some things that Scripture affirms about God do not mean what they seem to mean, and do mean what they do not seem to mean. That provokes the question: How can these statements be part of the *revelation* of God when they actually *misrepresent and so conceal* God? In other words, how may we explain these statements about God's grief and repentance without seeming to explain them away?

Surely we must accept Barth's insistence that at every point in his self disclosure God reveals what he essentially is, with no gestures that mystify. And surely we must reject as intolerable any suggestion that God *in reality* is different at any point from what Scripture makes him appear to be. Scripture was not written to mystify, and therefore we need to ask how we can dispel the contrary impression that the time-honored, orthodox line of explanation leaves.

Three things seem to be called for as means to this end.

First, we need *exegetical restraint* in handling Scripture's anthropomorphisms (phrases using human figures to describe God). Anthropomorphism is characteristic of the entire biblical presentation of God. This is so not because God bears man's image, but because man bears God's, and hence is capable of understanding God's testimony to the reasons for his actions. The anthropomorphisms are there to show us why God acted as he did in the biblical story, and how therefore he might act towards us in our own personal stories. But nothing that is said about God's negative or positive reactions to his creatures is meant to put us in a position where we can tell what it feels like to be God. Our interpretation of the Bible must recognize this.

Second, we need to guard against misunderstanding of God's *changelessness*. True to Scripture, this must not be understood as a beautiful pose, eternally frozen, but as the Creator's moral constancy, his unwavering faithfulness and dependability. God's changelessness is not a matter of intrinsic immobility, but of moral consistency. God is always in action. He enters into the lives of his creatures. There is change around him and change in the relations of men to him. But, to use the words of Louis Berkhof, "there is no change in his being, his attributes, his purpose, his motives of action, or his promises." When one conceives of God's immutability in this biblical way, as a moral quality that is expressed whenever God changes his way of dealing with people for moral reasons, the biblical reference to such change will cease to mystify.

Third, we also need to rethink God's *impassibility*. This conception of God represents no single biblical term, but was introduced into Christian theology in the second century. What was it supposed to mean? The historical answer is: Not impassivity, unconcern, and impersonal detachment in face of the creation. Not inability or unwillingness to empathize with human pain and grief, either. It means simply that God's experiences do not come upon him as ours come upon us. His are foreknown, willed, and chosen by himself, and are not involuntary surprises forced on him from outside, apart from his own decision, in the way that ours regularly are.

This understanding was hinted at earlier, but it is spelled out here because it is so important, and so often missed. Let us be clear: A totally impassive God would be a horror, and not the God of Calvary at all. He might belong in Islam; he has no place in Christianity. If, therefore, we can learn to think of the *chosenness* of God's grief and pain as the essence of his impassibility, so-called, we will do well.

Problems of Rationalism

The final step needed to spruce up traditional theism is to purge it of *elements of rationalism*. Just as the two-year-old son of a man with a brain like Einstein's could not understand all that was going on in his father's mind if his father told him, so it would be beyond us to understand all that goes on in the all-wise, and not in any way time-bound mind of God.

But, just as the genius who loves his boy will take care to speak to him at his own level, even though that means reducing everything to baby talk, so God does when he opens his mind and heart to us in the Scriptures. The child, though aware that his father knows far more than he is currently saying, may yet learn from him all that he needs to know for a full and happy relationship with Dad. Similarly, Scripture, viewed as *torah* (God's fatherly law), tells us all that we need to know for faith and godliness.

But we must never forget that we are in the little boy's position. At no point dare we imagine that the thoughts about God that Scripture teaches us take the full measure of his reality. The fact that God condescends and accommodates himself to us in his revelation certainly makes possible clarity and sureness of understanding. Equally certain, however, it involves limitation in the revelation itself.

But we forget this, or so it seems; and then appears the rationalism of which I am speaking. It is more, I think, a temper than a tenet, but it produces a style of speech that in effect denies that there is anything about God we do not know. By thus failing to acknowledge his incomprehensibility beyond the limits of what he has revealed, we shrink him in thought down to our size. The process is sometimes described as putting God in a box.

It is certainly proper to stress, as against the sleep of reason in the world and the zaniness of subjectivism in the church, that scriptural revelation is rational. But the most thorough-going Bible believers are sometimes required, like Job, to go on adoring God when we do not specifically understand what he is doing and why he is doing it.

We should avoid like the plague any talk that suggests that we have enlisted him on our side, and now have him in our pockets. Confidence in the teaching of God's written Word is to be maintained all the time. But this stance of theological triumphalism is something quite different, and is to be avoided.

God the Image Maker

This review of traditional theism, and suggestions for its possible refinement, has been heavy sledding. How can it all be pulled together? Can we focus our theism in a phrase? I welcome the suggestion that we should speak of God as the *image maker*.

This phrase binds together the main theistic thrusts that our secular world needs to face. Say "God," and you point to the infinite, eternal, self-existent, self-revealing Father, Son, and Holy Spirit. Say "Maker," and you point to the fundamental relationship between God and us. He is the Creator, we are his creatures.

Say "Image Maker," and you point to the basis and presupposition of our knowledge of God—namely, the fact that he made us like himself. Included in that image are rationality, relationality, and the capacity for that righteousness that consists of receiving and responding to God's revelation. We are able to know God because we are thinking, feeling, relating, loving beings, just as he is himself.

I am no prophet, nor a prophet's son, but it seems fairly clear to me that pressure on conservative theology is still building up from exponents of religious relativism and pluralism. This is so both within the church (where some think that the more theologies there are, the healthier and merrier we shall be) and outside it.

I expect over the next few decades to see the quest for a synthesis of world religions gain impetus, with constant attempts to assimilate Christianity into other faiths. We may expect a generation of debate on the program of moving through and beyond syncretism to a nobler religion than any that has yet been seen. That notion, which has emerged more than once in liberal circles, looks like an idea whose time, humanly speaking, has come; and countering it, I predict, will be the next round in the church's unending task of defending and propagating the gospel. If this guess is right, we shall be badly at a disadvantage if we have not taken pains to brush up our theism, since the question of theism—whether or not we are going to think about God the Christian way, or some other way—will be at the heart of the debate. So I hope we shall take time out to prepare ourselves along the lines suggested—just in case.

Chapter 35

THE REALITY CURE

*Christians often imagine themselves to
be strong, healthy, and holy.*

I opened my eyes to find myself lying on my back in a strange
bed. Because my head was raised, I could see into the semi-
darkness beyond the bed. My first thought was that I was in New
York's Grand Central railroad station at night. Then I saw, sitting
on the left-hand side of the bed, my mother. She was wearing the
big, flowered overall and dusting cap in which she used to clean
the house. Afterward they told me that I went straight back to
sleep.

As I learned when I woke, I was nowhere near Grand Central
station. I was in a hospital in my English hometown, having had
surgery for a depressed fracture of the skull, which was thought
to have damaged my brain. What I saw was partly a delusion. The
ward did not really look like the photos of Grand Central station
I had recently seen. The person keeping vigil by my bed had been
a nurse in uniform.

I saw what I saw (if I shut my eyes I can see it now), but I was not seeing what was there. My shocked and battered brain was playing tricks on me. Reality was different from what I thought it was.

All of that happened in 1933, when I was seven years old. Why do I now hark back to it? Because it illustrates two truths that I find I have to stress over and over again when talking to Christians today.

In God's Hospital

The first truth is that we are all invalids in God's hospital. In moral and spiritual terms, we are all sick and damaged, diseased and deformed, scarred and sore, lame and lopsided, to a far, far greater extent than we realize.

Under God's care we are getting better, but we are not yet well. Modern Christians egg each other on to testify that where once we were blind, deaf, and indeed dead so far as God was concerned, now through Christ we have been brought to life, radically transformed, and blessed with spiritual health. Thank God, there is real truth in that. But spiritual health means being holy and whole. To the extent that we fall short of being holy and whole, we are not fully healthy, either.

We need to realize that the spiritual health we testify to is only partial and relative, a matter of being less sick and less incapacitated now than we were before. Measured by the absolute standard of spiritual health that we see in Jesus Christ, we are all of us no more, just as we are no less, than invalids in process of being cured.

The old saying that the church is God's hospital remains true. Our spiritual life is at best a fragile convalescence, easily disrupted. When there are tensions, strains, perversities, and disappointments in the Christian fellowship, it helps to remember that no Christian, and no church, ever has the clean bill of spiritual health that would match the total physical well-being for which today's fitness seekers labor. To long for total spiritual well-being is right and natural, but to believe that one is anywhere near it is to be utterly self-deceived.

It is not always easy to grasp that one is ill. In the hospital in 1933 I was, so to speak, kept in cotton wool for several days by doctor's orders. I remember how hard it was to think of myself as sick, since at no stage did I feel any ill effects. For slipping out of bed to wander round, I was tongue-lashed, I recall, by the ward sister who upbraided me with Welsh eloquence for, in effect, putting my life at risk. After this I remained dutifully bedbound, according to instructions—but still without any conviction inside me that it needed to be that way.

In the same way, Christians today can imagine themselves to be strong, healthy, and holy when, in fact, they are still weak, sick, and sinful. Pride and complacency, however, blind us to this reality. We decline to be told when we are slipping; thinking we stand, we set ourselves up to fall, and predictably, alas, we do fall.

In God's hospital, the course of treatment that the Father, Son, and Holy Spirit, the permanent medical staff (if I dare so speak), are administering to us is called *sanctification*, which has as its goal our final restoration to the fullness of the divine image. It is a process that includes, on the one hand, medication and diet (in the form of biblical instruction and admonition coming in various ways to the heart) and, on the other hand, tests and exercises (in the form of internal and external pressures, providentially ordered, to which we have to make active response). The process goes on as long as we are in this world, which is something that God determines in each case. Like patients in any hospital, we are impatient for recovery. But God knows what he is doing; sometimes, for reasons connected with the maturity and ministry that he has in view for us, he makes haste slowly. That is something we have to learn humbly to accept. We are in a hurry; he is not.

Humble Self-Suspicion

Second truth: We are all prone to damaging delusions. On my first night in the hospital, the place was not where I thought it was, and the person by my bed was not who I thought it was: I was in a state of delusion. Next day I felt well and could not think of myself as ill, but that was delusion, too. In the same way, believers are often deluded about Christian faith and living.

There are the delusions of direct theological error about God's nature and character and ways and purposes. In liberal and modernist and process theology, to look no further, these abound.

There are the delusions of doubt and unbelief. Something horrible happens, and at once we conclude that God must have forgotten us or turned against us, or perhaps gone out of existence.

There are the delusions of self-confidence. We think we have finally licked some particular sin or weakness by which we were previously dragged down. We relax, and a sense of well-being, security, and triumph creeps over us. Then comes the double whammy of fresh external pressure and a renewed inner urge, and down we go.

There are also the delusions that disrupt relationships. We misunderstand each other's motives and purposes. We blame others for generating the hostility and are blind to our own part in provoking the difficulties.

There are delusions, too, resulting from failure to distinguish things that differ—for example, equating the biblical gospel with Jesus-centered legalism, Jesus-centered lawlessness, Jesus-centered socialism, or Jesus-centered racism; equating secular psychological counseling with biblical pastoral direction; or equating inner passivity as a formula for holiness with the biblical call to disciplined moral effort in the power of the Holy Spirit. All such delusions spell disaster.

Then there are delusions about the Christian life—that it will ordinarily be easy, successful, healthy, and wealthy, excitingly punctuated by miracles; that such acts as fornication and tax evasion will not matter as long as nobody finds out; that God always wants you to do what you feel like doing; and so on, and so on. Satan, the father of lies and a past master at deluding, labors constantly to mislead and muddle God's people. Thus humble self-suspicion and the commonsensical hard-headedness that used to be called prudence, and the habit of testing by Scripture things hitherto taken for granted, become virtues of great importance.

Our Physician's Bedside Manner

The sort of physician I appreciate takes the patient into his or her confidence and explains his or her diagnosis, prognosis, and treatment. Not all physicians behave this way, but the best do—and so does the Great Physician of our souls, our Lord Jesus Christ.

Our Lord's therapeutic style, if I may express it this way, is communicative from first to last. The Bible, heard and read, preached and taught, interpreted and applied, is both the channel and the content of his communication. It is as if Jesus hands us the canonical Scriptures directly, telling us that they are the authoritative and all-sufficient source from which we must learn both what we are to do to be his followers and also what he has done, is doing, and will do to save us from the fatal sickness of sin.

Think of your Bible, then, as Jesus Christ's gift to you; think of it as a letter to you from your Lord. Think of your name, written in front of it, as if Jesus himself had written it there. Think of Jesus each time you read your Bible. Think of him asking you, page by page and chapter by chapter, what you have just learned about the need, nature, method, and effect of the grace that he brings, and about the path of loyal discipleship that he calls you to tread. That is the way to profit from the Bible. Only when your reading of the written word feeds into your relationship with the living Word (Jesus) does the Bible operate as the channel of light and life that God means it to be.

In Scripture is revealed the whole work of divine grace in the individual, first to last. When we see what God through Christ and the Spirit has done for us and is doing in us, we shall be better placed for realism about our present spiritual condition and cooperation with God's purposes for our lives.

Chapter 36

———

ROME'S PERSISTENT

RENEWAL

R oman Catholics would be the first to declare that of all God's
twentieth-century surprises, none has startled them more
than the charismatic renewal in their own church during the past
25 years. Though its estimated 50-plus million adherents make
up less than a tenth of world Catholicism, they are probably more
than a fifth of the Pentecostal-charismatic constituency worldwide, and these numbers are very remarkable. So is the spread
of such a movement as this in a Catholic context.

Roman Catholics are not, of course, the only people whom the
emergence of the renewal has jolted. Many Protestants are still
unable to tune in to the new music, the singing in the Spirit, the
hand-and arm-waving in praise and prayer and orchestrated rituals of Spirit-baptism, exorcism, and healing, and the slayings in
the Spirit that have marked the movement wherever it has gone.
Some Protestants, like some Catholics, refuse to take these things
seriously, seeing them only as the crudities of an immature spiritual escapism. Others find the renewal disturbingly triumphalist,
unself-critical, and inward-looking; and most church leaders (not

all) seem currently to view it as a wayward development needing correction and control.

But the Catholic version of the renewal is especially astonishing, in two ways. First, it is mainly lay led, with priests and theologians following behind, rather than the other way about. Second, it is based on acceptance of an evangelical Protestant formula—the Pentecostal variant of John Wesley's doctrine of a post-conversion "second blessing" that raises one's Christian life to new heights of love, joy, and usefulness to God.

The Release of the Spirit

Can Catholic theology handle this? Yes, it can, and it does. Catholic theologians will explain both the first blessing (conscious conversion) and the second blessing (conscious Spirit-baptism) as the *release* of the Holy Spirit, whose indwelling presence was conferred in infant baptism and/or child confirmation. Protestants who expect Catholic sacramentalism to lead to a formal, mechanical piety in which the Holy Spirit is evidently uninvolved should note this development.

It is a fact that in charismatic Catholicism, joyful trust in Christ as one's sin-bearing Savior and loving fellowship with him in his risen life have shifted the traditional devotional focus away from the somber disciplines of self-denial and suffering and away, too, from the anxieties about merit and destiny to which the formulations of the Council of Trent naturally give rise. Does Catholic doctrine as Trent defined it permit assurance of salvation based on once-for-all justification through faith? Opinions, both Protestant and Catholic, differ about that. Nevertheless, Catholic charismatics do observably enjoy this assurance, while yet maintaining humility, a sense of sin, and a life of repentance often more successfully then do their Protestant counterparts. And Protestant and Catholic charismatic teaching on the

Christian life is to all intents and purposes identical. Is this not significant for the Christian future?

The Place of the Renewal

What place has the ongoing charismatic renewal in God's global strategy? Long-term, it is beyond us to tell; but as regards the short term, four things may be said with confidence.

1. The renewal is God's witness against the implicit *unitarianism* and explicit *pluralism* of much Protestant and Catholic theology, which reduces Jesus from a divine Savior to a God-filled model of human goodness, and the Spirit from a person to an urge, and Spirit-filled life in Christ to natural religiosity. God refutes these killing trends by renewing the knowledge of Christ and the new supernaturalized existence that the Spirit imparts. The refutation is conclusive: one cannot argue against the power of God.

2. The renewal is God's therapy for *formalism* in personal religion. It frees up God's "frozen chosen," both Catholic and Protestant, for spontaneous praise and love, deep penitence, and honest, self-humbling, truly Christ-centered relationships, and truly uninhibited witnessing. It confronts the world with the arresting transparency of lives turned gloriously upside-down. Hallelujah!

3. The renewal is God's cure for *clericalism*—that is, the historic conjunction of professional priestcraft with lay apathy, and passivity. Every-member ministry in the body of Christ, as each Christian's spiritual gifts are found and honed through open and enabling pastoral leadership, belongs to the renewal vision that both Protestants and Catholics share.

4. The renewal is God's summons to *grassroots cooperation* among lay people—clergy, too, so far as their separated church systems allow it—for advancing as much of God's truth and

righteousness as through renewal they now find they agree on—which is, in fact, a great deal.

What a momentous difference it would make if there were agreement on these four points!

Chapter 37

———

WHY I LEFT

I tell this story because I was asked to do so. It is an account of how, standing firm convictionally, I saw the leading organization of the world Christian-unity movement slide away from me. My attitude to it had then to change, just because my view of God's truth had not changed.

Once, perhaps pompously, I spoke of my relation to the World Council of Churches and local enterprises linked with it as one of qualified involvement. Now my understanding of biblical ecumenism requires me to stand outside those structures and speak of the need for repentance. I call my position, again perhaps pompously, one of prophetic detachment. My narrative is offered as a case study. It has three parts.

Doing the Do-Gooders Good

Part one began in 1944, when I was converted to Christ in my first term at Oxford. Both the student evangelical movement to which, under God, I owed my soul and the evangelical Anglicans, with whom, as a cradle Anglican, I then formed links, nurtured me in an isolationist mindset. I was taught to view professed Christians who were not wholly with us on matters like biblical inspiration and authority or personal conversion as hardly Christian at all. Against this my judgment slowly rebelled.

While I saw myself as much closer, doctrinally and devotionally, to evangelicals of other church allegiances than to non-evangelicals in my own denomination, I could also see that many "catholic" and "liberal evangelical" Anglicans loved my Lord, even though some of their beliefs made me wince. I became an ecumenical evangelical with a bilateral stance, stretching out my right hand to fellowship with the world evangelical movement, whatever its church affiliation (or lack of it), and extending my left hand to associate with Anglicans as such. So a concern for Christian unity—perhaps I should say *Christian* Christian unity— was born in me fairly early on.

When I was ordained and began my ministry in a church in 1952, my theology had settled down as creedal and Reformed, with a directly biblical and pastoral thrust, and my hopes and prayers centered on the need for a new evangelical revival in the Church of England.

As for the World Council of Churches, formed in 1948, with the powerful biblical theologian W. A. Visser't Hooft as general secretary, and the announced aim of advancing Christian unity and service to the world, I saw no reason not to wish it well. I knew about the Faith and Order and Life and Work movements (both launched in the 1920s) that were coming together in it. And while I regretted the Life and Work slogan "Doctrine divides; service unites," I thought, no doubt naively, that being tied in with Faith and Order would do the do-gooders good, and complement their agenda.

Alarm Bells Ringing

Part two of the story opens in the late fifties. An Anglican bureaucrat came to Bristol, where I was teaching in a theological college, to persuade me to set aside time to contribute to the work of various church commissions that were exploring new proposals about faith, order, and church relations. I said I would, and over the next 20 years I was involved in Anglican-Presbyterian and Anglican-Methodist unity talks, in the Archbishops' Doctrine Commission, and for more than a decade in the Faith and Order Advisory Group of the Church of England's General Synod, a body which, among other things, prepared responses to questions and documents sent from the WCC headquarters in Geneva. This obliged me to look more intentionally at what the WCC was doing, and I was not too happy with what I saw.

In the fifties, I had believed that the theological tools being forged by the "biblical theology" movement would be put to use in the WCC for purging and synthesizing in a directly biblical mold the many denominational traditions being brought together. The informal slogan of "biblical theology" was "read the Bible from within, in terms of its writers' own faith," and I was all for that (and still am). In the sixties, however, it became clear to me that the WCC was working not with a reformational but with a relativist agenda, based on the idea that the church should let the secular world rather than the Bible tell it what to think and speak about. Politicization, in the sense of seeking political influence and adjusting testimony and policy as a means to a political end, had thus begun. I found that very worrying.

In the fifties, "one world—one church" was an oft-used slogan, and suspicious critics alleged that the WCC was out to create a single global super-church, including all Roman Catholics, and headed by the pope. I never considered the criticism realistic, for the WCC was in no position to bring this ecumaniac's pipe dream to pass, and I thought the WCC's supposed commitment to "biblical theology" was in any case safeguard enough against it. In the sixties, however, while super-church talk dried up, so did "biblical theology" (academics were by then reacting against it), and the WCC now appeared as sponsoring a consensus theology that celebrated the Bible without encountering its authority. This theology seemed bent on reducing Christian tradition to secular concepts of "humanization." The cloven hoofs of North American liberal Protestantism and Latin American liberation theology were seen as the council began more explicitly to identify at official levels with socialist and revolutionary politics. In doing so, it acted as if it represented its member churches. It committed churches to these programs, or at the least promised to ensure that concern for peace and justice on earth would henceforth be the churches' top priority in this fallen world. The alarm bells in my mind were now ringing loud and clear.

What was the church's true priority? To evangelize the world, and thereby establish self-supporting, self-propagating churches everywhere. Where should "humanization" in the sense of philanthropy and social service come in? As supporting expressions of the neighbor-love of which evangelism is the primary expression. What was the WCC, which had absorbed the International Missionary Council in 1961, now saying about cross-cultural evangelism? That the church of the West should put into force a "moratorium" on it (that is, an indefinite suspension of the activity). Was the WCC assuming that universalism is true, so that all will be saved whether evangelized or not? Apparently so. Did the WCC then wish to redefine the Christian mission in a way that makes evangelism optional, or leaves it out of the picture altogether? Again, apparently so. Was not the WCC hereby disqualifying itself from the leadership it claimed in the ecumenical—that is, the world-Christian—sphere? I began to suspect so, and waited anxiously to see. So to part three of my story.

The Point of No Return

The cat finally came out of the bag at the Conference on World Mission held in Bangkok in 1973. I was not there, but the reports that reached me affected me like a kick in the stomach. Bangkok was deliberately structured as an experience of ideological group dynamics, orchestrated with the set purpose of browbeating participants into accepting a new account of the Christian world mission. This view equated present salvation with socio-politico-economic well-being. The sinner's reconciliation to God, sanctification by grace, and hope of eternal glory were no longer viewed as central; indeed, for all practical purposes they were pushed right out of the picture. Syncretistic humanization became the name of the WCC's game. The WCC leadership celebrated Bangkok as the close of the era of missions and the opening of the era of mission: truly a watershed event. For me, too, it was a watershed event, but one to be described in different terms.

Bangkok impressed me as a point of no return. It confirmed my worst fears about the way the WCC was going. Now the council had betrayed the true church by abandoning the true gospel and the true missionary task and, what was more, made it a virtue to have done so. I saw this as the nemesis of the WCC's politicization: seeking significance in the global power play, it had given up its trusteeship of truth. Its euphoria about Bangkok seemed spiritually unreal, if not indeed demonic. With all the charity in the world, I could not but see the WCC, ideologically speaking, as a juggernaut that had run off the road and totaled itself, becoming irrelevant to and useless in the furthering of the church's God-given role.

So since 1973 I have as a matter of conscience stood apart from the world of the WCC and done what I could for Christian unity and the Christian world mission under other auspices. I live in hope that the WCC might show some signs of going back on Bangkok, and I wish I could see some, but none has appeared as yet. Affirmations of evangelism have certainly been made since 1973, but they are clearly meant to be fitted into the Bangkok frame. Meanwhile, however, informal ecumenism flourishes among creedal Christians—Protestant, Orthodox, and Roman Catholic, all round the world. And in Asia, Africa, and Latin America, to look no further, church-planting evangelism prospers wonderfully. Christian unity and the Christian mission still go ahead, despite the debacle of the WCC, and in that I rejoice.

Chapter 38

WHAT IS AT STAKE?

When experts argue, it is often hard for laypeople to sort out what really matters from the finer details of the debate. Christianity Today *asked senior editor J. I. Packer to tell our readers what is at stake in the debate between Murray Harris and his critics.*

T he bodily rising from the dead of our Lord Jesus Christ is as crucial to Christianity as is the cross itself. Easter Day, when Christians traditionally tell each other "The Lord is risen!" is the highest of the high spots of the Christian year. Paul pointed to Jesus' resurrection as proof of his divine identity (Rom. 1:4), of the reality of atonement through his death (1 Cor. 15:17), and of the certainty that he will return for judgment (Acts 17:31). No Christian beliefs are more basic. A muddled witness to the nature and significance of the Resurrection must therefore be most damaging.

The Meaning of Change

In 1985, Murray Harris criticized England's bishop of Durham for muddling the resurrection witness by affirming Jesus' risenness while denying the empty tomb. Since 1987, Norman Geisler has been attacking Murray Harris for muddling this witness by affirming that Jesus' body was so changed in the event of his rising as to be henceforth invisible to human eyes, being no longer material, in the sense in which our present bodies are material.

Harris holds that in the resurrection appearances, Jesus resumed flesh, bones, a digestive system, and solid visibility as before, for the purpose of showing his disciples that he was the identical person who had been crucified (Luke 24:36–43, etc.). It is Harris's view that this is what the relevant Scriptures most naturally imply. Geisler contends that though the risen Jesus was certainly able to become invisible at will, any denial that flesh, bones, and a digestive system were part of his permanent make-up obscures the bodily character of his risen life in a way that is unacceptably unorthodox, if not indeed positively heretical.

Details of the Debate

The following points may be helpful.

1. What is at issue is the mode and details of Jesus' bodily resurrection, not the fact of it. Harris still negates the bishop of Durham's denial that Jesus rose in the flesh; his present concern is only to explicate that rising.

2. Teachers are free to explore any line of thought compatible with their institution's basis of faith, and the teacher who holds no opinions that his peers might challenge is rare indeed.

3. The nature of resurrection bodies is so mysterious, being right outside our present experience, that any theories about it must be tentative at best.

4. Harris's hypothesis does, in fact, fit all the relevant texts comfortably, as Harris, a highly skilled exegete, is able to show. It is not the only hypothesis that will fit these texts, but it cannot be dismissed as unbiblical.

5. Harris's hypothesis is not new: major scholars from Brooke Foss Westcott to George Ladd have maintained it during the past century, without their orthodoxy being questioned. It would seem therefore to merit careful consideration as a serious option rather than summary dismissal as an unorthodox freak.

6. In stating any position, the meaning of individual words and phrases must be determined by reference to the position as a whole. Harris has come under fire for a loose use of words, but there was never any lack of precision in his overall view.

7. A Christian opinion is orthodox if it squares with Scripture and with the consensus of the world church, as expressed in creeds, confessions, and a common mind. The essentials of orthodoxy on the Resurrection are that on the third day Jesus, who died on the cross, came forth bodily from the tomb and was exalted to the Father's throne, never to die again; that he showed himself repeatedly to his disciples during the 40 days preceding his ascension; and that in heaven his human body, however changed, along with his human mind, remains integral to his being forever. By this standard, both Harris and Geisler appear to be orthodox, and both of them equally so.

8. Harris's orthodoxy on the Resurrection has already been affirmed after inquiry both by the Evangelical Free Church of America, at whose seminary he teaches, and by his peers in Trinity Evangelical Divinity School itself. It is not now being challenged for the first time.

9. Harris's affirmation of the permanence of our Lord's glorified body negates the doctrine of such bodies as Jehovah's Witnesses, who affirm the entire dissolution of Jesus' body after

his resurrection. To accuse Harris of teaching cultic doctrine because his way of spelling out his affirmation matches one detail of Jehovah's Witnesses' ideas is unjust to Harris and confusing to the church.

An Ancient Debate

The present controversy is in many ways a rerun of an ancient debate.

During the second, third, and fourth centuries A.D., there were two opposing schools of thought regarding the nature of the future resurrection body. The Western, or Latin, school stressed the identity between the body that is buried and the body that is raised. At the resurrection, the material particles that composed the earthly body at the time of death will be reassembled by God's power to form the glorified flesh of the resurrection body. This view was formulated in opposition to pagans who disparaged the body and Gnostics who despised anything material. The corresponding creedal statement was "I believe in the resurrection of the flesh." Tertullian, a distinguished lawyer from North Africa, was the most noteworthy advocate of this position.

The other school, the Eastern, or Greek, emphasized the complete transformation that occurs when the body is raised. At the resurrection, the whole person, soul and body, is radically changed so as to form what Paul calls a "spiritual body," a body responsive to the spirit and suited to heaven. This view opposed the Docetists, who denied the reality of any resurrection, and the Latin School, with its materialistic view of resurrection. Those who espoused this belief favored the creed that affirmed, "I believe in the resurrection of the body," or "I believe in the resurrection of the dead." Origen, an Alexandrian exegete and polymath, was the principal exponent of their view.

Chapter 39

THE DEVIL'S DOSSIER

Before Christians engage the spiritual warfare, they
should know something about the Enemy.

"I hate the Devil!" yelled undergraduate and future missionary Paget Wilkes across an Oxford street a century ago to a friend walking on the opposite side. "So do I!" his friend roared back. Passersby were struck by the exchange, and maybe the memory of it did them good, for the sentiment was right. The Devil is hateful, and the Christian way is to hate him as heartily as one can.

Profile. Satan (his name means "adversary") hates humankind and seeks our ruin because he hates God, his and our Creator. He seeks only to thwart God's plans, wreck his work, rob him of glory, and in that sense master him. *Devil*, his descriptive title, means "slanderer," one who thinks, speaks, and plans evil against others.

Created good, he is the archetypal instance of good gone wrong. He heads a company of rebel angels, whose moral nature, like Adam's, was set in the mold of their first sin. This army of demons, as the Gospels call them, has "as king over them the angel of the Abyss, whose name in Hebrew is Abaddon, and in Greek, Apollyon" (Rev. 9:11)—both names meaning "destroyer."[1]

For his fierce, sustained, pitiless hatred of humanity, Satan is spoken of as a murderer, the evil one, a roaring and devouring lion, a great red dragon, and the accuser who constantly calls on God to banish his saints for their sins. For his habit of twisting truth as a means to his ends, he is called a liar and a deceiver. He is unimaginably malicious, mean, ugly, and cruel. His temptations are literally testings to destruction, and yielding to them is always the road to ruin.

Power. Like other angels, Satan's powers are more than human, though less than divine. He is at least multipresent if not omnipresent, and no member of the human race escapes his attention. Though not omniscient, he knows more of what is in us than we do ourselves. He is not omnipotent and functions only within bounds that God sets—he is, after all, in Luther's startling phrase, "God's devil," always on a chain, if a long one. Yet he has consummate power and skill to manipulate circumstances and inject thoughts into the human mind, as Paul's phrases, "a messenger of Satan" and "flaming arrows of the evil one" (2 Cor. 12:7; Eph. 6:16) show.

Satan controls all this rebel world apart from the church and the Christians who constitute it, and he is endlessly busy seeking to bring these latter back under his sway. Here, however, what he can do is limited on a day-to-day basis, for "God ... will not let you be tempted beyond what you can bear" (1 Cor. 10:13).

---

[1] Scripture quotations in this article are from the New International Version (1984).

Procedures. Satan's regular way of working is to deceive, and thereby get people to err without any suspicion that what they are thinking and doing is not right. He plays on our pride, willfulness, unrealism, addictions, stupidities, and temperamental flaws to induce all forms of mental and moral folly—fantasies, cults, idolatries, unbelief, misbelief, dishonesty, infidelity, cruelty, exploitation, and everything else that degrades and dehumanizes God's image bearers. Love, wisdom, humility, and pure-heartedness, four basic components of Christlikeness, are special objects of his attack.

Satanism is a corrupting superstition, offering spurious excitement, which he encourages. At the same time, the denial of his own existence by New Agers, materialists, and supposedly enlightened Christians is another superstition he encourages. In short, any fancy, feeling, or fashion that works against God and godliness and gives Satan himself room to work as the destroyer of truth, goodness, and beauty in God's world, among God's human creatures, will have full satanic backing.

Prospects. The Bible only tells us enough about Satan in order to detect and resist him, and many questions about him and the demonic hosts that follow him must remain unanswered. What is certain, however, is that through the sinless life, sacrificial death, and triumphant resurrection of the Lord Jesus Christ, Satan was decisively defeated and is now a beaten foe; that he will never be able finally to thwart God's purposes of salvation and restoration; that here and now Christians who take the armor of God to themselves can successfully withstand his attacks; and that he will spend eternity in "the lake of burning sulfur … tormented day and night forever and ever" (Rev. 20:10). Those who have learned to hate the Devil as Christians should rejoice and praise God that these things are so.

Chapter 40

——

PLEASURE PRINCIPLES

Why the Christian mission on earth is
not unrelieved heroic misery.

"What's your pleasure?" was, and is, a humane and cour-
teous question, for bestowing pleasure is one facet of
gracious living. Groucho Marx's brutal and discourteous answer
("Women. What's yours?") shows you why my mother would
never let me see any of the Marx Brothers' films; it also shows why
and how pleasure becomes a moral problem. Pursuing pleasure
can lead one sadly astray.

What does Scripture say to us about our pleasures? Does it, as
some imagine, tell us to give them all up, as having no place in holy
living? Certainly not! Scripture favors pleasure—"I commend the
enjoyment of life,"[1] says the wise man (Eccles. 8:15)—and only

---

[1] Scripture quotations in this article are from the New International Version
(1984).

forbids surrender to it as a lifestyle. But this has become an area of real difficulty for Christians in our day.

Since World War II, the West has grown affluent. Society now practices and promotes spending rather than saving, self-indulgence rather than self-discipline or self-improvement, and amusement at all costs. *Amusing Ourselves to Death* is the telling title of Neil Postman's 1985 assessment of American television: the same grim phrase might be used to describe the behavior that has led to the AIDS epidemic.

The ideology of pleasure is, in fact, global and has been so throughout history. To treat pleasure as a self-justifying value, and to run all sorts of risks and embrace all sorts of folly in order to get it, was always the way of the world. The modern West is simply doing this more blatantly than poorer communities are able to do, or than it could itself do in earlier times. Here, as elsewhere, there is nothing new under the sun.

Hedonism Enthroned

The philosophical name for the vision of life that we are looking at is *hedonism*. Hedonism means enthroning pleasure as life's supreme value and therefore as a goal everyone should pursue directly. Hedonism says, in effect, that pleasure-seeking is the height of wisdom and virtue, and that maximizing others' pleasure is the highest service we can render them. Popular Western culture is increasingly hedonist, and modern Christians are constantly exposed to its brainwashing influences, especially perhaps through the media ("Oprah," "Geraldo," game shows, soaps, and so forth) and the endless inflamings of desire crafted by the advertising industry.

That God wants us all to be pain-free and happy, right now; that total satisfaction is what Jesus offers, right now; that present healing of bodily discomforts is available to us all, right now;

that it is a good and godly thing to dismiss a spouse with whom one is not perfectly happy and marry someone else; that it is a good and godly thing to engage in genital homosexual behavior, if that gives you positive pleasure—all of these hedonistic notions have become familiar in the church in recent years. That leisure is entirely for pleasure and that improving one's lifestyle means simply increasing one's pleasures are unchallenged axioms not only in contemporary advertising, but are unquestioned assumptions among many professed Christians as well. There is a major problem here, for hedonism runs radically contrary to the Christian scale of values.

Recently the phrase *Christian hedonism* has gained prominence as a tag for the truth that the God who promises his people joy and delight in their relationship with him, both here and hereafter, does, in fact, fulfill his promise here and now. Christian hedonism speaks a word in season as a corrective of what we may call "Christian anti-hedonism"—the view that pleasure has no place in godly living, that God will always want us to do what we least want to do, and that the real Christian life on earth will always be, in Churchillian phrase, blood, toil, tears, and sweat—in short, sustained heroic misery.

In itself, however, *Christian hedonism* is not a good phrase for its purpose; for it seems to say that rating pleasure as life's supreme value is something that Christianity itself teaches us to do, and that is not so.

Biblical Christianity does not teach that any pleasure or good feelings, or any form of present ease and contentment, should be sought as life's highest good. What it teaches, rather, is that glorifying God by our worship and service is the true human goal, that rejoicing and delighting in God is central to worship, and that the firstfruits of our heritage of pleasures for evermore will be given us as we set ourselves to do this; but should we start to seek pleasure rather than God, we would be in danger of losing both. It is apparent that this is what the exponents of Christian hedonism do themselves think, so my difficulty with them is limited to their choice of words. Real hedonism must be avoided.

How should Christians react to a culture that is so set as ours on pursuing pleasure? Merely to emphasize work rather than leisure, activity rather than rest, and austerity rather than delight is not good enough. This has been done, and the results of doing it are evident all around us. Such teaching turns some Christians into workaholics while leading others to live with a split mind, not relating their enjoyments to their devotions but behaving as if their pleasures are their own business after work is over and have nothing to do with God. How many late-night pizza-poppers, Coke-guzzlers, and sports-watchers among God's people thank God for these relaxing delights? A positive theology of pleasure, showing its proper place in a holy life, is what we need and lack. Here, in outline, I propose one.

God's Pleasure Garden

What is pleasure? Webster defines it as "the gratification of the senses or of the mind; agreeable sensations or emotions; the feeling produced by enjoyment or the expectation of good." Like joy, it is a gift of God, but whereas joy is basically active (one rejoices), pleasure is basically passive (one is pleased). The chemistry of it is that morphinelike endorphins flood the brain, producing a euphoric glow at conscious level. Pleasures are feelings—feelings of stimulation or of tensions relaxed in the body, of realizations of something good in the mind, or of realized mastery in some performance or exercise of skill.

Pleasure belongs to God's plan for humankind. As God himself takes pleasure in being God and in doing what he does, so he means human beings to find pleasure in being his. Adam and Eve's state was all pleasure before they sinned (Eden, God's pleasure-garden, pictures that), and when the redemption of Christians is complete, pleasure—total, constant, and entire—will have become their permanent condition.

> Never again will they hunger;
>> never again will they thirst.
> The sun will not beat upon them,
>> nor any scorching heat.
> For the Lamb ... will be their shepherd;
>> he will lead them to springs of living water.
> And God will wipe away every tear from their eyes.
>> (Rev. 7:16–17, NIV)

Thus the words of Psalm 16:11, "You will fill me with joy in your presence, with eternal pleasures at your right hand," and Psalm 36:8, "You give them drink from your river of delights," will find fulfillment. God values pleasure, both his and ours, and it is his pleasure to give us pleasure as a fruit of his saving love.

Saints and Sadists

Pleasure is Janus-faced: as a human reality it may be good and holy, or it may be sinful and vile. This is not because of the nature of the pleased feeling itself, for that in itself is morally neutral; it is because of what produces it and what goes with it. Do saints find pleasure in praising God? Yes. Do sadists get pleasure from hurting people? Yes again.

If pleasure comes unsought, and if we receive it gratefully as a providential gift, and if it does no damage to ourselves or to others, and if it involves no breach of God's laws, and if the delight of it prompts fresh thanksgiving to God, then it is holy. But if the pursuit of one's pleasure is a gesture of egoism and self-indulgence whereby one pleases oneself without a thought as to whether one pleases God or anyone else, then, however harmless in itself the pleasure pursued may be, one has been entrapped by what the Bible sees as the pleasures of the world and of sin (see Luke 8:14; 2 Tim 3:4; Titus 3:3; Heb 11:25; James 4:3; 5:5; 2 Pet 2:13). The same experience—eating, drinking, making love, listening to music, painting, playing games, or whatever—will be good or bad, holy or unholy, depending on how it is handled.

In the order of creation, pleasures as such are meant to serve as pointers to God. Pleasure-seeking in itself sooner or later brings boredom and disgust, as the wise man testifies (Eccles. 2:1–11). Appreciating pleasures as they come our way, however, is one mark of a reverent, God-centered heart. A Jewish rabbi is credited with affirming that, on the day of judgment, God will hold us accountable for any neglect we have shown of pleasures he provided.

Christian teachers have insisted that contempt for pleasure, far from demonstrating superior spirituality, is actually an expression of the Manichean heresy (the view that the material world and everything it yields have no value and are indeed evil) and a manifestation of spiritual pride. Pleasure is divinely designed to raise our sense of God's goodness, deepen our gratitude to him, and strengthen our hope as Christians looking forward to richer pleasure in the world to come.

Escaping the Pleasure Grip

This truth about pleasure was not fully grasped in the first Christian centuries. The Greco-Roman world that the early church confronted was in the grip of a frenzied pleasure-seeking mentality, with overeating, drunkenness, and sexual shenanigans as preferred amusements, just like today; so it is no wonder that the early church fathers spent more time attacking sinful pleasures than celebrating godly ones, nor that this perspective was carried into the Middle Ages, in which the world-renouncing asceticism of the monastery was thought of as the highest form of Christianity. But through the Reformers' and the Puritans' appreciation of God's grace and insistence on the sanctity of secular life, the biblical theology of pleasure finally broke surface.

John Calvin states it best. In his *Institutes*, in a chapter entitled "How We Should Use This Present Life and Its Helps," he warns against the extremes of both overdone austerity and overdone indulgence. He affirms that not to use for pleasure those created realities that afford pleasure is ingratitude to the Creator. At the same time, however, he enforces Paul's admonition not to cling to sources of pleasure since we may one day lose them (1 Cor. 7:29–31); and he recommends moderation—that is, deliberate restraint—in availing ourselves of pleasures, lest our hearts be enslaved to them and we become unable cheerfully to do without them.

It is ironic that Calvin, who is so often considered the embodiment of gloomy austerity, should actually be a masterful theologian of pleasure. It is no less ironic that the Puritans, whose public image is of professional killjoys (H. L. Mencken defined Puritanism as the haunting fear that somewhere, somehow, somebody may be happy), should have been the ones who have insisted again and again that, in the words of Isaac Watts, their leading songster, "Religion never was designed / To make our pleasures less." And it is supremely ironic that, after two millennia of Christian culture, the West should now be plunging back into a self-defeating hedonism that is horribly similar to the barbaric pagan lifestyle of the first century, while decrying the Christian religion as basically antihuman because it does not set up pleasing oneself as life's highest value. But the wisdom about pleasure that Calvin voiced nearly five centuries ago remains basic to authentic Christian living, in this or any age.

———

Chapter 41

WHY I SIGNED IT

*The recent statement "Evangelicals and Catholics
Together"' recognizes an important truth: Those
who love the Lord must stand together.*

"Evangelicals and Catholics Together: The Christian Mission
in the Third Millennium" (ECT) is the title of a pro-
grammatic statement composed by eight Protestants (leader,
Charles Colson) and seven Roman Catholics (leader, Richard
John Neuhaus) and endorsed by 12 more Protestants and 13
more Roman Catholics. It appeared in the journal *First Things*
in May of this year [1994] and, shortened, in the Spring edition
of *Touchstone*.

The statement is not, of course, official, nor has it any more
authority than the personal credit of those who have put their
names to it. It does not commit the churches, institutions, and
organizations to which they belong: each subscriber speaks
simply for himself. The hope, however, clearly is that the document will make waves and change established behavior patterns.

In this way its strategic importance could be far-reaching, for the lead it gives has not been given before.

The plot-line of its 8,000 words is simply summarized. After stating that its concern is with "the relationship between evangelicals and Catholics, who constitute the growing edge of missionary expansion at present and, most likely, in the century ahead," it announces its composers' agreement on the Apostles' Creed and on the proposition that "we are justified by grace through faith because of Christ"; it affirms a commitment to seek more love, less misrepresentation and misunderstanding, and more clarity about continuing doctrinal differences between the two constituencies; then it declares war on anti-Christian statism and specifies social values that must be fought for; and it sketches out a purpose of nonproselytizing joint action for the conversion and nurture of outsiders. Grassroots "co-belligerence," to borrow Francis Schaeffer's word, is its theme. It identifies common enemies (unbelief, sin, cultural apostasy) and pleads that the counterattack be cooperative up to the limit of what conscience allows.

Hitherto, isolationism everywhere in everything has been the preferred policy of both Catholics and evangelicals, and a good deal of duplication and rivalry, fed by mutual suspicion and inflammatory talk, has resulted. This is particularly so in Latin America, where the Roman Catholic Church sometimes walks hand in hand with landowners and power brokers, and evangelicals multiply by the million, mostly through bringing true life in Christ to lapsed Catholics. But Latin America is not the only part of the world where isolationist animosities are strong. To transcend these tensions by undercutting isolationism itself is part of ECT's aim. So inevitably, ECT has run into trouble. Many isolationists are unwilling either to rethink or, under any circumstances, to change.

I was surprised at the violence of initial negative Protestant reaction, but I should not have been. Years ago, I came to realize that fear plays a larger part in North American motivation than is ever acknowledged. The sitting-on-a-volcano feeling is very American and is easily exploited. But fear clouds the mind and generates defensive responses that drive wisdom out of the window.

So I ought to have anticipated that some Protestants would say bleak, skewed, fearful, and fear-driven things about this document—for instance, that it betrays the Reformation; that it barters the gospel for a social agenda; that it forfeits the right to share Christ with nominal Roman Catholics; that by saying "we are justified by grace through faith because of Christ" it abandons justification by faith alone; and that its backers should be dropped from evangelical fellowship. All these untrue things have been said—and it is time, I think, to set the record straight.

What I write has inevitably a personal angle, for though I was not a drafter of the document, I endorsed it. Why? Because it affirms positions and expresses attitudes that have been mine for half a lifetime, and that I think myself called to commend to others every way I can. Granted, for the same half lifetime I have publicly advocated the Reformed theology that was first shaped (by Calvin) in opposition to Roman teaching about salvation and the church and that stands opposed to it still—which, I suppose, is why some people have concluded I have gone theologically soft, and others think I must be ignorant of Roman Catholic beliefs, and others guess that I signed ECT without reading it. But in fact, while maintaining what Reformed theology has always said about the official tradition of the Church of Rome, I have long thought that informal grassroots collaboration with Roman Catholics in ministry is the most fruitful sort of ecumenism that one can practice nowadays. And it is that, neither more nor less, that ECT recommends.

Perhaps I should say this more bluntly. I could not become a Roman Catholic because of certain basic tenets to which the Roman system, as such, is committed. Rome's claim to be the only institution that can without qualification be called the church of Christ is theologically flawed, for it misconceives the nature of the church as the New Testament explains it. The claim is historically flawed, too, for the papacy, which is supposed to be of the church's essence, was a relatively late development; if pipeline continuity of priestly orders and a sacramentalist soteriology are of that essence, then Eastern Orthodoxy's claim to be Christ's one church is stronger.

Also, developed Roman teaching on the Mass and on merit cuts across Paul's doctrine of justification in and through Christ by faith. And all forms of the Mary cult, the invoking of saints, the belief in purgatory, and the disbursing of indulgences (which still goes on) damp down the full assurance to which, according to Scripture, justification should lead through the ministry of the Holy Spirit.

Finally, the infallibility claimed for all conciliar and some papal pronouncements, and the insistence that the faithful should take their beliefs from the church as such rather than from the Bible as such, make self-correction, as ordinarily understood, impossible. The assumption that the church is never wrong on basics is very cramping.

So I find the Roman communion, as it stands, unacceptable, just as more than four-and-a-half centuries of Protestants did before me.

Why, then, should any Protestant, such as myself, want to maximize mission activity in partnership with Roman Catholics? Traditionally, Protestants and Catholics have kept their distance, treating each other as inferiors; each community has seen the other as out to deny precious elements in its own faith and practice, and so has given the other a wide berth. There are sound reasons why this historic stance should be adjusted.

First: Do we recognize that good evangelical Protestants and good Roman Catholics—good, I mean, in terms of their own church's stated ideal of spiritual life—are Christians together? We ought to recognize this, for it is true.

I am a Protestant who thanks God for the wisdom, backbone, maturity of mind and conscience, and above all, love for my Lord Jesus Christ that I often see among Catholics, and who sometimes has the joy of hearing Catholics say they see comparable fruits of grace in Protestants. But I am not the only one who is thus made aware that evangelicals and Catholics who actively believe are Christians together. The drafters of ECT declare that they accept Jesus Christ as Lord and Savior, affirm the Apostles' Creed, "are justified by grace through faith because of Christ," understand the Christian life from first to last as personal conversion to Jesus Christ and communion with him, know that they must "teach and live in obedience to the divinely inspired Scriptures, which are the infallible Word of God," and on this basis are "brothers and sisters in Christ." Though Protestant and Catholic church systems stand opposed, and bad—that is, unconverted—Catholics and Protestants are problems on both sides of the Reformation divide, good Protestants and Catholics are, and know themselves to be, united in the one body of Christ, joint-heirs not only with him but with each other.

Now, this mutual acknowledgment brings obligations, and one of these is observance of the so-called Lund principle, formulated decades ago in light of Jesus' high-priestly prayer for the unity of all his disciples. This prayer clearly entails the thought that God's family here on earth should seek to look like one family by acting as one family; and the Lund principle is that ecclesiastically divided Christians should not settle for doing separately anything that their consciences allow them to do together. The implication is that otherwise we thwart and grieve the Lord. Where there is fellowship in faith, fellowship in service should follow, and the cherishing of standoffishness and isolationism becomes sin. So togetherness in mission is appropriate.

Second: do we recognize that the present needs of both church and community in North America (not to look further for the moment) cry out for an alliance of good evangelical Protestants with good Roman Catholics (and good Eastern Orthodox, too)? We ought to recognize this, for it, too, is true.

Vital for the church's welfare today and tomorrow in the United States and Canada is the building of the strongest possible transdenominational coalition of Bible-believing, Christ-honoring, Spirit-empowered Christians who will together resist the many forms of disintegrative theology—relativist, monist, pluralist, liberationist, feminist, or whatever—that plague both Protestantism and Catholicism at the present time. Such a coalition already exists among evangelicals, sustained by parachurch organizations, seminaries, media, mission programs and agencies, and literature of various kinds. It would be stronger in its stand for truth if it were in closer step with the parallel Catholic coalition that has recently begun to grow.

Time was when Western Christendom's deepest division was between relatively homogeneous Protestant churches and a relatively homogeneous Church of Rome. Today, however, the deepest and most hurtful division is between theological conservatives (or "conservationists," as I prefer to call them), who honor the Christ of the Bible and of the historic creeds and confessions, and theological liberals and radicals who for whatever reason do not; and this division splits the older Protestant bodies and the Roman communion internally. Convictional renewal within the churches can only come, under God, through sustained exposition, affirmation, and debate, and since it is substantially the same battle that has to be fought across the board, a coalition of evangelical and Catholic resources for the purpose would surely make sense.

It is similarly vital for the health of society in the United States and Canada that adherents to the key truths of classical Christianity—a self-defining triune God who is both Creator and Redeemer; this God's regenerating and sanctifying grace; the sanctity of life here, the certainty of personal judgment hereafter, and the return of Jesus Christ to end history—should link up for the vast and pressing task of re-educating our secularized communities on these matters. North American culture generally has lost its former knowledge of what it means to revere God, and hence it has lost its values and standards, its shared purposes, its focused hopes, and, in a word, its knowledge of what makes human life human, so that now it drifts blindly along materialistic, hedonistic, and nihilistic channels. Again, it is the theological conservationists, and they alone—mainly, Roman Catholics and the more established evangelicals—who have resources for the rebuilding of these ruins, and their domestic differences about salvation and the church should not hinder them from joint action in seeking to re-Christianize the North American milieu.

In its section titled "We Contend Together," ECT spells out a resolve to uphold religious freedom, sanctity of life, family values, parental choice in education, moral standards in society, and democratic institutions worldwide. This should be as much an agenda for all evangelicals as it is for any Catholic, and these contendings are crucial at present; but they will only gain credibility if the view of reality in which they are rooted takes hold of people's minds. Propagating the basic faith, then, remains the crucial task, and it is natural to think it will best be done as a combined operation. So togetherness in witness is timely.

Third: do we recognize that in our time mission ventures that involve evangelicals and Catholics side by side, not only in social witness but in evangelism and nurture as well, have already emerged? We ought to recognize this, for it is a fact.

From the many available examples, I take three. Among them, they illustrate the point sufficiently. The late Francis Schaeffer focused the concept of co-belligerence, that is, joint action for agreed objectives by people who disagree on other things, and then implemented it by leading evangelicals into battle alongside Roman Catholics on the abortion front, where—thank God!—they remain. Billy Graham's cooperative evangelism, in which all the churches in an area, of whatever stripe, are invited to share, is well established on today's Christian scene. And so are charismatic get-togethers, some of them one-off, some of them regular, and some of them huge, where the distinction between Protestant and Catholic vanishes in a Christ-centered unity of experience. So the togetherness that ECT pleads for has already begun.

ECT, then, must be viewed as fuel for a fire that is already alight. The grassroots coalition at which the document aims is already growing. It can be argued that, so far from running ahead of God, as some fear, ECT is playing catch-up to the Holy Spirit, formulating at the level of principle a commitment into which many have already entered at the level of practice; and certainly, the burden of proof must rest on any who wish to deny that this is so.

I conclude, then, on grounds of biblical principle, reinforced by current pressures and precedents, that ECT's modeling of an evangelical–Roman Catholic commitment to partnership in mission within set limits and without convictional compromise is essentially right, and I remain glad to endorse it. In the days when Rome seemed to aim at political control of all Christendom and the death of Protestant churches, such partnership was not possible. But those days are past and after Vatican II can hardly return. Whatever God's future may be for the official Roman Catholic system, present evangelical partnership with spiritually alive Roman Catholics in communicating Christ to unbelievers and upholding Christian order in a post-Christian world needs to grow everywhere, as ECT maintains. This should be beyond question.

Concerning ECT itself, however, questions remain, and it is time to turn to them. Whether it was wisest to write this document in a flowing, rhetorical, open-textured way, so that it reads like a political speech; whether it would have helped to have professional evangelical theologians involved in the drafting process (there were none); and whether any particular rearrangements, additions, and tightenings up would make ECT more persuasive to its suspicious critics—all are questions we may leave on one side. ECT's tone and thrust are right, and anyone who has learned not to rip phrases out of their context will see well enough what is intended.

Some, however, denounce ECT as a sellout of evangelical Protestantism and conclude that the evangelical team was incompetent, irresponsible, and outmaneuvered. The difficulties these critics feel raise issues of importance.

First: Does it not always put you in a false position to work with people with whom you do not totally agree? Not if you agree on the specific truths and goals the proposed collaboration involves, and if the points of nonagreement and therefore the limits of togetherness in action are well understood. Here, I judge, ECT, fairly read, passes muster.

Second: May ECT realistically claim, as in effect it does, that its evangelical and Catholic drafters agree on the gospel of salvation? Yes and no. If you mean, could they all be relied on to attach the same small print to their statement, "we are justified by grace through faith because of Christ," no. (The Tridentine assertion of merit and the Reformational assertion of imputed righteousness can hardly be harmonized.) If you mean, do all present-day Catholics focus on the living Christ, Lord, Savior, and coming King as the direct object of the sinner's faith and hope in the way ECT does, doubtless no again. (I imagine some traditional Catholics have problems with ECT at this point, though today's Catholic theologians observably do not.) But if you mean, does ECT's insistence that the Christ of Scripture, creeds, and con- fessions is faith's proper focus, and that "Christian witness is of necessity aimed at conversion," not only as an initial step but as a personal life-process, and that this constitutes a sufficient account of the gospel of salvation for shared evangelistic min- istry, then surely yes. What brings salvation, after all, is not any theory about faith in Christ, justification, and the church, but faith itself in Christ himself. Here also ECT, fairly read, seems to me to pass muster, though the historic disagreements at theory level urgently now need review.

Third: Does not ECT treat baptismal regeneration, which Catholics affirm and evangelicals deny, as acceptable doctrine? No. Its logic (smudged somewhat by loose drafting, but clear enough to fair readers) is that agreement on the necessity of personal conversion makes evangelistic cooperation viable, in principle and in practice, despite this continuing disagreement. ECT clearly envisages an evangelism that, by requiring transac- tional trust in the living Christ, rules out all thought of baptism without faith saving anyone.

Fourth: Does not ECT imply that Protestants should stop trying to evangelize Roman Catholics, or make Protestants out of them? No. ECT walks a tightrope here, as follows: "We condemn the practice of recruiting people from another community for purposes of denominational or institutional aggrandizement. ... It is neither theologically legitimate nor a prudent use of resources for one Christian community to proselytize among active adherents of another Christian community. ... Those converted ... must be given full freedom and respect as they discern and decide the community in which they will live their new life in Christ."

It is clear that sharing Christ with inactive, nominal, lifeless-looking adherents of any communion is permitted by this wording; so is explaining the pros and cons of choosing a church, and the importance, for growth, of being under faithful ministry of the word. What is ruled out is associating salvation or spiritual health with churchly identity, as if a Roman Catholic cannot be saved without becoming a Protestant or vice versa, and on this basis putting people under pressure to change churches.

The flow of thought in the above extract shows that "theologically legitimate" means "theologically appropriate." This is not the only example of loose phrasing in ECT. But all comes clear if one follows the flow of ideas.

So I find that ECT is not at all a sellout of Protestantism, but is in fact a well-judged, timely call to a mode of grassroots action that is significant for furthering the kingdom of God.

To be sure, ECT is only a beginning. Those for whom anti-Romanism or anti-Protestantism is part of their identity and ministry will need more than ECT to alter their mindset, as will those Protestants who deny that Roman Catholics can be Christians without leaving Rome. There needs now to be a rigorous review of how the theological questions that have thus far divided the Catholic and Protestant churches look in light of the new ECT commitment. Well does ECT say, "The differences and disagreements ... must be addressed more fully and candidly in order to strengthen between us a relation of trust in obedience to truth." Without this ECT will get nowhere, nor will it deserve to.

To help shape this proposed study of the historic disagreements, Michael Horton and I put together some agenda suggestions that are printed in *Modern Reformation* (July–August 1994). What is important, however, is not that the work be done our way, but that the work be done as distinct from not done; for such study is the necessary next step.

But ECT is a good beginning, and for it I continue to thank God.

Chapter 42

———

THANK GOD FOR
OUR BIBLES

*While Scripture comes in many flavors today, we can
still trust these translations to give us God's Word.*

I n one respect, today's English-reading believers are the most
privileged Christians of all time. Available to us are more ver-
nacular versions of Holy Scripture than any generation before us
had, and all the mainline ones are good. (I am not considering
here such renderings as the Jehovah's Witnesses' *New World
Version.*) It is important, however, to grasp that they are good in
different ways, according to how each seeks to impact its targeted
readership. The goal is still Luther's and Tyndale's goal, that ordinary people might clearly understand the Word of God, but it is
pursued by different routes.

Versions is an umbrella word that covers all the products of
the two main translation methods currently in use. Some versions opt for grammatical equivalence, that is, a word-for-word
and clause-for-clause correspondence with the original as far

as possible. The risk here is stiffness of style, unnatural English, and consequent obscurity. Other versions aim at dynamic equivalence, that is, a rendering that conveys the substance and force of the original, though at the cost of periodic paraphrase. The risk here is a woolly superficiality that keeps readers from deep and exact understanding. The ideal would be an equivalence that was fully literal and fully dynamic too, but that is not always possible, because the usage of pre-Christian Hebrew and first-century Greek does not always match that of modern English. So tradeoffs are inescapable in the translation process, and here the versions fan out into three main types.

Some prefer verbal equivalence, even if awkward, over punchy vividness in places where you cannot have both. Examples of this are the New King James Version (NKJV) and the New American Standard Bible (NASB). Instances of the opposite choice carried through are the Living Bible (LB), the New Century Version (NCV), Today's English Version (TEV; also called the Good News Bible), God's Word (GW), and the Contemporary English Version (CEV). In between come compromise renderings that aim at the best of both worlds, as much grammatical literalness and punchy vividness combined as they can manage. Here the Revised Standard Version (RSV), now off the market, and the New International Version (NIV) have established themselves as the top products of this type, with the NIV currently the best-selling of all the translations. Whether the recently arrived New Revised Standard Version (NRSV) and the yet more recent New Living Translation (NLT), both of which exemplify the balanced tradeoff mode, will ever displace the NIV remains to be seen.

Do we need so many versions? Probably, yes, for our world is split into many subcultures, each with its own linguistic and reading habits and shifting wavelengths of comprehension. Shakespeare lovers and connoisseurs of Milton and Bunyan still appreciate the stately King James Version of 1611 (KJV), as do elderly folk brought up on it. But tabloid readers and teens get further faster with the brasher liveliness of the NLT or CEV, or Eugene Peterson's *The Message*. The American cultural kaleidoscope that has made niche marketing necessary in retail trade has also made necessary "niche rendering" in the world of Bible translation. So it should cause no pain or consternation to learn that one's own favorite version rings no bells with someone else who likes a version that rings no bells with you.

When in Doubt, Lean Literal

Translators of the spoken word, in preaching, diplomacy, business, or any other field, are rightly called interpreters, for all translation is interpretation to some extent. Translators decide what a speaker means and how to convey it most clearly in the other language and are rated according to their skill in doing this. So it is with written material, and signally so with the text of Scripture, in which much of God's teaching is carried by choice of words and phrases and by significant verbal echoes. Paraphrase renderings can be a problem here, because they make the original wording inaccessible and give only the translator's view of what it all adds up to; and that view may be disputable.

This is illustrated by the recent debate about inclusive-language versions. It was urged that rendering *brothers* in the New Testament as *brothers and sisters* (which secular Greek usage allows, though Old Testament thought-forms hardly encourage) and cutting out the generic masculine *he* (which is standard in Greek and Hebrew, as it has been in English and most other languages) would make translations more accurate by showing that God in Scripture addresses women as well as men. It was assumed that nothing of theological significance hangs on these changes.

But is this inclusive masculine part of a pervasive biblical and general-revelation witness to a male priority (headship, however precisely defined) in the order of creation? There are those who think so; and while the debate about this continues, and everyone understands, even if some do not like, the inclusive masculine, the wise way is not to paraphrase it out—certainly not to cut it out of any version that currently displays it, as if any such display is a defect. The rule should surely be: where there is doubt or dispute about the significance of the data, render literally so that readers have access to the wording of the original and so can engage with the problem directly. To paraphrase out a disputed feature would be, from one standpoint, to slant the version, and from another, to undertranslate.

Undertranslation, in pursuit of an easy English flow, can be more of a problem than is sometimes realized. Two examples show this. First, in Ephesians 4:13 most modern versions (NIV, RSV, NRSV, GW, NLT for starters) make Paul say that through reaching unity in the faith and in the knowledge of the Son we are to become mature, or to reach mature manhood, the fullness of Christ being the standard of our maturity. Only the KJV and NASB let us know that Paul actually wrote of reaching "a mature man." The paraphrasing translations take the "mature man" to be either a full-grown Christian or Christ himself, both of which find support in the commentaries. But, as John Stott observes, the context points to a corporate understanding of the "mature man" as the "one new man" of Ephesians 2:15, the Jewish-Gentile church that Paul pictures as Christ's body, building, and bride. Paul's point then is that only through the maturing of the whole worldwide, multinational, multicultural Christian community will the fullness of Christ—that is, all that he is and gives—find full expression. No single one of us can embody it all! But the translations mentioned conceal from us the possibility that this is Paul's meaning by putting "manhood" where he put "man," or indeed by dropping "man" altogether. This is undertranslation.

Second, in James 2:1, most modern translations, including the NASB, give us the phrase "our glorious Lord Jesus Christ." James, however, wrote "our Lord Jesus Christ, *the glory*" (or "the Lord of the glory," as the KJV and RSV less naturally render the words). "The glory" in the Old Testament was the bright light that signified God's presence to bless, and what James seems to be saying is that our Lord Jesus Christ is precisely that—God present with us through his Spirit to bless us according to his revealed character and promises and purpose. But "glorious" fails to catch this, and so is undertranslation.

Paraphrasing out such semitechnical New Testament terms as *propitiation, justification, redemption, reconciliation,* and *righteousness* keeps the readers from realizing that these were among the apostolic teachers' keywords, and thus is a further instance of undertranslation.

These examples show that it is no more possible to produce a translation of the Bible that caters to all the concerns of all Bible readers than it is to square the circle. My opening statement that all the current versions are good did not mean that any of them was perfect, only that all of them do surprisingly well in terms of their own ground rules. So we should thank God for the scholarly labor that gives us so rich a range of options for our Bible reading and show our gratitude by soaking ourselves in the version or versions that suit us best. A comparison of the time we spend daily with the newspaper and with the Bible would put some of us to shame. We should banish the irrational though widespread suspicion that the multiplicity of versions means that none of them can be trusted; we should acknowledge (for this is the truth) that each of the best of them from time to time throws greater light on the detailed meaning of the text than do the others; and we should make Bible reading a life priority, as our Christian forefathers did. To read through the Bible annually, ringing the changes perhaps on a grammatical-equivalent, a dynamic-equivalent, and a middle-of-the-road version, would be a good goal for us all.

The Bible presented to the sovereign in the British coronation service is there described as "the most valuable thing that this world affords ... the lively oracles of God." This witness is true, and it will be well for us if we learn to behave as those who believe it.

Chapter 43

STILL SURPRISED BY LEWIS

Yes, I was at Oxford in Lewis's day (I went up in 1944); but *no*, I never met him. He was regularly on show as the anchorman of the Socratic Club, which met weekly to discuss how science, philosophy, and current culture related to Christianity; but as a young believer, I was sure I needed Bible teaching rather than apologetics, so I passed the Socratic by. The nearest I ever got to Lewis was hearing him address the Oxford theologians' society on Richard Hooker, about whom he was writing at that time for his assigned volume of the Oxford History of English Literature, the "Oh-Hell" as for obvious reasons he liked to call it. He spoke with a resonant Anglicized accent (you would never have guessed he was Irish), and when he said something funny, which he did quite often, he paused like a stage comedian for the laugh. They said he was the best lecturer in Oxford, and I daresay they were right. But he was not really part of my world.

Yet I owe him much, and I gratefully acknowledge my debt.

First of all, in 1942–43, when I thought I was a Christian but did not yet know what a Christian was—and had spent a year verifying the old adage that if you open your mind wide enough much rubbish will be tipped into it—*The Screwtape Letters* and the three small books drat [*sic*] became *Mere Christianity* brought me, not indeed to faith in the full sense, but to mainstream Christian beliefs about God, man, and Jesus Christ, so that now I was halfway there.

Second, in 1945, when I was newly converted, the student who was discipling me lent me *The Pilgrim's Regress.* This gave me both a full-color map of the Western intellectual world as it had been in 1932 and still pretty much was 13 years later, and also a very deep delight in knowing that I knew God, beyond anything I had felt before. The vivid glow of Lewis's scenic and dramatic imagination, as deployed in the story, had started to grab me. *Regress*, Lewis's first literary effort as a Christian, is still for me the freshest and liveliest of all his books, and I reread it more often than any of the others.

Third, Lewis sang the praises of an author named Charles Williams, of whom I had not heard, and in consequence I picked up *Many Dimensions* in paperback in 1953 and had one of the most overwhelming reading experiences of my life—though that is another story.

Fourth, there are stellar passages in Lewis that for me, at least, bring the reality of heaven very close. Few Christian writers today try to write about heaven, and the theme defeats almost all who take it up. But as one who learned long ago from Richard Baxter's *Saints' Everlasting Rest* and Bunyan's *Pilgrim's Progress* the need for clearly focused thought about heaven, I am grateful for the way Lewis helps me along here.

The number of Christians whom Lewis's writings have helped, one way and another, is enormous. Since his death in 1963, sales of his books have risen to 2 million a year, and a recently polled cross section of CT readers rated him the most influential writer in their lives—which is odd, for they and I identify ourselves as evangelicals, and Lewis did no such thing. He did not attend an evangelical place of worship nor fraternize with evangelical organizations. "I am a very ordinary layman of the Church of England," he wrote; "not especially 'high,' nor especially 'low,' nor especially anything else." By ordinary evangelical standards, his idea about the Atonement (archetypal penitence, rather than penal substitution), and his failure ever to mention justification by faith when speaking of the forgiveness of sins, and his apparent hospitality to baptismal regeneration, and his noninerrantist view of biblical inspiration, plus his quiet affirmation of purgatory and of the possible final salvation of some who have left this world as nonbelievers, were weaknesses; they led the late, great Martyn Lloyd-Jones, for whom evangelical orthodoxy was mandatory, to doubt whether Lewis was a Christian at all. His closest friends were Anglo-Catholics or Roman Catholics; his parish church, where he worshiped regularly, was "high"; he went to confession; he was, in fact, anchored in the (small-c) "catholic" stream of Anglican thought, which some (not all) regard as central. Yet evangelicals love his books and profit from them hugely. Why?

As one involved in this situation, I offer the following answer.

In the first place, Lewis was a *lay evangelist*, conservative in his beliefs and powerful in his defense of the old paths. "Ever since I became a Christian," he wrote in 1952, "I have thought that the best, perhaps the only service I could do for my unbelieving neighbors was to explain and defend the belief that has been common to nearly all Christians at all times." To make ordinary people think about historic Christianity, and to see and feel the strength and attraction of the case for it, was Lewis's goal throughout. All through his writings runs the sense that moderns have ceased to think about life and reality in a serious way and have settled instead for mindless drift with the crowd, or blind trust in technology, or the Athenian frivolity of always chasing new ideas, or the nihilism of knee-jerk negativism toward everything in the past. The Christian spokesman's first task, as Lewis saw it, is to put all this into reverse and get folk thinking again.

So his immediate goal in a sustained flow of didactic books, opinion pieces, children's stories, adult fiction and fantasy, autobiography, and poems, along with works of literary history and criticism, spread out over more than 30 years, was to stir up serious thought. About what? About the Christian values and perspectives that the people he once labeled the Clevers had left behind, and about the morasses one gets bogged down in once the Christian heritage is abandoned; and on from there. He would have agreed with the often-stated dictum of fellow evangelist Martyn Lloyd-Jones that the Christian is and must be the greatest thinker in the universe, and that God's first step in adult conversion is to make the person think.

Lewis was clear that, as he has Screwtape tell us in many different ways, thoughtlessness ruins souls; so he labored mightily by all kinds of stimulating persuasives—witty, argumentative, pictorial, fanciful, logical, prophetic, and dramatic by turns—to ensure, so far as he could, that death-dealing thoughtlessness would not flourish while he was around. His constant pummelling of his reader's mind was neither Ulster temperament nor Oxford didacticism, but the urgent compassionate expression of one who knew that the only alternative to grasping God's truth and seeing everything by its light is idiocy in one form or another.

And he believed, surely with reason, that his credibility as a Christian spokesman in an anticlerical age was enhanced by the fact that he had no professional religious identity but was just an Anglican layman earning his salt by teaching English at Oxford. As G. K. Chesterton was to himself simply a journalist with a significant Christian outlook, so Lewis was to himself simply an academic with a significant spare-time vocation of Christian utterance. Evangelicals appreciate lay evangelists of Lewis's kind.

Second, Lewis was a *brilliant teacher.* His strength lay not in the forming of new ideas but in the arresting simplicity, both logical and imaginative, with which he projected old ones. Not wasting words, he plunged straight into things and boiled matters down to essentials, positioning himself as a common-sense, down-to-earth, no-nonsense observer, analyst, and conversation partner. On paper he had a flair, comparable to that of the great evangelists in the pulpit (Whitefield, Spurgeon, Graham, for example), for making you feel he is in personal conversation with you, searching your heart and requiring of you total honesty in response. Never pontifical, never browbeating, and never wrapping things up, Lewis achieved an intimacy of instruction that is very unusual. Those who read today what he wrote half a century ago find him engaging and holding their attention, and when the reading is over, haunting them, in the sense that they do not forget what he said. At his best, Lewis is a teacher of great piercing power. What is his secret?

The secret lies in the blend of logic and imagination in Lewis's make-up, each power as strong as the other, and each enormously strong in its own right. In one sense, imagination took the lead. As Lewis wrote in 1954:

> The imaginative man in me is older, more continuously operative, and in that sense more basic than either the religious writer or the critic. It was he who made me first attempt (with little success) to be a poet. ... It was he who after my conversion led me to embody my religious belief in symbolic or mythopoeic forms, ranging from Screwtape to a kind of theologized science-fiction. And it was of course he who has brought me, in the last few years, to write the series of Narnia stories for children ... because the fairy tale was the genre best fitted for what I wanted to say.

The best teachers are always those in whom imagination and logical control combine, so that you receive wisdom from their flights of fancy as well as a human heartbeat from their logical analyses and arguments. This in fact is human communication at its profoundest, for in the sending-receiving process of both lobes of the brain (left for logic, right for imagination) are fully involved, and that gives great depth and strength to what is heard. The teaching of Jesus presents itself as the supreme example here. Because Lewis's mind was so highly developed in both directions, it can truly be said of him that all of his arguments (including his literary criticism) are illustrations, in the sense that they throw light directly on realities of life and action, while all his illustrations (including the fiction and fantasies) are arguments, in the sense that they throw light directly on realities of truth and fact.

G. K. Chesterton, Charles Williams, and to some extent Dorothy L. Sayers exhibit the same sort of bipolar mental development, and what I have said of Lewis's writings can be said of theirs, too. Such minds will always command attention, and when possessed, as the minds of these four were possessed, by the values and visions of Christian faith and Christian humanism, they will always make an appeal that is hard to resist; and that appeal will not diminish as the culture changes. Visionary didacticism, as in Plato, Jesus, and Paul (to look no further) is transcultural, and unfading in its power. Bible-loving evangelicals, who build their whole faith on the logical-visionary teaching of God himself via his servants from Genesis to Revelation, naturally seek and appreciate this mode of communication in their latter-day instructors, and the consensus among them is that no twentieth-century writer has managed it so brilliantly as did C. S. Lewis.

Third, Lewis projects a *vision of wholeness*—sanity, maturity, present peace and joy, and finally fulfillment in heaven—that cannot but attract, willy-nilly, the adult children of our confused, disillusioned, alienated, and embittered culture: the now established culture of the West, which we shall certainly take with us (or maybe, I should say, which will certainly take us with it) into the new millennium. Both Lewis's didactic expositions (think of *The Problem of Pain, The Screwtape Letters, Mere Christianity, Miracles, The Four Loves, Letters to Malcolm: Chiefly on Prayer,* and *Reflections on the Psalms)* and his fiction (think of the three Ransom stories, the seven Narnia tales, *The Great Divorce,* and *Till We Have Faces)* yield a vision of human life under God (or Maleldil, or Aslan, or the unnamed divinity who confronts Orual) that is redemptive, transformational, virtue-valuing, and shot through with hints and flashes of breathtaking glory and eternal delight in a world to come. To be sure, the vision is humbling, for the shattering of all egoistic pride, all Promethean heroics, and all the possessive perversions of love is part of it. In the text of all his Christian writings, and in the subtext, at least, of all his wider literary work, Lewis rings endless changes on the same story: a story of moral and intellectual corruption, embryonic or developed, being overcome in some way, whereby more or less disordered human beings, victims of bad thinking and bad influences from outside, find peace, poise, discernment, realism, fulfillment, and a meaningful future. Evangelicals love such writing: who can wonder at that?

Here we are at the deepest level of Lewis's creative identity. At bottom he was a mythmaker. As Austin Farrer, Lewis's closest clerical friend and Oxford's most brilliant theologian at that time, observed, in Lewis's apologetics "we think we are listening to an argument; in fact, we are presented with a vision; and it is the vision that carries conviction." Myth is perhaps best defined as a story that projects a vision of life of actual or potential communal significance by reason of the identity and attitudes that it invites us to adopt. Lewis had loved the pre-Christian god-stories of Norse and Greek mythology, and the thought that did most to shape his return to Christianity and his literary output thereafter was this: In the Incarnation, a myth that recurs worldwide, the myth of a dying and rising deity through whose ordeal salvation comes to others, has become a space-time fact. Both before Christ, in pagan mythology, and since Christ, in imaginative fiction from Christian and para-Christian Westerners, versions of this story in various aspects have functioned as "good dreams," preparing minds and hearts for the reality of Christ according to the gospel. With increasing clarity, Lewis saw his own fiction as adding to this stock of material.

Lewis knew that by becoming fact in Christ, the worldwide myth had not ceased to be a story that, by its appeal to our imagination, can give us "a taste for the other"—a sense of reality, that is, which takes us beyond left-brain conceptual knowledge. He found that what he now knew as the fact of Christ was generating and fertilizing within him stories of the same shape—stories, that is, that picture redemptive action in worlds other than ours, whether in the past, present, or future. In the fantasy novels (*Out of the Silent Planet, Perelandra, That Hideous Strength, Till We Have Faces*, and the seven Narnias) he became what Tolkien called a "sub-creator," producing good dreams of his own that, by reflecting Christian fact in a fantasy world, might prepare hearts to embrace the truth of Christ. The vision of wholeness that these myths project, and of the God-figures through whom that wholeness comes (think here particularly of Aslan, the Christly lion), can stir in honest hearts the wish that something of this sort might be true, and so beget, under God, readiness to accept the revelation that something of this sort is true, as a matter of fact.

Lewis once described *The Lion, the Witch and the Wardrobe* as giving an answer to the question, "What might Christ be like if there really were a world like Narnia and he chose to be incarnate and die and rise again in that world as he actually has done in ours?" All the Narnia books elaborate that answer: Aslan's doings are a reimagining in another world of what Jesus Christ did, does, and will do in this one. George Sayer, Lewis's finest biographer, ends his chapter on Narnia by telling how "my little stepdaughter, after she had read all the Narnia stories, cried bitterly, saying, 'I don't want to go on living in this world. I want to live in Narnia with Aslan' "—and then adding the five-word paragraph: "Darling, one day you will." The power of Lewisian myth as Christian communication could not be better shown, and countless believers who have nourished their children on Narnia will resonate with Sayer here.

Nor is that all. Over and above its evangelistic, or pre-evangelistic, role, Lewisian myth has an educating and maturing purpose. Lewis's 1943 Durham University lectures, published as *The Abolition of Man* (whew!) with the cooler academic subtitle, "Reflections on education with special reference to the teaching of English in the upper forms of schools," is a prophetic depth charge (it has been called a harangue) embodying his acute concern about our educational and cultural future. Lewis's educational philosophy called for imaginative identification on the part of young people, with paths of truth and value foreshadowed in the Platonic tradition, focused in the biblical revelation, and modeled in such writings as Spenser's *Faerie Queene* and his own stories; and *The Abolition of Man* was the waving of a red flag at an oncoming juggernaut that would reduce education to the learning of techniques and so dehumanize and destroy it, tearing out of it that which is its true heart. (Could he inspect public education today, a half-century later, he would tell us that what he feared has happened.) His fiction, however, was meant to help in real education, moral aesthetic and spiritual—value-laden education, in other words—and it is from that standpoint that we look at it now.

A close-up on Lewis's philosophy of education is needed here. Its negative side is hostility to any reductionist subjectivizing of values, as if the words that express them signify not realities to discern and goals to pursue, but just feelings of like and dislike that come and go. As a long-term Platonist and now a Christian into the bargain, Lewis had for some time been troubled by the lurching of twentieth-century philosophy into this subjectivism, and *The Abolition of Man* begins as his assault on a school textbook that assumed it. Such subjectivizing, he says, produces "men without chests"; that is, adults who lack what he calls "emotions organized by trained habit into stable sentiments"—what we would call moral formation and moral character.

Positively, Lewis calls for adherence to the Tao (his term: *Tao* means *way*). The Tao is the basic moral code (beneficence, obligations and respect within the family, justice, truthfulness, mercy, magnanimity) that all significant religions and all stable cultures maintain, and that Christians recognize from the first two chapters of Romans as matters of God's general revelation to our race. Lewis sees this code as a unity, and as time-honored and experientially verified wisdom, and as the only safeguard of society in this or any age, so it is no wonder that he states its claim emphatically. Commenting on the fact that would-be leaders of thought dismiss some or all of the Tao in order to construct alternative moralities (think of Nietzsche, for instance), he declares:

> This thing which I have called for convenience the Tao, and which others may call Natural Law or Traditional Morality or the First Principles of Practical Reason or the First Platitudes is not one among a series of possible systems of value. It is the sole source of all value judgments. ...

The effort to refute it and raise a new system of value in its place is self-contradictory. ... What purport to be new systems or (as they now call them) 'ideologies', all consist of fragments from the Tao itself, arbitrarily wrenched from their context in the whole and then swollen to madness in their isolation, yet still owing to the Tao and to it alone such validity as they possess. If my duty to my parents is a superstition, then so is my duty to posterity. ... If the pursuit of scientific knowledge is a real value, then so is conjugal fidelity. The rebellion of new ideologies against the Tao is a rebellion of the branches against the tree: if the rebels could succeed they would find that they had destroyed themselves.

Lewis's novel *That Hideous Strength*, which tells of a devilish research organization called the N.I.C.E. taking over a British university in order to take over Britain in the name of science, seems to me as to others an artistic failure, but it is a striking success in the way that it pictures this process of moral rebellion and the self-destruction to which it leads—and that, I suspect, was the only success that Lewis cared about when he wrote it.

Now, Tao-orientation is an internalized mindset that has to be learned. Lewis invokes Plato on this: "The little human animal will not at first have the right responses. It must be trained to feel pleasure, liking, disgust and hatred at those things which really are pleasant, likable, disgusting, and hateful." Yes, but how? Partly, at least, through stories that model the right responses: poems like Spenser's *Faerie Queene*, one of Lewis's lifelong favorites (best read, he once affirmed, between the ages of 12 and 16), novels like those of George MacDonald, and myths like the Chronicles of Narnia. Doris Myers urges that the chronicles are a more or less conscious counterpart to the *Faerie Queene*, modeling particular forms of virtue in a Tao frame with Christian overtones across the spectrum of a human life. Affirming that "the didacticism of the Chronicles consists in the education of moral and aesthetic feelings ... to prevent children growing up without Chests," Myers reviews them to show how in each one "a particular virtue or configuration of virtues is presented, and the reader is brought to love it through participating in the artistry of the tale." The child will thus absorb the Tao by osmosis through enjoying the story.

Specifically: in the first chronicle, *The Lion, the Witch and the Wardrobe*, Lewis works to "strengthen the Chest" by inducing an emotional affirmation of courage, honor, and limitless kindness, with an emotional rejection of cowardice and treachery. In *Prince Caspian*, the second, he highlights joy within responsible self-control, in courtesy, justice, appropriate obedience, and the quest for order. In the third, *The Voyage of the Dawn Treader*, the endragoning and dedragoning of Eustace, "the Boy without a Chest," is flanked by vivid images of personal nobility (Reepicheep the Mouse) and public responsibility (Caspian the captain), while a tailpiece tells us how Eustace after his dedragoning was seen to be improved—"you'd never know him for the same boy." (The image, of course, is of Christian conversion.) Numbers four and five (*The Silver Chair* and *The Horse and His Boy*) teach lessons on managing one's thoughts and feelings as one nears adulthood; number six (*The Magician's Nephew*) invites hatred for the life-defying development of knowledge and use of power apart from the Tao; and number seven (*The Last Battle*) inculcates bravery in face of loss and death.

Thus Lewis's Narnia links up with his attempt, in *The Abolition of Man*, to recall education to its Tao-grounded roots. The attempt was ignored, and today we reap the bitter fruits of that fact. The inner desolation and desperation that young people experience as subjectivist relativism and nihilism are wished upon them in schools and universities is a tragedy. (If you do not know what I am referring to, listen to the pop singers; they will tell you.) Yet Lewis's imaginative presentation in his tales of a life of wholeness, maturity, sanity, honesty, humility, and humaneness, fictionally envisaged in order that it might be factually realized, still has great potency for both conversion and character building, as Narnia lovers most of all will testify. And evangelical believers greatly appreciate potency of this kind.

This brings us to the fourth factor in evangelical enthusiasm for C. S. Lewis: namely, the power with which he communicates not only the goodness of godliness, but also the *reality of God*, and with that the reality of the heaven that exists in the fullness of God's gracious presence.

Lewis's power here stemmed from his own vivid *experience*. From childhood he knew stabbing moments of what he called *joy*, that is, intense delightful longing, Sweet Desire (his phrase), that nothing in this world satisfies, and that is in fact a God-sent summons to seek the enjoyment of God and heaven. The way he describes it is calculated (Lewis, like other writers, could calculate his effects) to focus in our minds an awareness that this experience is ours too, so that Augustine was right to say that God made us for himself and our hearts lack contentment till they find it in him, in foretaste here and in fullness hereafter. Having found Sweet Desire to be an Ariadne's thread leading him finally to Christ (the autobiographical *Surprised by Joy* tells us how), Lewis holds our feet to the fire to ensure, if he can, that the same will happen to us. "If we consider the unblushing promises of reward and the staggering nature of the rewards promised in the Gospels, it would seem that Our Lord finds our desires, not too strong, but too weak. We are half-hearted creatures, fooling about with drink and sex and ambition when infinite joy is offered us

... We are far too easily pleased." Nothing must be allowed to distract us from staying the course with Sweet Desire.

Lewis's power to communicate God and heaven's reality was exerted through his marvelously vivid *rhetoric*. Rhetoric—that is, the art of using words persuasively—ran in the Lewis family, and C. S. Lewis himself was a prose poet whose skill with simple words, like Bunyan's, enabled him to suggest ineffable things to our imaginations with overwhelming poignancy. Thus, in *The Voyage of the Dawn Treader*, a momentary breeze brought the three children

> a smell and a sound, a musical sound. Edmund and Eustace would never talk about it afterwards. Lucy could only say, "It would break your heart." "Why," said I, "was it so sad?" "Sad!! No," said Lucy.
>
> No one in that boat doubted that they were seeing beyond the End of the World into Aslan's country.

And this is how *The Last Battle* ends:

> "There *was* a real railway accident," said Aslan softly. "Your father and mother and all of you are—as you used to call it in the Shadowlands—dead. The term is over: the holidays have begun. The dream is ended: this is the morning."
>
> And as He spoke He no longer looked to them like a lion; but the things that began to happen to them after that were so great and beautiful that I cannot write them ... we can most truly say that they all lived happily ever after. ... All their life in this world and all their adventures in Narnia had only been the cover and the title page now at last they were beginning Chapter One of the Great Story which no one on earth has read: which goes on forever: in which every chapter is better than the one before.

The knockout quality of such writing is more than words can express.

The combination within him of insight with vitality, wisdom with wit, and imaginative power with analytical precision made Lewis a sparkling communicator of the everlasting gospel. Matching Aslan in the Narnia stories with (of course!) the living Christ of the Bible and of Lewis's instructional books, and his presentation of Christ could hardly be more forthright. "We are told that Christ was killed for us, that His death has washed out our sins, and that by dying he disabled death itself. That is the formula. That is Christianity. That is what has to be believed." Then, on the basis of this belief and the future belief that he is risen and alive and so is personally *there* (that is, everywhere, which means *here)*, we must "put on," or as Lewis strikingly renders it, "dress up as" Christ—that is, give ourselves totally to Christ, so that he may be "formed in us," and we may henceforth enjoy in him the status and character of adopted children in God's family, or as again Lewis strikingly puts it, "little Christs." "God looks at you as if you were a little Christ: Christ stands beside you to turn you into one." Precisely.

Not just evangelicals, but all Christians, should celebrate Lewis, "the brilliant, quietly saintly, slightly rumpled Oxford don" as James Patrick describes him. He was a Christ-centered, great-tradition mainstream Christian whose stature a generation after his death seems greater than anyone ever thought while he was alive, and whose Christian writings are now seen as having classic status.

Long may we learn from the contents of his marvelous, indeed magical, mind! I doubt whether the full measure of him has been taken by anyone as yet.

Chapter 44

WISDOM IN A TIME OF WAR

*What Oswald Chambers and C. S. Lewis teach us about
living through the long battle with terrorism.*

S o we are at war. The United States leads a loose international coalition pledged to destroy the worldwide terrorist
networks, which produced the 19 young men who on September
11 randomly killed thousands of civilians and destroyed billions
of dollars worth of flagship property.

America's war aim is not just retributive justice (though it
certainly is that, as far as the terrorists are concerned). It is pri-
marily to prevent such attacks in the future by eliminating their
source. War is always evil, but in our nightmare scenario, where
more terrorism as a follow-up is confidently promised, a war of
suppression appears to most as the lesser evil. However burden-
some, it is surely the best and only rational course.

We need to be clear that terrorism, whether religiously, politically, or ideologically motivated, begins as a mindset—what the
Bible calls a thought of the heart. In this case, alienated persons

are driven by bitterness at real or fancied wrongs, by some form of racial or class hatred, and by utopian dreams of better things after the present order has been smashed. This is an explosive mix.

Terrorists think of themselves as both victims and avenging angels. They act out their self-justifying heartsickness in a way that matches Cain killing Abel. They see themselves as clever heroes, outsmarting their inferiors by concealing their real purpose and by overthrowing things they say are contemptible. So their morale is high, and conscience does not trouble them. Gleeful triumphalism drives terrorists on; they are sure they cannot lose. This is what the anti-terrorism coalition is up against. It is only realistic to anticipate that ridding the world of terrorism will be a long job.

Terrorism is something countries like Ireland and Israel know all about, having lived with local forms of it for decades, and now America must face it too. It would be silly to deny that the prospect is daunting, indeed traumatic. Jesus spoke of a day when men's hearts would faint with fear and foreboding of what was about to come on the world (Luke 21:26). Such a day may not be far off. Here and there, it seems a measure of panic has already begun to appear.

Where may we find godly wisdom to face days like these? One source is the teaching of two 20th-century British veterans of the Cross. One was a Baptist minister, Oswald Chambers, who died in 1917 at age 43 of complications following an appendectomy. At the time, he was serving as a YMCA chaplain with the British Commonwealth forces in Egypt. The other was an Oxford don, C. S. Lewis, who was in the trenches during the first World War and who, during World War II, taught basic Christianity to the troops, to Oxford undergraduates, and to the whole English nation by a series of books, broadcasts, and addresses. He died of kidney failure in 1963 at age 64. Chambers, little known in his own lifetime, became a Christian icon only when his widow compiled and published *My Utmost for His Highest* in 1927; Lewis gained that status with the success of *The Problem of Pain*, published in 1940.

Chambers and Lewis might seem an odd couple to pair up, but they had much in common. As their admirers already know, each had a brilliant mind, a stout faith, an uncannily empathetic and perceptive imagination, and a masterful way with words. Each was a teacher by instinct and gift. Each was spiritually honest and down-to-earth to an almost frightening degree. Each was well versed in the Western theological heritage, and in Western philosophy, literature, and history. Each adored the Lord Jesus Christ unstintingly as his Savior and Master. And each had a similar approach to the nitty-gritty of living through a war.

To be sure, Lewis, the Anglo-Catholic, would not have endorsed Chambers's acceptance of the Wesleyan belief in entire sanctification; and Chambers, the evangelical, would have felt that Lewis's treatments of biblical inspiration and the Atonement were a bit loose. But that is irrelevant here. The two men shared a full belief in the triune God, original sin, redemption and regeneration through Jesus Christ, and in the reality of God's sovereign control of all that happens. Against this background, the convergence of their thinking about spiritual life when surrounded by war is less surprising.

For any who wish to verify what I am about to report, the main evidence on Chambers is in the volume of his *Complete Works*, published in 2000, and in David McCasland's *Oswald Chambers: Abandoned to God* (1993). Lewis's thoughts are most clearly focused in *The Screwtape Letters* (1942) and his Oxford sermon, "Learning in War-time," which he preached in October 1939.

The war itself was never the subject of what Lewis and Chambers said, only part of the predicate. As neither politicians nor prophets but Christian nurturers, they took people in perplexity of need as their subject. They discussed war, with its unforeseeable outcomes and certain distresses, as only one of life's incidentals (granted, a huge one) with which we must learn to deal.

What, then, did they have to say about living with war? Basically, it was the same as they regularly said to help people live for God in this fallen world. It can be set out thus:

First, we must think. It is no surprise that Lewis, a university teacher, should have cast all he said as a Christian spokesman and apologist as an argument. (See *Mere Christianity*, *The Problem of Pain*, *Miracles*, and *God in the Dock* for starters.) Demanding critical thought for the developing of discernment is, after all, what Oxbridge education was (and still is) all about. It is more surprising that Chambers, long the chief speaker for the League of Prayer, a body promoting a second-blessing experience, should have stressed so constantly the need to grapple with life's big questions and urged so strongly that thinking was vital for spiritual growth and maturity.

The truth is that Chambers and Lewis were teachers to their fingertips. They knew that the unthinking—professed Christians no less than others—live perforce on prejudices, moods, and knee-jerk reactions that keep them from wisdom. They believed that informed thought is integral to the process of discipleship.

And so Chambers's word to a man who read only the Bible and books about it, and who felt stuck and inarticulate, was: "The trouble is you have allowed part of your brain to stagnate for want of use." The man later wrote, "There and then, [Chambers] gave me a list of over 50 books, philosophical, psychological, theological, covering almost every phase of modern thought," leading to "a revolution which can only be described as a mental new birth"— just as Chambers had hoped.

Conversely, Lewis's didactic devil Screwtape warns his naïve nephew and protégé, Wormwood, that humans must at all costs be distracted from pursuing truth by active thought. "The trouble about argument is that it moves the whole struggle onto the Enemy's own ground. ... By the very act of arguing, you awake the patient's reason; and once it is awake, who can foresee the result?" Serious thinking about life's basic questions is never ultimately on the devil's side; Lewis knows this and makes Screwtape acknowledge it.

Second, we must think about our own lives. Both teachers agreed that:

- God gives us life to live for his glory.

- Since the Fall, tragedy, distortion, frustration, and waste have been the regular marks of life in this world.

- Reason (with a capital R) cannot save us, as its secular worshipers thought it could.

- Knowing and serving Jesus Christ the Redeemer and his Father, who through Christ is now our Father, is the only thing that gives life meaning.

- "Human life has always been lived on the edge of a precipice" (Lewis), sometimes with danger to the body and always with danger to the spirit.

- Death is inescapable and wisdom requires us to remember this and live our lives accordingly.

- While God protects his people against spiritual shipwreck, he often puts them through pain for their spiritual progress and sometimes permits and uses war to that end.

- Christians are called not to understand everything God is doing but to be faithful to him.

All of this, to be sure, is mere mainstream Christianity, but it is worth underlining that Chambers the Baptist and Lewis the Anglican were at one in stressing it all.

Third, we must think directly about war. "War is the most damnably bad thing," Chambers said in Egypt three months before his death. "Because God overrules a thing and brings good out of it does not mean that the thing itself is a good thing. ... [However,] if the war has made me reconcile myself with the fact that there is sin in human beings, I shall no longer go with my head in the clouds, or buried in the sand like an ostrich, but I shall be wishing to face facts as they are." And that will be a good thing, for "it is not being reconciled to the fact of sin that produces all the disasters in life."

Lewis's Screwtape knows this to be true. He tells Wormwood not to hope for too much from the war, for it will not destroy the faith of real believers and will under God produce a measure of realism about life, death, and the issues of eternity that was not there before. "One of our best weapons, contented worldliness, is rendered useless," moaned Screwtape. "In wartime not even a human can believe that he is going to live forever."

"War," said Lewis the preacher, "makes death real to us; and that would have been regarded as one of its blessings by most of the great Christians of the past." Then he told his audience of undergraduates that they were at Oxford to study, that the values of being educated were not affected by the fact of war, and so they should get on with their academic work. Thus they would glorify

God. For trusting God for the future, and attending to present daily duties and tasks, is the way to honor God in wartime, as at all other times.

Lewis sharply denies that the experience of war in any form changes everything, as some have been saying that September 11 did. Writing half a century ago of nuclear war, he risked sounding unfeeling in order to enforce the way of wisdom:

> Believe me, dear sir or madam, you and all whom you love were already sentenced to death before the atomic bomb was invented; and quite a high percentage of us were going to die in unpleasant ways. ... It is perfectly ridiculous to go about whimpering and drawing long faces because the scientists have added one more chance of painful and pre-mature death to a world which already bristled with such chances and in which death itself was not a chance but a certainty. ... Let that bomb when it comes find us doing sensible and human things—praying, working, teaching, listening to music, bathing the children, playing tennis, chatting to our friends over a pint and a game of darts—not huddled together like frightened sheep and thinking about bombs. They may break our bodies (any microbe can do that) but they need not dominate our minds.

In other words, despite the threat of war, let life—God-given life—go on.

What then of America's present fears—of more targeted destructions and random explosions, of germ and chemical war-fare, and of other science-fiction fantasies becoming grim fact? Many feel panic at this moment, and it is clear, I think, what our teachers would have said to us had they foreseen such things.

Here is Chambers on fear:

It is the most natural thing in the world to be scared, and the clearest evidence that God's grace is at work in our hearts is when we do not get into panics. ... The remarkable thing about fearing God is that when you fear God you fear nothing else, whereas if you do not fear God you fear everything else.

And Lewis wrote:

You needn't worry about not feeling brave. Our Lord didn't—see the scene in Gethsemane. How thankful I am that when God became man he did not choose to become a man of iron nerves. ... Especially don't worry about being brave over merely possible evils in the future. ... If and when a horror turns up you will then be given Grace to help you. I don't think one is usually given it in advance. "Give us our daily bread" (not an annuity for life) applies to spiritual gifts too; the little daily support for the daily trial. Life has to be taken day by day and hour by hour.

In light of all this, I guess that Chambers and Lewis, were they back with us, would direct us as follows: Accept tightened security. Take all precautions that are responsibly certified as reasonable and desirable. While keeping watch and being careful, always remember that God is in charge and Romans 8:28 is true—he is working for the good of all those who love him. And, finally, pray for courage to cope with whatever comes, in the confidence that Isaac Watts was right when he wrote:

Should all the hosts of death
And powers of hell unknown
Put their most dreadful forms
Of rage and malice on,
I shall be safe, for Christ displays
Superior power and guardian grace.
Here, surely, is the wisdom and comfort we all need today.

Chapter 45

———

WHY I WALKED

Sometimes loving a denomination requires you to fight

In June 2002, the synod of the Anglican Diocese of New Westminster authorized its bishop to produce a service for blessing same-sex unions, to be used in any parish of the diocese that requests it. A number of synod members walked out to protest the decision. They declared themselves out of communion with the bishop and the synod, and they appealed to the Archbishop of Canterbury and other Anglican primates and bishops for help.

J. I. Packer, an executive editor of Christianity Today, *was one of those who walked out. Many people have asked him why. Though one part of his answer applies specifically to Anglicans, his larger argument should give guidance to any Christians troubled by developments in their church or denomination.*

W hy did I walk out with the others? Because this decision, taken in its context, falsifies the gospel of Christ, abandons the authority of Scripture, jeopardizes the salvation of fellow human beings, and betrays the church in its God-appointed role as the bastion and bulwark of divine truth.

My primary authority is a Bible writer named Paul. For many decades now, I have asked myself at every turn of my theological road: Would Paul be with me in this? What would he say if he were in my shoes? I have never dared to offer a view on anything that I did not have good reason to think he would endorse.

In 1 Corinthians we find the following, addressed it seems to exponents of some kind of antinomian spirituality:

> Do you not know that the unrighteous will not inherit the kingdom of God? Do not be deceived: neither the sexually immoral, nor idolaters, nor adulterers, nor men who practice homosexuality, nor thieves, nor the greedy, nor drunkards, nor revilers, nor swindlers will inherit the kingdom of God. And such were some of you. But you were washed, you were sanctified, you were justified in the name of the Lord Jesus and by the Spirit of our God (6:9–11, ESV).

To make sure we grasp what Paul is saying here, I pose some questions.

First: What is Paul talking about in this vice list? Answer: Lifestyles, regular behavior patterns, habits of mind and action. He has in view not single lapses followed by repentance, forgiveness, and greater watchfulness (with God's help) against recurrence, but ways of life in which some of his readers were set, believing that for Christians there was no harm in them.

Second: What is Paul saying about these habits? Answer: They are ways of sin that, if not repented of and forsaken, will keep people out of God's kingdom of salvation. Clearly, self-indulgence and self-service, free from self-discipline and self-denial, is the attitude they express, and a lack of moral discernment lies at their heart.

Third: What is Paul saying about homosexuality? Answer: Those who claim to be Christ's should avoid the practice of same-sex physical connection for orgasm, on the model of heterosexual intercourse. Paul's phrase, "men who practice homosexuality," covers two Greek words for the parties involved in these acts. The first, *arsenokoitai*, means literally "male-bedders," which seems clear enough. The second, *malakoi*, is used in many connections to mean "unmanly," "womanish," and "effeminate," and here refers to males matching the woman's part in physical sex.

In this context, in which Paul has used two terms for sexual misbehavior, there is really no room for doubt regarding what he has in mind. He must have known, as Christians today know, that some men are sexually drawn to men rather than women, but he is not speaking of inclinations, only of behavior, what has more recently been called acting out. His point is that Christians need to resist these urges, since acting them out cannot please God and will reveal lethal impenitence. Romans 1:26 shows that Paul would have spoken similarly about lesbian acting out if he had had reason to mention it here.

Fourth: What is Paul saying about the gospel? Answer: Those who, as lost sinners, cast themselves in genuine faith on Christ and so receive the Holy Spirit, as all Christians do (see Gal. 3:2), find transformation through the transaction. They gain cleansing of conscience (the washing of forgiveness), acceptance with God (justification), and strength to resist and not act out the particular temptations they experience (sanctification). As a preacher friend declared to his congregation, "I want you to know that I am a non-practicing adulterer." Thus he testified to receiving strength from God.

With some of the Corinthian Christians, Paul was celebrating the moral empowering of the Holy Spirit in heterosexual terms; with others of the Corinthians, today's homosexuals are called to prove, live out, and celebrate the moral empowering of the Holy Spirit in homosexual terms. Another friend, well known to

me for 30 years, has lived with homosexual desires all his adult
life, but remains a faithful husband and father, sexually chaste,
through the power of the Holy Spirit, according to the gospel. He
is a model in every way. We are all sexually tempted, one way or
another, yet we may all tread the path of chastity through the
Spirit's enablement, and thereby please God.

Missing Paul's Point

As one who assumes the full seriousness and sincerity of all who
take part in today's debates among Christians regarding homosexuality, both in New Westminster and elsewhere, I now must
ask: how can anyone miss the force of what Paul says here? There
are, I think, two ways in which this happens.

One way, the easier one to deal with, is the way of special exegesis: I mean interpretations that, however possible, are artificial and
not natural, but that allow one to say, "What Paul is condemning is
not my sort of same-sex union." Whether a line of interpretation
is artificial, so constituting misinterpretation, is, I grant, a matter
of personal judgment. I do not, however, know how any reasonable person could read Robert A. J. Gagnon's 500-page book, *The
Bible and Homosexual Practice: Texts and Hermeneutics* (Abingdon,
2001), and not conclude that any exegesis evading the clear meaning of Paul is evasive indeed. Nor from now on can I regard anyone
as qualified to debate homosexuality who has not come to terms
with Gagnon's encyclopedic examination of all the relevant passages and all the exegetical hypotheses concerning them. I have
not always agreed with James Barr, but when on the dust jacket he
describes Gagnon's treatise as "indispensable even for those who
disagree with the author," I think he is absolutely right.

The second way, which is harder to engage, is to let experience judge the Bible. Some moderns, backed by propaganda from
campaigners for homosexual equality, and with hearts possessed

by the pseudo-Freudian myth that you can hardly be a healthy human without active sexual expression, feel entitled to say: "Our experience is—in other words, we feel—that gay unions are good, so the Bible's prohibitions of gay behavior must be wrong." The natural response is that the Bible is meant to judge our experience rather than the other way around, and that feelings of sexual arousal and attraction, generating a sense of huge significance and need for release in action as they do, cannot be trusted as either a path to wise living or a guide to biblical interpretation. Rhyming the point to make what in my youth was called a grook: the sweet bright fire / of sexual desire / is a dreadful liar. But more must be said than that.

Two Views of the Bible

At issue here is a Grand Canyon–wide difference about the nature of the Bible and the way it conveys God's message to modern readers. Two positions challenge each other.

One is the historic Christian belief that through the prophets, the incarnate Son, the apostles, and the writers of canonical Scripture as a body, God has used human language to tell us definitively and transculturally about his ways, his works, his will, and his worship. Furthermore, this revealed truth is grasped by letting the Bible interpret itself to us from within, in the knowledge that the way into God's mind is through that of the writers. Through them, the Holy Spirit who inspired them teaches the church. Finally, one mark of sound biblical insights is that they do not run counter to anything else in the canon.

This is the position of the Roman Catholic and Orthodox churches, and of evangelicals and other conservative Protestants. There are differences on the place of the church in the interpretive process, but all agree that the process itself is essentially as described. I call this the *objectivist* position.

The second view applies to Christianity the Enlightenment's trust in human reason, along with the fashionable evolutionary assumption that the present is wiser than the past. It concludes that the world has the wisdom, and the church must play intellectual catch-up in each generation in order to survive. From this standpoint, everything in the Bible becomes relative to the church's evolving insights, which themselves are relative to society's continuing development (nothing stands still), and the Holy Spirit's teaching ministry is to help the faithful see where Bible doctrine shows the cultural limitations of the ancient world and needs adjustment in light of latter-day experience (encounters, interactions, perplexities, states of mind and emotion, and so on). Same-sex unions are one example. This view is scarcely 50 years old, though its antecedents go back much further. I call it the *subjectivist* position.

In the New Westminster debate, subjectivists say that what is at issue is not the authority of Scripture, but its interpretation. I do not question the sincerity of those who say this, but I have my doubts about their clear-headedness. The subjectivist way of affirming the authority of Scripture, as the source of the teaching that now needs to be adjusted, is precisely a denying of Scripture's authority from the objectivist point of view, and clarity requires us to say so. The relative authority of ancient religious expertise, now to be revamped in our post-Christian, multifaith, evolving Western world, is one view. The absolute authority of God's unchanging utterances, set before us to be learned, believed, and obeyed as the mainstream church has always done, never mind what the world thinks, is the other.

What are represented as different "interpretations" are in fact reflections of what is definitive: in the one view, the doctrinal and moral teaching of Scripture is always final for Christian people; in the other view, it never is. What is definitive for the exponents of that view is not what the Bible says, as such, but what their own minds come up with as they seek to make Bible teaching match the wisdom of the world.

Each view of biblical authority sees the other as false and disastrous, and is sure that the long-term welfare of Christianity requires that the other view be given up and left behind as quickly as possible. The continuing conflict between them, which breaks surface in the disagreement about same-sex unions, is a fight to the death, in which both sides are sure that they have the church's best interests at heart. It is most misleading, indeed crass, to call this disagreement simply a difference about interpretation, of the kind for which Anglican comprehensiveness has always sought to make room.

Spiritual Dangers

In addition, major spiritual issues are involved. To bless same-sex unions liturgically is to ask God to bless them and to enrich those who join in them, as is done in marriage ceremonies. This assumes that the relationship, of which the physical bond is an integral part, is intrinsically good and thus, if I may coin a word, *blessable*, as procreative sexual intercourse within heterosexual marriage is. About this assumption there are three things to say.

First, it entails *deviation* from the biblical gospel and the historic Christian creed. It distorts the doctrines of creation and sin, claiming that homosexual orientation is good since gay people are made that way, and rejecting the idea that homosexual inclinations are a spiritual disorder, one more sign and fruit of original sin in some people's moral system. It distorts the doctrines of regeneration and sanctification, calling same-sex union a Christian relationship and so affirming what the Bible would call salvation in sin rather than from it.

Second, it threatens *destruction* to my neighbor. The official proposal said that ministers who, like me, are unwilling to give this blessing should refer gay couples to a minister willing to give it. Would that be pastoral care? Should I not try to help gay people change their behavior, rather than to anchor them in it? Should I not try to help them to the practice of chastity, just as I try to help restless singles and divorcees to the practice of chastity? Do I not want to see them all in the kingdom of God?

Third, it involves the *delusion* of looking to God—actually asking him—to sanctify sin by blessing what he condemns. This is irresponsible, irreverent, indeed blasphemous, and utterly unacceptable as church policy. How could I do it?

Changing a Historical Tradition

Finally, a major change in Anglicanism is involved: Writing into a diocesan constitution something that Scripture, canonically interpreted, clearly and unambiguously rejects as sin. This has never been done before, and ought not to be done now.

All the written standards of post-Reformation Anglicanism have been intentionally biblical and catholic. They have been biblical in terms of the historic view of the nature and authority of Scripture. They have been catholic in terms of the historic consensus of the mainstream church.

Many individual eccentricities and variations may have been tolerated in practice. The relatively recent controversial permissions to remarry the divorced and make women presbyters arguably had biblical warrant, though minorities disputed this. In biblical and catholic terms, however, the New Westminster decision writes legitimation of sin into the diocese's constitutional standards.

It categorizes the tolerated abstainers as the awkward squad of eccentrics rather than the mainstream Anglicans that they were before. It is thus a decision that can only be justified in terms of biblical relativism, the novel notion of biblical authority that to my mind is a cuckoo in the Anglican nest and a heresy in its own right. It is a watershed decision for world Anglicanism, for it changes the nature of Anglicanism itself. It has to be reversed.

Luther's response at Worms when he was asked to recant all his writings echoes in my memory, as it has done for more than 50 years.

> Unless you prove to me by Scripture and plain reason that I am wrong, I cannot and will not recant. My conscience is captive to the Word of God. To go against conscience is neither right nor safe [it endangers the soul]. Here I stand. There is nothing else I can do. God help me. Amen.

Conscience is that power of the mind over which we have no power, which binds us to believe what we see to be true and do what we see to be right. Captivity of conscience to the Word of God, that is, to the absolutes of God's authoritative teaching in the Bible, is integral to authentic Christianity.

More words from Luther come to mind.

> If I profess with the loudest voice and clearest exposition every portion of the truth of God except precisely that little point that the world and the devil are at the moment attacking, *I am not confessing Christ*, however boldly I may be professing Christ. Where the battle rages is where the loyalty of the soldier is proved, and to be steady on all the battlefield besides is merely flight and disgrace if he flinches at that point.

Was the protest in order? Was "no" the right way to vote? Did faithfulness to Christ, and faithful confession of Christ, require it? It seems so. And if so, then our task is to stand fast, watch, pray, and fight for better things: for the true authority of the Bible, for the "true truth" of the gospel, and for the salvation of gay people for whom we care.

Chapter 46

THE JOY OF ECCLESIASTES

How a wizened sage tamed my youthful cynicism.

C hristians like to quiz each other about their favorite book
in the Bible. Finding out how people experience Scripture—
especially those who write books about the Bible—is a natural
interest to us. When asked which Bible book is my favorite, I say
Ecclesiastes. Should people raise their eyebrows and ask why, I
give them two reasons.

First, it is a special pleasure to read an author with whom one
resonates. That is how the writer, who called himself Qohelet—
Hebrew for "Gatherer," a title that in Greek became Ecclesiastes,
the "Assembly-man"—strikes me. I see him as a reflective senior
citizen, a public teacher of wisdom, something of a stylist and
wordsmith. As his official testimonial or third-person testimony
(it might be either) in 12:10 shows, this man took his instructional
task very seriously and labored to communicate memorably.
Whether he was the Solomon of history or someone imperson-
ating him—not to deceive but to make points in the most effective

way—we do not know. All I am sure of is that each point has maximum strength if it comes from the real Solomon at the end of his life.

Whoever he was, Qohelet was a realist about the many ways in which this world gives us a rough ride. But while temperamentally inclined to pessimism and cynicism, I think, he was kept from falling into either of those craters of despair by a strong theology of joy.

How far this matches the way people see me, I do not know, but this is how I want to see myself—and why I warm to Ecclesiastes as a kindred spirit. (One main difference, of course, is that his thinking is all done within the framework of Old Testament revelation.)

Second, looking back to my late-teens conversion, I see myself as having received from Ecclesiastes wisdom that I needed badly. When Jesus Christ laid hold of me, I was already well on my way to becoming a cynic. But by God's grace, I was tamed thoroughly, and I see Ecclesiastes—the man and his book—as having done much of that taming.

Cynics are people who have grown skeptical about the goodness of life, and who look down on claims to sincerity, morality, and value. They dismiss such claims as hollow and criticize programs for making improvements. Feeling disillusioned, discouraged, and hurt by their experience of life, their pained pride forbids them to think that others might be wiser and doing better than they themselves have done. On the contrary, they see themselves as brave realists and everyone else as self-deceived. Mixed-up teens slip easily into cynicism, and that is what I was doing.

I was reared in a stable home and did well at school, but, being an introvert, I was always shy and awkward in company. Also, I was barred from sports and team games by reason of a hole in my head—literally, just over the brain—that I had acquired in a road accident at age 7. For years I had to cover the hole, where there was no bone, by wearing an aluminum plate, secured to my head by elastic. I could never get my body to learn to swim or dance.

Being an isolated oddity in these ways was painful to me, as it would be to any teen. So I developed a self-protective sarcasm, settled for low expectations from life, and grew bitter. Pride led me to stand up for Christian truth in school debates, but with no interest in God or a willingness to submit to him. However, becoming a real as distinct from a nominal Christian brought change, and Ecclesiastes in particular showed me things about life that I had not seen before.

Learning to Live

Waiting for me in the pages of Ecclesiastes was a view of reality very different from my junior-level cynicism.

Ecclesiastes is one of the Old Testament's five wisdom books. It has been said that the Psalms teach us how to worship; Proverbs, how to behave; Job, how to suffer; Song of Solomon, how to love; and Ecclesiastes, how to live. How? With realism and reverence, with humility and restraint, coolly and contentedly, in wisdom and in joy.

People who may not have read beyond chapter 3 might think of Ecclesiastes as voicing nothing more than bafflement and gloom at the way everything is. But 2:26 already goes beyond this: "to the one who pleases him God has given ... joy" (ESV, used throughout). In Ecclesiastes, joy is as central a theme, and as big and graciously bestowed a blessing, as it is in, say, Philippians.

Ecclesiastes is a flowing meditation on the business of living. It has two halves. Each is a string of separate units juxtaposed without connectives in a loose-looking way, which yet links them logically and theologically by subject matter. And binding everything together are three recurring imperatives:

Revere God: *fear* in Ecclesiastes, as in Proverbs, means "trust, obey, and honor," not "be terrified" (3:14; 5:7; 7:18; 8:12–13; 12:13). Recognize good things in life as gifts from God and receive them accordingly, with enjoyment (2:24–26; 5:18–19; 8:15; 9:7–9). Remember that God judges our deeds (3:17; 5:6; 7:29; 8:13; 11:9; 12:14).

There are two further unifying features. The first is the book-end sentence, "Vanity of vanities, says the Preacher. ... All is vanity"—the opening words in 1:2 and the closing words in 12:8. *Vanity* literally means "vapor" and "fog," and appears more than two dozen times to convey emptiness, pointlessness, worthlessness, and loss of one's way. "Striving after wind"—that is, trying to catch hold of it—is an image of parallel meaning (1:14, 17; 2:11, 17, 26; 4:4; 6:9). Both metaphors point to fruitless effort, of which the world is full, says the writer.

The second unifying feature is the phrase "under the sun." It specifies the standpoint and pinpoints the perspective of no less than 29 verdicts on how things appear when assessed in this-worldly terms, without reference to God.

The first half of Ecclesiastes, chapters 1–6, is in effect a downhill slide "under the sun" into what we may call the darkness of vanity. The natural order, wisdom in itself, uninhibited self-indulgence, sheer hard work, money-making, public service, the judicial system, and pretentious religiosity—are all canvassed to find what meaning, purpose, and personal fulfillment they yield. The reason for enquiring is given: Deep down in every human heart, God has put "eternity" (3:11)—a desire to know, as God knows, how everything fits in with everything else to produce lasting value, glory, and satisfaction. But the inquiry fails:

It leaves behind only the frustration of having gotten nowhere. The implication? This is not the way to proceed.

The second half, chapters 7–12, is somewhat discursive—we might even say meandering. It labors to show that despite everything, the pursuit and practice of modest, quiet, industrious wisdom is abundantly worthwhile and cannot be embarked on too early in life. After comparing old age to a house falling to pieces (12:1–7), the writer works up to a solemn conclusion:

> The end of the matter; all has been heard. Fear God and keep his commandments, for this is the whole duty of man.

That last phrase is elusive; duty may be its focus, or the phrase could be carrying the thought "the completeness of the human person," which the Good News Bible has neatly rendered:

> Fear God and keep his commands, because this is all that man was created for. God is going to judge everything we do. (12:13–14)

How then should we finally formulate the theology of joy that runs through and undergirds the entire book? Christian rejoicing in Christ and in salvation, as the New Testament depicts, goes further. But in celebrating joy as God's kindly gift, and in recognizing the potential for joy of everyday activities and relationships, Ecclesiastes lays the right foundation.

> There is nothing better for a person than that he should eat and drink and find enjoyment in his toil. This also, I saw, is from the hand of God. (2:24)

> I commend joy. (8:15)

> Enjoy life with the wife whom you love, all the days of your vain life that he has given you under the sun. (9:9)

Being too proud to enjoy the enjoyable is a very ugly short-coming, and one that calls for immediate correction. Let it be acknowledged that, as I had to learn long ago, discovering how under God ordinary things can bring joy is the cure for cynicism.

Part 3

—

GOOD QUESTIONS

Chapter 47

———

CAN THE DEAD BE CONVERTED?

*Hebrews 9:27 says, "Man is destined to die once and after
that to face the judgment." Does Scripture say why God
ends choice for/against Jesus as Savior at physical death?
If God were to extend the opportunity for even 30 seconds
after physical death, what a difference that might make!*

—Paul Gavitt, Tucson, Arizona

When the writer of Hebrews speaks of dying "once," he uses a word that means not once merely as distinct from two or more times, but "once and for all." The adverb (*hapax* in Greek) points to the decisiveness of the event it qualifies; by happening once, the event changes things permanently so that the possibility of it happening again is removed. That is what the word means when it is applied in verses 26 and 28 to Jesus' atoning sacrifice of himself on the cross, and in verse 27 it means the same when applied to the event of our own heartstop and brainstop and the separating of the self from the corpse.

The unrepeatable reality of physical death leads directly to reaping what we sowed in this world. So Jesus taught in his tale of the callous rich man and Lazarus the beggar (Luke 16:19–31), and when he spoke of dying in one's sins as something supremely dreadful (John 8:21–23). So Paul taught when he affirmed that, on judgment day, all received a destiny corresponding to their works; that is, to the decisive direction of their lives (Rom. 2:5–16; Gal. 6:7–8; 2 Cor. 5:10). The New Testament is solid in viewing death and judgment this way.

Modern theologians are not all solid here. Some of them expect that some who did not embrace Christ in this life may yet do so savingly in the life to come. Some who expect this are evangelicals who think that the God of grace owes everyone a clear presentation of the gospel in terms they understand. Others who expect an exercise of postmortem faith are universalists, for whom it is axiomatic that all humans will finally enjoy God in heaven, and therefore that God must and will continue to exert loving pressure till all have been drawn to Christ. So John Hick posits as many postmortem lives for each non-Christian as is necessary to this end, and Nels Ferré describes hell as having "a school and a door" in it: when those in hell come to their senses about Christ they may leave, so that the place ends up empty. But this is nonscriptural speculation, and reflects an inadequate grasp of what turning to Christ involves.

What sort of event is "choice for/against Jesus as Savior?" The phrase might suggest it is like choosing the preferred dish from a menu—a choice where you opt for what strikes you as the best of the bunch, knowing that if your first choice is not available, a second is always possible. But coming savingly to Christ is not like that. When it occurs, there is a sense of inevitability about it, springing from three sources: the pressure of gospel truth that feels too certain to be denied, plus the sense of God's presence forcing one to face the reality of Jesus Christ, plus the realization that without him, one is lost, currently ruining oneself and desperately needing to be changed. This sense is generated by God's prevenient grace—his action of making the first move. There is no commitment to Christ (no "choice for Jesus," if one prefers to say it that way) apart from this convicting divine action. The nature and necessity of regeneration (for that is what this is) was never a matter of dispute between Puritan Calvinists and Wesleyan Arminians.

The act of the heart in choosing Jesus Christ is not always performed in a single moment, nor is it always performed calmly and clear-headedly. At surface level there are often crosscurrents of reluctance. C. S. Lewis, dissecting his own conversion story, wrote of "the steady, unrelenting approach of him whom I so earnestly desired not to meet," and scoffed at the idea that anyone really seeks the real God and the real, living Christ, with their dominating, dictatorial demands for discipleship. ("You might as well speak of the mouse's search for the cat.") But in every real conversion, prevenient grace (meaning, as is now clear, the Holy Spirit) ensures a real change of heart through the Calvary love of Christ becoming irresistible.

How a just-dead person's perceptions differ from what they were before is more than we have been told. But Scripture says nothing of prevenient grace triggering postmortem conversions, and that being so, we should conclude that the unbeliever's lack of desire for Christ and the Father and heaven remains unchanged. So for God to extend the offer of salvation beyond the moment of death, even for thirty seconds, would be pointless. Nothing would come of it.

Chapter 48

———

DID GOD DIE ON
THE CROSS?

*Since Jesus was divine, how do we explain
his death? Can the eternal God die?*
—James Miller, Lexington, Kentucky

T he background to this question is today's post-Christian perplexity as to whether physical death is the end of the person
who lived in (or, more accurately, through) the now-defunct body.

All brands of materialists—scientific, philosophical, theo-
retical Marxist, secular irreligious, and antireligious European
and American—say it is. Everyone else, from ancient Egyptians,
Greeks, and Norsemen to every form of religion and tribal culture
the world has ever seen, has always been sure it isn't. Historic,
Bible-based Christianity is part of this consensus. On the nature
of postmortem life there are great differences, but on its reality,
agreement has been so widespread that current Western skepticism about survival seems a mere local oddity.

So the first thing to say is that all human selves, with all the powers of remembering, relating, learning, purposing, and enjoying that make us who we are, survive death, and by dying are actually set free from all shrinkings of personal life due to physical factors—handicaps, injuries, and deteriorations of body and mind; torture and starvation; Alzheimer's disease, Down syndrome, AIDS, and the like. This was true for both Jesus and the believing criminal to whom he said, as crucifixion drained their lives away, "Today you will be with me in paradise"[1]; and it will be just as true for you and me.

To be sure, the ugliness and pain and aftermath of dying as we know it is the penalty of sin. For anyone unconverted in heart, who is thus already "dead in transgressions" (Eph. 2:5), dying means entering more deeply into the death state (meaning, separation from that sharing with God that Scripture calls "life"). We need to be clear that as our penal substitute, Jesus "tasted death" (Heb. 2:9) in this deep sense precisely to ensure that we would never have to taste it. The natural view of his cry from the cross, "My God, my God, why have you forsaken me?" (first words of Ps. 22; Matt. 27:46), is that he was telling the bystanders, and through them the world, that in fulfillment of prophecy he was already undergoing deep death, as we may call it, during those dark hours. Godforsakenness was the hell into which Jesus entered on the cross; as Rabbi Duncan once told a class, with tears in his eyes, "it was *damnation*, and he took it *lovingly*".

Incarnation gave the eternal Son of God capacity for this experience. "The Word became flesh" in the sense that without ceasing to be anything that he was before, he added to himself all that humanness in this world involves—namely, life through a body

---

[1] Unless otherwise noted, all Scripture quotations in part 3 are from the English Standard Version.

bounded by space and time, with all the glories, limitations, and vulnerabilities that belong to our everyday existence, including in due course leaving behind the body through which one has consciously lived all along. Shakespeare, we know, acted in the plays he authored and produced, and that is a faint parallel to the co-Creator living an ordered creaturely life within his own created world.

There are mysteries here beyond our grasp—how, for instance, the sense of human and of divine identity meshed; how the Son controlled his divine powers so as not to overstep the limits of human finiteness; how entire dependence on his Father's leading for every word and deed made him the most unnerving initiative taker ever seen; and so on. But the certain fact is that as his life was a divine person's totally human life, so his dying was a divine person's totally human death.

Nor was Jesus' dying the end of the story. His rising from the dead, of which Scripture speaks as the work of all three persons of the Trinity (John 10:17–18; Acts 13:30; 1 Pet. 3:18), was a fresh exercise of the power that made the world and effected the Incarnation, leading on to the further work of power whereby the Son was glorified and enthroned, now to live as the God-Man in unbroken fellowship with his Father forever (Rom. 6:9–10). His resurrection and glorification is the prototype of what awaits all believers, and his experience of dying guarantees that when it is time for us to leave this world his loving, supportive, sympathizing presence with us will, as William Williams's hymn puts it, "land me safe on Canaan's side." Such is God's great grace.

Theology is not for casual curiosity, but for heartfelt doxology, and never more so than when Christ's death is the theme. So Williams's contemporary Charles Wesley was really giving our question a perfect and final answer when he wrote:

'Tis mystery all! The Immortal dies:
  Who can explore his strange design?
 In vain the first-born seraph tries
  To sound the depths of love divine.
'Tis mercy all! let earth adore,
  Let angel minds inquire no more.

Chapter 49

IS SATAN OMNIPRESENT?

If not, how does he tempt many people at one time?
—Barry Wolfe, Lancaster, Pennsylvania

The first principle of sound demonology is that you cannot have a more adequate idea of Satan than you have of God. That is because Satan is God's creature, and creatures must be understood in relation to their Creator.

Today's Western world, having lost the knowledge of God, is currently in process of losing the knowledge of man and of Satan. Man is thought of as no more than a sort of ape, Satan is seen as no more than a medieval bugaboo (i.e., a sick fancy), and temptation is reduced to conflict between our higher and lower natures (Freud's *ego* and *id*). We need biblical clarity, and we must start with getting our minds straight about God himself.

How, biblically, should we think of God's omnipresence? The word means that God knows exhaustively, and upholds and touches continually, every single item in the universe he has made, from the tiniest genes and electrons to the most massive stars in the expanding universe to the most complex mind-body interactions in the psyche of over 6 billion people. God is here, there, and everywhere, and his mind and hand are on everything. We are never out of his sight (Ps. 139), and we cannot get away from him (John 1). Wherever we are, he is there too. This is not simply a matter of transcending spatial confines. Strictly speaking, God has no spatial location at all, for space belongs to the created order and exists in him rather than he in it. Such is the omnipresence of God.

What to think, then, of "your enemy, the devil" (1 Pet. 5:8)? "Devil" means *slanderer*, through malice and misrepresentation; "Satan" means *adversary*. He is called the evil one and an enemy (Matt. 13:19), a murderer and the father of lies (John 8:44), who "has been sinning from the beginning" (1 John 3:8). He is an angel, one of the nonembodied personal creatures God made for the joy he and they would find in their worship, fellowship, and service. (To that end, he also made humans.)

But Satan is a rebel and corrupt. He leads the angels who, according to 2 Peter 2:4 and Jude 6–7, are now under restraint in "dungeons" and "chains" and face the judgment of eternal fire for their sins (Matt. 25:41). These fallen angels, whose character is set in the mold of their first transgression as later Adam's would be, are called *demons* in the New Testament. God restrains them to limit what they can do, but their hostility toward God and the godly has no limits. Wrecking God's work, thwarting his grace, and bringing us to spiritual ruin is their common goal with Satan.

Called "the tempter" in 1 Thessalonians 3:5, Satan seeks to trap God's servants into doing evil, thinking it to be good, and lapsing into unbelief that makes obedience impossible and disobedience inevitable. Thus he assaults all Christians (Eph. 6:11–13). Believers walk into Satan's war with God and should not wonder when he turns his fire on them.

Satan tempts many people simultaneously—does that mean he is omnipresent? No. Omnipresence, as we saw, is unique to the Creator. Satan comes and goes (Matt. 4:3, 11; Job 1:7–12). So how does he manage these multiple temptations? Scripture does not say, but two theories are common.

Theory one, recognizing that all angels have powers beyond ours to move around and see into people, posits that Satan has the power of "multipresence"—not "omnipresence," but not as spacially limited as humans.

Theory two, surely the more natural, is that the New Testament writers do what we do when speaking of wars—that is, ascribe all the hostile action to the opposing leader. "Hitler (or Napoleon or Saddam) attacked," we say, when in fact subordinates acted at their leader's command. Most Christians, like C. S. Lewis in *The Screwtape Letters*, hold some form of this view, and have always done so.

Either way, James's admonition, "Resist the devil, and he will flee from you" (4:7), explodes any idea of Satan's omnipresence by promising moments when he will *not* be with us. Jesus knew such moments (Luke 4:13)—and so may we.

Chapter 50

—

HELL'S FINAL ENIGMA

Won't heaven's joy be spoiled by our awareness
of unsaved loved ones in hell?

—William P. Bunnell, Redlands, California

First, I resonate with the question to the depths of my soul. Loved ones of my own, some living, some dead, have not shared my faith in Christ. That is painful.

Second, belief in the outright annihilation of nonbelievers after final judgment (as opposed to an eternal punishment) seems to me biblically illegitimate. I suspect some Christians whose loved ones die without accepting Christ are tempted to embrace the annihilationist view. Scripture, however, seems to show that one aspect of human dignity is that we are built to last. Whether for joy or for sorrow, our souls are eternal.

Third, Scripture and good biblical theology indicate that none will be in hell who did not effectively choose it by following in the footsteps of Adam and preferring their own way to God's. In some fashion, God reveals himself and his will to everyone, and everyone responds in one way or another (see Rom. 1:18–2:16). But nonbelievers universally make the anti-God choice, and hell is God giving people what they chose. That is reality—retributive reality—and an abiding consequence of following our heart and doing what we want to do; I wish I could persuade more people to face this seriously.

Now pose the question in its toughest form. Imagine a believing spouse or parent who loved, prayed for, and agonized over a dear one who resisted the gospel and died suddenly in an accident. There are no grounds for thinking that this or any other memory will be erased in heaven. So how can it not keep the bereaved one from heaven's total joy?

Significantly, this is not a Bible problem; instead, Scripture rules out all thought of it ever becoming anyone's problem. For it tells us that God the Father (who now pleads with mankind to accept the reconciliation that Christ's death secured for all) and God the Son (our appointed Judge, who wept over Jerusalem) will in a final judgment express "wrath" and administer justice against rebellious humans. God's holy righteousness will hereby be revealed; God will be doing the right thing, vindicating himself at last against all who have defied him, and there is no hint that this hurts the Judge more than it hurts the sinner. (Read through Matt. 25; John 5:22–29; Rom. 2:5–16; 12:19; 2 Thess. 1:7–9; Rev. 18:1–19:3; 20:11–15, and you will see that clearly.) God will judge justly, and all angels, saints, and martyrs will praise him for it. So it seems inescapable that we shall, with them, approve the judgment of persons—rebels—whom we have known and loved.

That sounds appalling; how can it be? Remember, in heaven our minds, hearts, motives, and feelings will be sanctified, so that we are fully conformed to the character and outlook of Jesus our Lord. This will happen at or before our bodily resurrection. How we shall then think and feel is really beyond our knowing, just as a chrysalis could not know what it feels like to be a butterfly till it becomes one.

But certainly the promise that God will wipe away every tear from believers' eyes (Rev. 7:17) will find its fulfillment as one aspect of this transformation. In heaven, glorifying God and thanking him for everything will always absorb us. All our love for and joy in others who are with us in heaven will spring from their doing the same, and love and pity for hell's occupants will not enter our hearts. Their hell will not veto our heaven.

Granted, this sounds to us more like hard-heartedness than Christlikeness, yet Christlikeness is precisely what it will be. Our difficulty is that we cannot now conceive the heavenly condition in a full way.

Wrote Richard Baxter: "My knowledge of that life is small, / The eye of faith is dim; / But it's enough that Christ knows all, / And I shall be with him."

Chapter 51

TEXT CRITICISM
AND INERRANCY

How can I reconcile my belief in the inerrancy of Scripture
with comments in Bible translations that state that a
particular verse is not 'in better manuscripts'?
—Carol Stanley, Manchester, New Hampshire

T he answer to this question parallels that of Charles Spurgeon who, when asked to reconcile human freedom with divine predestination, said, "I never reconcile friends." He maintained that the two realities fit together. So here.

Manuscripts first. The New Testament books first circulated in hand-copied form, and hand-copying by monks went on till Gutenberg invented the printing press in the 15th century. Anyone who has copied by hand knows how easily letters, words, and even whole lines get dropped out or repeated. The New Testament manuscript tradition was not exempt from this.

Also, it is clear that some copyists facing what they thought were miscopyings made what they thought were corrections.

Some of these copyists added in the margin amplifying words and sentences that the next copyist put into the text itself, thinking that was where they belonged. Because the copying was done reverently and with professional care, manuscripts vary little overall, except for the occasional slippages of this kind. Manuscript comparison reveals many passages that clearly need correcting at this level of detail.

The King James Version New Testament was translated from the "received text"—the dominant manuscript tradition at the time—and published in 1516. New manuscript discoveries have led to minor adjustments to that text, and where uncertainty remains about exact wording or authenticity, the margins of honest modern versions will tell us so. The New King James, for instance, while still following the received text, notes these things conscientiously as it goes along. Other things being equal, manuscripts are "better" when they are nearer to the original—that is, earlier in date.

In the New Testament only one word per 1,000 is in any way doubtful, and no point of doctrine is lost when verses not "in better manuscripts" are omitted. (As examples, see Matt. 6:13b; 17:21; 18:11; Mark 9:44, 46, 49; 16:9–20; Luke 23:17; John 5:4; and Acts 8:37.) Such has been God's "singular care and providence" in preserving his written Word for us (Westminster Confession I.viii).

So how does all this bear on the Christian's very proper faith in biblical inerrancy—that is, the total truth and trustworthiness of the true text and all it teaches?

Holy Scripture is, according to the view of Jesus and his apostles, God preaching, instructing, showing, and telling us things, and testifying to himself through the human witness of prophets, poets, theological narrators of history, and philosophical observers of life. The Bible's inerrancy is not the inerrancy of any one published text or version, nor of anyone's interpretation, nor of any scribal slips or pious inauthentic additions acquired during transmission.

Rather, scriptural inerrancy relates to the human writer's expressed meaning in each book, and to the Bible's whole body of revealed truth and wisdom.

Belief in inerrancy involves an advance commitment to receive as from God all that the Bible, interpreting itself to us through the Holy Spirit in a natural and coherent way, teaches. Thus it shapes our understanding of biblical authority.

So inerrantists should welcome the work of textual scholars, who are forever trying to eliminate the inauthentic and give us exactly what the biblical writers wrote, neither more nor less. The way into God's mind is through his penmen's minds, precisely as expressed, under his guidance, in their own words as they wrote them.

Text criticism serves inerrancy; they are friends. Inerrancy treasures the meaning of each writer's words, while text criticism checks that we have each writer's words pure and intact. Both these wisdoms are needed if we are to benefit fully from the written Word of God.

Chapter 52

PRAYERS FOR SALVATION

The Bible tells us that anything we ask according to his will, we shall have (1 John 5:14–15). How is it, then, that not all prayers for the salvation of others are answered?
—Amy Lynn Nuttall, Brooklyn, New York

All Christians, I suppose, like myself, have prayed for the conversion of loved ones without seeing it happen. So did Paul (Rom. 9:1–3, 10:1), and so did prayer giant George Müller in at least one case (though the prayed-for person came to Christ at Müller's funeral).

Much is uncertain here; we cannot tell, for instance, how God may deal with holdouts who, as we say, "know it all" in the moments of their dying. But we know the pain of the love that makes us pray for them, and while they continue impervious to Christ, the pain stays.

Now, our heavenly Father is indeed a promise-keeping God who answers all proper prayer in positive terms. Proper prayers flow from faithful, obedient hearts bringing to God real needs that we beg him to meet. His answer may be "Yes, here and now, as requested," or "Yes, but in a better way than you asked," or "Yes, but you must wait—I will take the right action at the right time, which is not yet."

God, the perfect Father, loves to give good gifts to his children but reserves the right to give only the best, and only in the best way. What he gives, therefore, is not always what the praying believer had in mind.

But proper prayers are made according to his will; what does that mean? The Lord's Prayer shows. All our requests are to be a spelling out of our motive, purpose, and desire, which matches God's own, for the hallowing (honoring, glorifying) of his name (that is, of God himself as revealed in the Bible and its Christ).

The bottom line here must ever be that God's will (command and plan) be done—not just in others' lives but in ours too. In our lives God may have lessons for us in the way he answers our askings.

As children growing up in God's family, we are to work out what we think will most advance the divine glory, and pray for that (as did Paul when he asked that his thorn in the flesh be healed). Then we must wait and watch to see what God, in his greater wisdom, does in answer (as when he strengthened Paul to live with the thorn unhealed).

But, given all that, does not God categorically state in 2 Peter 3:9 that he wants everyone on Earth to come to repentance? Well, no; not there, anyway. "The Lord," says Peter, "is patient toward you (my Jewish-Christian fellow believers, whom I am addressing), not wishing that any (of you) should perish, but that all (of you) should reach repentance." Texts must be understood in context, which often limits their application, as it does here.

But does not God call everyone who hears the gospel to come to Christ and be saved? Yes, but be careful; there is mystery here, the mystery of God's sovereignty. The gospel message is a *bona fide*, good faith, "whosoever will" invitation to Christ, who is truly present to save all who truly turn to him in faith and repentance.

To us who thus turn, the New Testament explains that God reached out to open our eyes, renew our hearts, and raise us from spiritual death into new birth and new life. Hence he is to be praised no less for our conversion than for providing our Savior. But not all turn, and the unbelief of those who do not is diagnosed as their own fault. Beyond this, the mystery of some-but-not-others is left unexplained, and humbly we have to settle for that.

Yet, though our prayers do not make God dance to our tune, they do make a difference. When, as so often, those who have come to faith learn that someone was praying for them, they know that they owe their salvation, under God, to that person.

And when God moves me to love and pray for someone (with verbal witness to them also, as God gives opportunity), I should assume that God means to bless that person. He is privileging me to be a link in the chain and will answer my prayer in positive terms, whether or not I see how.

Keep loving, then, keep praying, keep expecting, keep trusting God to know what he is doing, and keep praising him for his unsearchable wisdom. So did Paul (Rom. 9–11, especially 11:33–36), and so should we.

53

——

EXPERIENCING
GOD'S PRESENTS

Is every believer guaranteed at least one spiritual gift?

Tracie N. Moore, Springfield Gardens, New York

T he short answer is yes—at least one, perhaps more. But let us be clear what we are talking about. What are spiritual gifts? None of the New Testament passages that speak of them (Rom. 12:3–8; 1 Cor. 12–14; Eph. 4:11–16; 1 Pet. 4:10–11) define them. Since these passages all come from letters to churches where gifts were already in use, and the only question was whether they were being used well, that need not surprise us. But constructing a definition is not hard.

Gifts are manifestations of the Holy Spirit (1 Cor. 12:4–11), given to build up the church (12:7, 14:4) and the individuals within it. It is only through Christ, in Christ, and by learning and responding to Christ that anyone is ever edified. Therefore, gifts should be defined in terms of him—as powers of expressing, celebrating, displaying, and obeying Christ. Gifts communicate his reality through word or action in service of God and others (fellow believers and non-Christians too).

Gifts vary. There are gifts of speech and of Samaritanship; Paul's flitting to and fro between the two kinds in his gift lists (Rom. 12:6–8; 1 Cor. 12:8–10) shows that there is no scale of values attached to them. There is no pecking order between helping, serving, giving, administering, encouraging, and being kind, on the one hand, and preaching, teaching, leading, and exhorting, on the other, let alone such "sign-gifts" as healing, speaking in tongues, and interpreting tongues.

The key truth is that in the church, which is one body in Christ, we're all members—that is, body parts of Christ, and, in him, of each other.

Among the variety of God's gifts, some are natural abilities and character qualities sanctified, while others correspond to nothing that was previously seen in the person's life. That the gift is from the Holy Spirit is more evident in the latter case than in the former, but the reality is that all our capacities for expressing Christ are spiritual gifts. By means of them, Christ from his throne uses us as his hands, feet, and mouth, even his smile, and speaks, meets, loves, saves, and sustains.

As the test of whether you are a leader or teacher is that others follow you or learn from you, so the test of whether you are exercising a spiritual gift is that people in the church feel the influence of Christ through what you say and do. Natural abilities, however spectacular, are not spiritual gifts as such, whereas diffident clumsiness of word and gesture is no sign that a spiritual gift is not in action.

That the indwelling Holy Spirit imparts to every Christian believer at least one gift appears both from Paul's image of the body growing toward the full stature of Christ, its head, "when [and clearly only when] *each part* is working properly" (Eph. 4:16), and from his emphatic declaration: *"To each* is given the manifestation of the Spirit for the common good" (1 Cor. 12:7, cf. 11). It is plain that every-member ministry in the body of Christ is Paul's, and therefore Christ's own, ideal.

The church is not to be like a bus, where passengers sit quietly and let someone else do the driving, but like an anthill, where everybody is at work. Not everyone who thus ministers will be a church officer, nor will the service they render always be appreciated. But just as every bit of that fabulous complex, the human body, has a job to do, so it is with each of us who believe.

How can Christians identify their own gift or gifts? By trying themselves out in paths of service that attract them, or that others, who know them well enough to discern their potential, urge upon them. The presence or absence of a gift will quickly become apparent.

When, as sometimes happens, all attention focuses on the spectacular "sign-gifts" that, over and above their benefit to the church, specifically authenticated the apostles' personal ministry, the truth about gifts is skewed. God seems to have given some renewal of "sign-gifts" in recent years (though some doubt this), but it is clear that, as in New Testament times, not all Christians become channels of these manifestations (see 1 Cor. 12:29–30). Most are gifted in less eye-catching and more unobtrusive ways.

Paul told the Corinthians to seek the best gifts. Other things being equal, the best gifts will always be those that express most love and do most good to most people.

Chapter 54

———

REFLECTED GLORY

What does Genesis mean by man being made in the image of God?
—Robert Lal, Gorakhpur, India

T he Bible indicates that my body, though not me, is integral to my humanity, which would be reduced without it. Scripture promises me resurrection. Plato thought I would be better off without a body, as many think today, but that is wrong.

I have a mind, including a conscience; also feelings and desires, along with my powers of mental and physical action. Thus endowed, I read the Bible as God's Word, teaching me what I should think and do about this puzzling, complex reality that I know myself to be.

Genesis 1:26–27 declares that God created mankind of both sexes, male and female, in his image and likeness. *Image* and *likeness* were once thought to express different things, but they mean about the same. This passage shows us, first, our unique and special dignity (God speaks of no creature other than man as his image-bearer), and, second, how we are meant to live.

Image means representative likeness—which tells us at once that we should be reflecting, at our creaturely level, what Genesis 1 shows God is and does. Therefore we should always act with resourceful rationality and wise love, making and executing praiseworthy plans just as God did in creation. He generated value by producing what was truly good; so should we. We should be showing love and goodwill toward all other persons, as God did when he blessed Adam and Eve (1:28). And in fellowship with God, we should directly honor and obey him by the way we manage and care for that bit of the created order that he gives us to look after, according to his dominion mandate (26, 28).

For us, then, as for Adam and Eve before the Fall, and for the Lord Jesus himself—the incarnate Son whom Paul hails as the Father's true image (2 Cor. 4:4; Col. 1:15)—being the image of God means actually living this way, moment by moment and day by day.

But, like Adam and Eve and everyone else save Jesus, we fail here constantly, however good our intentions as believers. And so, in spades, do all unbelievers who, being under the power of the anti-God force Paul calls sin (Rom. 3:9), lack good intentions (Eph. 2:1–3, 4:17–24). That does not mean, of course, that they are all as bad as they could be; it simply means that sin in the human system, our legacy from Adam, drives us all the time to be self-centered and self-seeking, and so robs us of the power to love God with all our heart, mind, and strength.

So a distinction has to be drawn. We still bear the image of God *formally*—that is, we still have in us the abilities that, if rightly harnessed, would achieve a fully righteous, Godlike life—and so the unique dignity of each human being must still be recognized and respected (Gen. 9:6; James 3:9), as a gesture of honor to our maker. But we have lost the image *substantially*, and it takes God's grace-gift of union with Christ to restore it fully. Through this gift we share his resurrection life in regeneration, sanctification, and glorification.

Hereby we "put on the new self, created after the likeness of God in true righteousness and holiness" (Eph. 4:24), and are progressively transformed into the image of the Lord Jesus, "from one degree of glory to another" (2 Cor. 3:18). Thus the *substantial* image is renewed.

God's work of restoring the image starts in the heart, with inward illumination, our embrace of Christ, and motivational change at the core of our being (2 Cor. 4:4, 6, 5:17). Born-again believers want God more than they want anything else. In daily life our strongest desire is to love and worship and serve and please and honor and glorify the Father and the Son, who saved us.

Also, we find ourselves wanting to do good to others every way we can, and most of all to share with others our knowledge of new life with God in Christ.

Thus all our duty becomes all our delight at the deepest level, and from our new motivation comes that imitation of God and of Christ that is every Christian's calling (1 Cor. 4:16; Eph. 5:1; 1 Thess. 1:6)—and which is precisely expressing the image of God in daily life. True imaging of God in Christlike action starts with the Christlike motivation of the regenerate, Spirit-indwelt heart.

Two humans, living in God's image, were the crown of God's creation. Our fallen race, acting out the image of Satan, ruins his creation. A new humanity, the company of believers recreated in Christ's image, will adorn and enjoy the new heaven and earth that are promised. Praise God!

Chapter 55

INCARNATE FOREVER

*What is the scriptural and theological support for the teaching
that Jesus, the God-man, remains eternally incarnate?*
—Terry M. Horvath, Winter Springs, Florida

T his question is part of a bigger one: How do we understand
the mystery of the Incarnation itself? When I say *mystery*,
I'm using theology's label for any divine reality that we know is
actual (because the Bible tells us so) while not knowing how it is
possible (since it outstrips our minds). We know it by faith, taking
God's Word for it, and see it as above (but not against) reason. The
Trinity, God's sovereignty over human freedom, and our union
with the risen Christ in new birth are examples. So is the incarnation of the Son of God.

The Incarnation, meaning "en-fleshing," is the event that the
Apostle John announced by saying "the Word became flesh" (Jn.
1:14). The concept is not that the Son put on a human body as
one puts on an overcoat, nor that a human being and a divine
person lived together under one skin, nor that a divine person

came to possess two sets of powers (natures), each of which he could switch on or off as he chose.

It is, rather, that first in Mary's womb, and then in this world, and now forever in heaven, the Son lives life through the mind-body complex that constitutes humanity—bypassing none of it, even when drawing directly on divine power or intuiting directly the Father's mind and will. Without diminishing his divinity, he added to it all that is involved in being human.

When Jesus is hailed as one person in two natures, according to the Council of Chalcedon in 451, this is what is meant. So by incarnation the Son became more than he was before, and a human element became integral to the ongoing life of the Triune God. Being as fully human as divine became one strand of the Son's identity, destiny, and glory. Evangelicals, Orthodox, and Catholics unite in believing this.

The biblical and theological warrant for affirming the permanence of the incarnate state lies in more than the absence from Scripture of any hint of transitoriness. It even lies in more than single texts like Hebrews 13:8, "Jesus Christ is the same yesterday [when on earth] and today [now as we read] and forever." The weightiest warrant is that New Testament teaching on the key gospel themes—mediation, faith, and hope—otherwise collapses.

Mediation. The Son was incarnate in order to become the "one mediator between God and man, *the man* Christ Jesus" (1 Tim. 2:5). *Christ* meaning the prophesied Messiah, and *Jesus* being his God-given human name (Matt. 1:21). Mediatorial messiahship involved three roles: prophet (channel of divine instruction), priest (self-sacrificing intercessor), and king (lord and protector). These three, as personal relationships between each believer and Jesus Christ, never end.

The visions of eternity in Revelation clearly assume that Jesus, the Lion who is the Lamb, the Amen, Faithful and True, the First and the Last, will always be to his people all that he is now. The work of the kingdom—that is, the perfecting of the church—will finish, but "the man Christ Jesus" will be our beloved prophet, priest, and king forever.

Faith. Hebrews lays before converted Jews, under pressure to return to Judaism, the abiding reality of the Son who declares and is God's last word to man. He is the royal high priest, now enthroned, who mediates the better covenant, with its better promises and better hope, that his better sacrifice established (Heb. 1:1–2:4; 7:19, 22; 8:6; 9:23).

We sinners should trust the abiding faithful mercy of our enthroned forerunner. His human experience on earth prompts sympathy for our weakness, and he gives "grace to help in time of need" (see 2:17–18; 4:14–16; 5:7–9; 7:24–25; 12:2–3). Glorified, he remains all that he was, with sympathy for strugglers undiminished.

Hope. Christ's exaltation did not abolish his humanity, but glorified it. So it will be for us. If alive when Christ returns, we shall be transformed, body and soul, into his image directly; if already dead, re-embodiment will begin the process (see Rom. 8:17, 29; 1 Cor. 15:42–54; 2 Cor. 3:18; 4:14; 5:1–4; Ph. 3:21). Christ will still be our life (Col. 3:4); the vital union that undergirds our fellowship with him will continue, literally forever.

So Christ's glorified humanity, which is the template and link for the glorification that is ours, must go on forever too. If the hope of our faith is to be like Jesus in his glory, that glory must be permanent.

Chapter 56

———

ALL SINS ARE NOT EQUAL

Are all sins weighed equally, or is one
more important than another?

—Linda Linton, Celina, Ohio

T his question leads into what for many evangelicals has become uncharted territory. We think of conversion as the moment when the guilt of all our sins—past, present, and future—is washed away by the atoning blood of Christ. As sinners justified by faith and heirs of promised glory, we rejoice in salvation and think no more about our continued shortcomings and how God might "weigh" them.

If asked, we explain our attitude as true evangelical assurance. But is it?

The Puritans of history were evangelicals too, but on this point they differed from us considerably. They remembered that Christ taught us to pray daily for forgiveness. One of their spiritual disciplines (not yet one of ours, generally) was self-examination each evening to discern what actions in particular, done or left undone, they needed to ask pardon for.

In the forefront of their minds was the holiness of God, the awfulness of his anger, and his amazing patience in nurturing and correcting his irresponsible, recalcitrant children. These were the realities framing their certainty that the precious blood of Christ cleanses faithful repenters from all sin. Most later evangelicals were with them until the 20th century. We are the ones out of step.

Scripture shows that in God's estimate some sins are worse and bring greater guilt than others, and that some sins do us more damage. Moses rates the golden calf debacle a *great* sin (Ex. 32:30). Ezekiel in his horrific allegory says that after Oholah (Samaria) had ruined herself by unfaithfulness to God, Oholibah (Jerusalem) "became *more* corrupt ... in her lust and in her whoring, which was *worse* than that of her sister" (Ezek. 23:11, ESV). John distinguishes sins that do and do not inevitably lead to death (1 John 5:16), picking up Jesus' warning about the unforgivable sin (Mk. 3:28–30).

Answers 151 and 152 of the *Westminster Larger Catechism*, a Puritan product, bring clarity by analyzing *aggravations* of sins, thus providing a means for discerning their gravity and guilt. On one level, all sins are equal in that no matter how trivial they seem, they all deserve God's "wrath and curse, both in this life, and that which is to come, and cannot be expiated but by the blood of Christ." No sins are small when committed against a great and generous God. Beyond this, however, the gravity of each transgression depends on varying factors.

First is the extent to which the *transgressors* know better, are in the public eye, and are objects of public trust, "guides to others, and whose example is likely to be followed by others." For instance, there is Solomon in 1 Kings 11:9–10 and the unwise servant in Luke 12:48–49—trusted persons knowingly sinning; Nathan describing David's sin with Bathsheba in 2 Samuel 12:7–10; and Jews who set themselves up as guides to godliness in Romans 2:17–23.

Second come transgressions categorized by *persons offended*, ranging from the Father, the Son, and the Spirit to "any of the saints, particularly weak brethren." For example, there are those publicly dishonoring Christ in Hebrews 10:28–29; and those who cause people to stumble in Matthew 18:6, Romans 14:13–15, and 1 Corinthians 8:9–12.

Third comes the extent to which, defying conscience and censures from others, the transgressors *act* "deliberately, willfully, presumptuously, impudently, boastfully, maliciously, frequently, obstinately, with delight, continuance, or relapsing after repentance." Thus we find cumulative defiance of God in Jeremiah 5:8 and Amos 4:8–11; disregard of conscience and correction in Romans 1:32 and Matthew 18:15–17; and falling from grace in 2 Peter 2:20–22.

Fourth is *"circumstances* of time and place," which make the bad worse—for example, joining sin with hypocritical religiosity in Ezekiel 23:37–39, and involving others in one's sin in 1 Samuel 2:22–24.

Finally, there is the unforgivable sin—such resistance to the light of Spirit-taught truth about the deity and grace of Jesus Christ as rules out all possibility of faith and repentance, hence its lethal consequence. Its nature is evident from Matthew 12:31–32 and Mark 3:28–30.

We must learn to think of sin clear-headedly, to deal with it in ourselves realistically, and to negate and hate it everywhere wholeheartedly.

Chapter 57

———

SALVATION SANS JESUS

*"The Gospel of Jesus Christ: An Evangelical Celebration" states
that sincere worshipers of other religions will not be saved—does
that also refer to Moses and other Old Testament faithful?*

—Ty Conley, Salem, Oregon

The cited document, under "Affirmations and Denials," No. 4,
states: "The Bible offers no hope that sincere worshipers
of other religions will be saved without personal faith in Jesus
Christ."

The direct answer to the reader's question is no. The words
quoted speak only of our own era, the almost two millennia since
our Lord Jesus Christ lived, died, rose, and ascended. Moses
appears in Hebrews 11:24–29 as a hero of faith, along with Abel,
Enoch, Noah, the patriarchs, his own parents, and others. These
Old Testament believers, so we read, looked for "a better country,
that is, a heavenly one ... a better life" (vs. 16, 35), which God had
planned for them with us (v. 40). They trusted God's promises,
which included indicators of the coming Christ, and their faith

now stands as a model for us all. I, for one, expect to meet them in the world to come.

This question, however, reflects deep-rooted concern about sincere adherents of non-Christian faiths today. At a time when Hindus, Buddhists, and Muslims, along with our Jewish friends, work beside us each day, something would be very wrong with us if we did not feel such concern.

The first thing to say, and with emphasis, is that beyond the stark factual statement ("the Bible offers no hope"), all is speculation. The stark statement is certainly correct. The New Testament, exegeted rationally and without reading into it what cannot be read out of it, tells us that the Christian faith is true for everybody, and that all need God's forgiveness and rescue from the power of sin and Satan. All are called to turn to Jesus Christ and so become God's adopted children, and eternal life comes only to those who do this.

Also, it tells us that on a coming day of judgment God will "render to each one according to his works" (Rev. 22:12), God's true servants receiving one destiny and his opponents another. These certainties evidently underlie Jesus' Great Commission (Mt. 28:19–20), Paul's missionary outreach (Col. 1:27–29), and Luke's missionary outlook reflected in the storyline of Acts.

Despite this background, some pursue two lines of speculation. The first is *universalism*, the belief that despite the New Testament witness to the contrary, God will somehow bring all who leave this world as nonbelievers to share the inheritance of those who die living in Christ. This requires successful postmortem evangelism for some and heartchanging corrective discipline for others, and raises at least these questions:

When Jesus and the apostles warned people of eternal loss if they did not repent (Lk. 13:3, 5; Acts 26:16–20), were they bluffing? Do we in fact know more about God's purpose of grace than they did?

When James Denney said, a century ago, "I dare not say to myself that if I forfeit the opportunity this life affords, I shall ever have another; and therefore I dare not say so to another man," was he wrong? Or does every Christian conscience, when challenged, say the same?

The second speculation is *inclusivism*, positing a possibility of salvation for sincere devotees of faiths in which Jesus Christ is either unknown or is rejected as the divine Savior. On what, biblically speaking, might this possibility be based? Not, clearly, on sincerity or devotion as such, nor on personal merit (no one has any), nor on any intrinsic efficacy of unchristian rituals. On what then?

It has been urged that if non-Christian devotees come to know themselves as guilty, defiled, and unworthy, and to confess and renounce their sins, asking mercy from whatever gods there may be, they will receive the forgiveness they seek because of the Jesus they do not yet know, but will know hereafter. God forbid we should dispute this. But have we reason to think there are such people? The New Testament only speaks of penitents being saved through knowing about, and coming to trust, the crucified and risen Lord; which is the point that the statement paraphrased in the question is making.

Both speculations, biblically, must be judged failures.

Conclusion

—

COUNT YOUR SURPRISES

The high spots of my life have been anything but expected.

I t has been a full quarter-century since the long-haired clergyman with the ukulele drilled the church's children in singing,
"God is a surprise, right before your eyes, God is a surprise." But
the words stayed with me because, now as then, they match my
own vivid experience.

The high spots of my life present themselves in retrospect as
a series of surprises—happy surprises, from the hand of a very
gracious God. Is that unusual? I doubt it. But I also doubt that
we dwell on the happy surprises as often and as thoughtfully as
we should. There is great wisdom in the elderly children's chorus,
"Count your blessings—name them one by one—and it will surprise you what the Lord has done."

Recently, at only a few minutes' notice, I realized that I was
expected to reply to some kind things being said about me by
saying something personal and also devotional. Off the cuff I

listed some of the happiest of the happy surprises that have come my way, and the story came out more or less as follows.

It was a happy surprise when God made me a Christian, after two years during which I had kidded myself that I was one already, since I went to church and argued at school for the truth of the Apostles' Creed. Jesus Christ broke into my life, claimed me as his own, and made me a different person, all in the space of about 20 minutes during the second half of an evangelistic sermon. I remember the experience as if it were yesterday. At the time it was a shattering surprise, but *happy* is my word for it now.

Happy too is my word today for the surprise of realizing, about a year after my conversion, in my second year at university, that God was calling me to a life of ministry, as an undershepherd for his sheep. Being in those days an odd person, somewhat solitary and, as I thought and felt, very poor at human relationships, I fought the call, but God—I have to use the word—overpowered me, telling me I must trust him and go ahead. It was unnerving at the time, but God knew what he was doing, and my call to shepherd souls has shaped my life's activities throughout.

I had arranged to go straight on to seminary in Oxford, where I was already studying. But it proved to be another happy surprise when in the final term of my first degree, having suddenly found in myself a strong desire to get away from Oxford for a time, I was in effect drafted out of the blue as a supply teacher of Latin, Greek, and philosophy—my degree subjects—to spend a year in a theological school in London. There, I found I had a gift for teaching adults and a passion for educating ministers, and I went back to Oxford knowing that educational work of that kind would be central in fulfilling my pastoral call.

Then, shortly before my ordination to a parish, I met a young lady at a retreat that neither of us by rights should have been at. Two days and one sleepless night later, I knew we were meant for each other, and soon she knew it too. Looking back over our 55 years together, I declare that this was God engineering another of his wonderfully happy surprises; but this is not the place to celebrate that further.

Soon came the happy surprise of becoming a published author. Asked to write up a talk at pamphlet length, six or seven thousand words perhaps, I struggled for a year and boldly, perhaps bumptiously, came up with a book of sixty thousand: *Fundamentalism and the Word of God*, which is still in print half a century later. Its success showed me that writing must henceforth have a central place in the educational work through which I sought to fulfill my pastoral call. The further happy surprise of finding that when I turned some magazine articles into the book *Knowing God*, it became a nurturing tool for the Christian world, served only to confirm this.

The final surprise in this story was to be "headhunted," as we say nowadays, by my oldest Oxford friend, James Houston, to join the faculty of Regent College, Vancouver, of which he was the founder-principal. Nothing was further from my mind at that time than leaving England, despite some awkwardnesses there, and I had already turned down some invitations to relocate. But Principal Houston's approach led to a move into a situation in which I have spent, beyond all question, the best 28 years of my life so far. Finding that God was calling me to do what I can do as a British immigrant in Canada—British by genes, now Canadian by choice, as I sometimes express it—was startling, but has proved to be yet another of God's very happy surprises.

These were the turning points in my life that I reeled off to illustrate the truth that believers serve a God of happy surprises, which is what I sought to tell the meeting. Straight after I had finished, the program required us all to sing "All the Way My Savior Leads Me." Victorian hymns rarely do much for me (I am a Watts,

Wesley, and Newton man), but, having through my own fault had to formulate on the fly and wing it verbally, and having, I thought, been helped in doing this, these words came as so true a theological interpretation of what I had just been through and the 63 years as a Christian that I had been talking about, that my heart was squeezed and I was almost in tears. In itself, the moment was yet another happy surprise, this time one of unexpected divine confirmation.

Paul, discipling converts, harps constantly on the virtue, duty, and (by implication) blessing of constant giving of thanks to God. "Be filled with the Spirit ... always giving thanks to God the Father for everything" (Eph. 5:18, 20).[2] "So then, just as you received Christ Jesus as Lord, continue to live in him, rooted and built up in him ... and overflowing with thankfulness" (Col. 2:6–7). "Give thanks in all circumstances, for this is God's will for you in Christ Jesus" (1 Thess. 5:18). Paul himself, in all his hardships, found matter for repeated thanksgiving in the privilege of his own ministry (1 Tim. 1:12–14), in the work of grace that he saw through his evangelism, and in the churches' ongoing life.

Glum Christians who say they have not much to give thanks for are wrong. Some of the specifics of my experience, narrated above, are no doubt peculiar to me, but I cannot believe that the quality of my experience is in any way special. So I say: Look for the happy surprises, for they will help you to keep expressing proper gratitude to God all your days.

---

[2] Scripture quotations in this article are from the New International Version (1984).

Epilogue

THE LAST PURITAN

*James Packer has had a considerable influence
in America because he has written and said what
evangelicals have most needed to hear.*

" I love pregnant brevity, and some of my material is, I know,
packed tight (Packer by name, packer by nature)." So says
James Innell Packer about his writing style, to which he adds this
apology: "I ask my readers' pardon if they find obscurity due to
my overindulging this love of mine" *(God's Word: Studies of Key
Bible Themes*, 1981).

He need not worry. Packer's ability to address immensely
important subjects in crisp, succinct sentences is one of the
reasons why, as both author and speaker, he has played such an
important role among American evangelicals for four decades.

It is not easy to assess the exact nature of his impact on
American evangelicals or the reasons for it. For one thing, Packer

has never lived in the United States. Since 1958, his books and essays have been widely read in the States, and he has traveled extensively to address American audiences; yet his activity has proceeded from outside the United States—first from a variety of posts in England, and since 1979 from his position as professor of theology at Regent College in Vancouver, British Columbia, Canada.

Further, his wide-ranging labor has aimed directly at the shadowy intersection between popular and academic concerns. He is a scholar who found his vocation in popular communication, a popular communicator who never abandoned scholarship.

Complex as it is to assess the impact of this multi-gifted contemporary, the effort is worthwhile. Learning about him may assist us in learning something about ourselves. And making such an effort may even illuminate the cause of Christian truth to which Packer has devoted his adult life.

The Making of the Wordsmith

J. I. Packer was born in Gloucestershire, England, 70 years ago this past July. At Oxford University he earned B.A. degrees in the classics and theology and a D.Phil. in theology. Important as Oxford was for him academically, it was even more important for his faith: here he fully encountered the Christian gospel and was converted; and from Oxford he set out on his life's course as an interpreter of Scripture and a promoter of classical evangelical theology.

The link between Packer the scholar and Packer the young Christian was his fascination with the Puritans. The Puritans provided for him a subject for doctoral studies, a model for Christian life, and (many years later) the subject matter for one of his most important books, *A Quest for Godliness: The Puritan Vision of the Christian Life* (1990).

After graduate studies at Oxford, Packer filled a number of posts at Tyndale Hall and College (Bristol) and Latimer House (Oxford), both institutions associated with the evangelical wing of the Church of England. In 1979 he moved to Canada as a professor of theology at Regent College (Vancouver). By that time, however, he was established as a widely read author, and he had already embarked on a far-flung ministry that had taken him to Australia, New Zealand, and many points in North America.

The Packing of Words

Packer's reputation, early and late, has rested on an ability to penetrate contested issues lying at the heart of Christian faith, and to do so with clarity, profundity, charity, and the benefits of historical learning. The book that first won him a hearing in the United States was *'Fundamentalism' and the Word of God: Some Evangelical Principles* (1958), which he published in the wake of controversy over Billy Graham's landmark visit to Great Britain in 1955. His conclusion for this substantial but pithy volume marked out a path from which he has never deviated. Packer recognized merit in criticism of evangelicalism, but he did not waver from expressing clear, evangelical convictions: "We must keep before us the real issues in this debate ... the authority of Christ and of Scripture; the relation between the Bible and reason; the method of theology, and the meaning of repentance; the choice between Evangelicalism and Subjectivism."

In the steady stream of books and articles that followed, the one with the broadest impact had the most compact title. *Knowing God* (1973) began with a memorable first line: "As clowns yearn to play Hamlet, so I have wanted to write a treatise on God." Packer hastened to say that "this book, however, is not it," and was "at best a string of beads: a series of small studies of great subjects." Yet *Knowing God* has served an immense throng of readers as a compelling account of God's character, purpose, and intentions. So too has it encouraged believers to live under the reality of God's supernal goodness.

As of early 1995, Packer's publications included 165 separate books, pamphlets, and articles in books, plus nearly that many more journal or periodical articles. About 65 of the books and pamphlets were published only in the United Kingdom, slightly more than those published only in the U.S.

The major books are well known in both the U.K. and the U.S.: *'Fundamentalism' and the Word of God* (1958), *Evangelism and the Sovereignty of God* (1961), *Knowing God* (1973), *A Quest for Godliness* (U.S.) or *Among God's Giants* (U.K.) (1991). Beyond these titles a pattern emerges. Someone who wants to read all of Packer's writings on the Puritans, or on sacraments, church order, and historical confessions should do so from a British library strong in contemporary Anglican writing. By contrast, someone who wishes to explore Packer's convictions on the gifts of the Spirit, the use of the Bible, or the meaning of justification by faith should pursue those inquiries in a North American library strong in materials from evangelical, interdenominational publishers.

One measure of Packer's influence is the number of his books sold. Counting just 18 different titles from five American publishers—Crossway, Eerdmans, Harold Shaw, InterVarsity Press, and Tyndale House—came to sales of slightly more than one and three-quarter million by the middle of 1995. *Knowing God* (IVP) accounted for over half that total; over 200,000 copies of *Evangelism and the Sovereignty of God* (IVP) have been distributed since its release in 1961; two IVP pamphlets, *Meeting God* and *Finding God's Will*, had both topped the 100,000 figure; and *'Fundamentalism' and the Word of God* (Eerdmans) and *I Want to Be a Christian* (Tyndale) have gone over the 50,000 mark.

That is a lot of books. Yet the figures are not as impressive as the numbers sold by some of Packer's publishing contemporaries like Hal Lindsey, Frank Peretti, or Marjorie Holmes. What is notable about the sale of Packer's books is that they combine very solid sales for volumes on practical spirituality and on sturdy theological topics.

The Peripatetic Packer

Remarkably, Packer has been able to maintain a brutal travel and guest lecture schedule while still writing steadily, supporting many theological and practical parachurch agencies, teaching at Regent, and participating in the parish life of Saint John's (Shaughnessy) Anglican Church in Vancouver (where he is an honorary assistant rector).

Besides his work at Regent, he has also served stints as a visiting lecturer at eight seminaries in the United States and Canada. The collective identity of these institutions is strikingly different from the British institutions where Packer was employed before migrating to North America. The British posts were Anglican, the North American posts have been Reformed, evangelical, or evangelical and Reformed.

Packer has also actively supported several other enterprises in the American evangelical world. He has not only written frequently for, but consulted regularly with, *Christianity Today* and its sister publications. He has served several terms on the board of the Institute for Advanced Christian Studies. He also has played an important part in many collaborative book projects. So it was that Packer made special contributions to several of Carl Henry's memorable evangelical symposia in the 1950s and 1960s, to several books on biblical inerrancy from the 1970s and 1980s, and to several general collections on theology and spirituality in the 1980s and 1990s.

Many of Packer's contributions to these institutional and collaborative projects feature his characteristic concentrations on churchly, historical, and confessional matters. But, with the exception of a few of the specifically Reformed enterprises, very few of the forums themselves can be said to be overwhelmingly historical, confessional, or churchly in their intents. Packer's identity as an Anglican has not loomed large in his North American career, where assistance to the Anglican Church of Canada and the American Episcopal Church has not been nearly as visible as his contributions to transdenominational evangelicalism.

Packer the Practical Theologian

As a thinker and theologian, Packer has offered American evangelicals exactly what they have needed. American evangelicalism can be best defined by its traditional activistic pietism (or "experiential biblicism"). It has been profoundly marked by an eager ability to mobilize for specific, tangible tasks like evangelism, institution building, and political action (sometimes for ill, but often for good). The other side of this activism has been an underemphasis on the historical, contemplative, mediating, and complex expressions of the faith. If that analysis is correct, Packer's influence on American evangelicalism has been as critical as it is broad.

Packer has exerted that influence by combining characteristics rarely joined in America: he is an educated, Reformed, Anglican evangelical, with each of the four ascriptions vital as a counterweight to the other three. As the history of Christianity in America has shown so often, any of these commitments by itself can easily become a threat to clarity of Christian thought and integrity of Christian activity. Together, at least as embodied in Packer's writing and speaking, they are water for a parched and weary landscape.

As a well-educated person grounded in both classical theology and the classics more generally, Packer readily perceives how complex many spiritual and intellectual problems really are. He has assumed that he has something to learn from authorities beyond his own inner circle. And he instinctively realizes that the canons of various academic disciplines have intrinsic value, but also that perceptive canon-criticism is a requirement for self-critical wisdom. At the same time, he has displayed these scholarly virtues as a part of, rather than in revolt against, his Reformed, Anglican, and evangelical identities. He has shown how learning can not only flourish with Reformed, Anglican, and evangelical convictions, but can flourish to honor God and build up the church.

As a Calvinist, Packer has embodied the virtues of a weighty theological tradition. He has demonstrated the profundity to be found in embracing one of the three or four truly consequential theological traditions in the Christian history of the last several centuries. His self-conscious Reformed theology has been displayed to best advantage in his explicitly biblical work—as careful exegete, resolute defender of the authority and inerrancy of Scripture, and self-conscious hermeneutical theorist. Against the widely prevailing, but intellectually suicidal, American tendency to act as if exegesis, hermeneutics, and dogmatizing on the doctrine of Scripture take place in a vacuum, Packer has offered the principled thinking of a sturdy Calvinist.

By comparison with American theologians, Packer most resembles B. B. Warfield, the great Princeton exegete, polemicist, and historically informed theologian who was active from the 1870s to the early 1920s. Like Warfield, Packer has sustained organic connections between a high doctrine of the Bible, careful methods of exegesis, and Reformed exegetical conclusions. And yet Packer the Calvinist has been simultaneously Packer the evangelical and Packer the Anglican, with each of the latter commitments taking the self-satisfied, triumphalist, and intellectualist edges off the spirit that so often has characterized Calvinism in America. (I can say these things about American Calvinists because I am one of them myself.)

As an Anglican, Packer is moderate and orthodox in the classical sense of holding to the great Trinitarian creeds. He is self-critical and historical and is open to theological insight from other points on the ecclesiastical compass (including the Roman Catholic and the Pentecostal). There are Episcopalians or Anglicans in the United States and Canada who share these virtues, but none (to my knowledge) who do so along with such obvious commitments to Reformed and evangelical convictions. He embodies the distilled wisdom of the ecclesiastical ages, but he has not scrupled to fellowship with those whose churches were founded yesterday.

Finally, in all things, Packer is an evangelical. He knows, teaches, and lives the truth that knowledge of God must be personal, that the work of Christ was a ransom to be actively embraced, and that the Holy Spirit is alive and active even today. At the end of *Knowing God*, Packer's evangelical convictions blend seamlessly with his recommendation of classical orthodoxy. Besides knowing what the Scriptures say about God, besides knowing that humans are sinners in need of divine grace, "we saw that knowing God involves a personal relationship whereby you give yourself to God on the basis of His promise to give Himself to you. Knowing God means asking His mercy, and resting on His undertaking to forgive sinners for Jesus' sake. Further, it means becoming a disciple of Jesus, the living Saviour who is 'there' today, calling the needy to Himself as He did in Galilee in the days of His flesh. Knowing God, in other words, involves faith—assent, consent, commitment—and faith expresses itself in prayer and obedience."

The diction is British, the sentiment is evangelical. The unusual quality of Packer's evangelicalism, however, is precisely that it is so organically linked to his education, his Calvinism, and his Anglicanism. This combination keeps it from the excesses that a largely un-historical, mostly antitraditional, and often anti-intellectual evangelicalism has suffered in American history.

If the full extent of Packer's influence cannot yet be adequately judged, the outlines of that influence are clear. The influence has been considerable, in part because of the gifts, wisdom, and innate abilities Packer has brought to the task. However, Packer has had a considerable influence because he has written and said what American evangelicals have needed to hear, not least about the holiness, goodness, mercy, and love of God.

—Mark A. Noll

SOURCES

1. Packer, J. I. "From the Senior Editors: Satan Scores Twice." *Christianity Today* 29.12 (September 6, 1985): 12.

2. Packer, J. I. "From the Senior Editors: 'Tecs, Thrillers, and Westerns." *Christianity Today* 29.16 (November 8, 1985): 12.

3. Packer, J. I. "From the Senior Editors: A Bad Trip." *Christianity Today* 30.4 (March 7, 1986): 12.

4. Packer, J. I. "From the Senior Editors: The Unspectacular Packers." *Christianity Today* 30.8 (May 16, 1986): 12.

5. Packer, J. I. "From the Senior Editors: Great George." *Christianity Today* 30.13 (September 19, 1986): 12.

6. Packer, J. I. "From the Senior Editors: All That Jazz." *Christianity Today* 30.18 (December 12, 1986): 15.

7. Packer, J. I. "From the Senior Editors: An Accidental Author." *Christianity Today* 31.8 (May 15, 1987): 11.

8. Packer, J. I. "From the Senior Editor: Decadence À La Mode." *Christianity Today* 31.14 (October 2, 1987): 13.

9. Packer, J. I. "From the Senior Editors: What Lewis Was and Wasn't." *Christianity Today* 32.1 (January 15, 1988): 11.

10. Packer, J. I. "From the Senior Editors: It's Wrong to Eat People." *Christianity Today* 32.6 (April 8, 1988): 11.

11. Packer, J. I. "From the Senior Editors: Nothing Fails like Success." *Christianity Today* 32.11 (August 12, 1988): 15.

12. Packer, J. I. "From the Senior Editors: John's Holy Sickness." *Christianity Today* 32.16 (November 4, 1988): 11.

13. Packer, J. I. "From the Senior Editors: Hype and Human Humbug." *Christianity Today* 33.3 (February 17, 1989): 11.

14. Packer, J. I. "From the Senior Editors: Mistaking Rome for Heaven." *Christianity Today* 33.8 (May 12, 1989): 15.

15. Packer, J. I. "From the Senior Editors: The Prayboy Club." *Christianity Today* 33.15 (October 20, 1989): 11.

16. Packer, J. I. "From the Senior Editors: Klaus Bockmuehl's Rich Legacy." *Christianity Today* 34.3 (February 19, 1990): 9.

17. Packer, J. I. "From the Senior Editors: Why I like My Pie in the Sky." *Christianity Today* 34.9 (June 18, 1990): 11.

18. Packer, J. I. "From the Senior Editors: Humor Is a Funny Thing." *Christianity Today* 34.15 (October 22, 1990): 15.

19. Packer, J. I. "From the Senior Editors: Fan Mail to Calvin." *Christianity Today* 35.1 (January 14, 1991): 11.

20. Packer, J. I. "From the Senior Editors: How Will I Be Remembered?" *Christianity Today* 35.7 (June 24, 1991): 11.

21. Packer, J. I. "From the Senior Editors: Surprised by Graphics." *Christianity Today* 35.13 (November 11, 1991): 15.

22. Packer, J. I. "From the Senior Editors: God's Plumber and Sewage Man." *Christianity Today* 36.4 (April 6, 1992): 15.

23. Packer, J. I. "From the Senior Editors: Bungee-Jumping, Anyone?" *Christianity Today* 36.11 (October 5, 1992): 17.

24. Packer, J. I. "From the Senior Editors: Packer the Picketed Pariah." *Christianity Today* 37.1 (January 11, 1993): 11.

25. Packer, J. I. "From the Senior Editors: The Whale and the Elephant." *Christianity Today* 37.11 (October 4, 1993): 11.

26. Packer, J. I. "From the Senior Editors: Fear of Looking Forward." *Christianity Today* 38.14 (December 12, 1994): 13.

27. Packer, J. I. "When Prayer Doesn't 'Work,'" *Christianity Today* 41.1 (January 6, 1997): 29.

28. Packer, J. I. "Fundamentalism: The British Scene." *Christianity Today* 2.25 (September 29, 1958): 3–6.

29. Packer, J. I. "Christianity and Non-Christian Religions." *Christianity Today* 4.6 (December 21, 1959): 3–5.

30. Packer, J. I. "Charismatic Renewal: Pointing to a Person and a Power." *Christianity Today* 24.5 (March 7, 1980): 16–20.

31. Packer, J. I. "Walking to Emmaus with the Great Physician." *Christianity Today* 25.7 (April 10, 1981): 20–23.

32. Packer, J. I. "Poor Health May Be the Best Remedy." *Christianity Today* 26.10 (May 21, 1982): 14–16.

33. Packer, J. I. "How to Recognize a Christian Citizen." *Christianity Today* 29.7 (April 19, 1985): 4–8.

34. Packer, J. I. "What Do You Mean When You Say God?" *Christianity Today* 30.13 (September 19, 1986): 27–31.

35. Packer, J. I. "The Reality Cure." *Christianity Today* 36.10 (September 14, 1992): 34–35.

36. Packer, J. I. "Rome's Persistent Renewal." *Christianity Today* 36.7 (June 22, 1992): 19.

37. Packer, J. I. "Why I Left." *Christianity Today* 37.4 (April 5, 1993): 33–35.

38. Packer, J. I. "What Is at Stake?" *Christianity Today* 37.4 (April 5, 1993): 64–65.

39. Packer, J. I. "The Devil's Dossier." *Christianity Today* 37.7 (June 21, 1993): 24.

40. Packer, J. I. "Pleasure Principles." *Christianity Today* 37.14 (November 22, 1993): 24–26.

41. Packer, J. I. "Why I Signed It." *Christianity Today* 38.14 (December 12, 1994): 34–37.

42. Packer, J. I. "Thank God for Our Bibles." *Christianity Today* 41.12 (October 27, 1997): 30–31.

43. Packer, J. I. "Still Surprised by Lewis." *Christianity Today* 42.10 (September 7, 1998): 54–60.

44. Packer, J. I. "Wisdom in a Time of War." *Christianity Today* 46.1 (January 7, 2002): 45–49.

45. Packer, J. I. "Why I Walked: Sometimes Loving a Denomination Requires You to Fight." *Christianity Today* 47.1 (January 2003): 46–50.

46. Packer, J. I., and Jill de Haan. "The Joy of Ecclesiastes." *Christianity Today* 59.7 (September 2015): 56–59.

47. Packer, J. I. "Directions: Can the Dead Be Converted?" *Christianity Today* 43.1 (January 11, 1999): 82.

48. Packer, J. I. "Directions: Did God Die on the Cross?" *Christianity Today* 43.4 (April 5, 1999): 70.

49. Packer, J. I. "Good Question: Is Satan Omnipresent?" *Christianity Today* 44.10 (September 4, 2000): 115.

50. Packer, J. I. "Good Question: Hell's Final Enigma." *Christianity Today* 46.5 (April 22, 2002): 84.

51. Packer, J. I. "Good Question: Text Criticism and Inerrancy." *Christianity Today* 46.11 (October 7, 2002): 102.

52. Packer, J. I. "Good Question: Prayers for Salvation." *Christianity Today* 47.4 (April 2003): 100.

53. Packer, J. I. "Good Question: Experiencing God's Presents." *Christianity Today* 47.8 (August 2003): 55.

54. Packer, J. I. "Good Question: Reflected Glory." *Christianity Today* 47.12 (December 2003): 56.

55. Packer, J. I. "Good Question: Incarnate Forever." *Christianity Today* 48.3 (March 2004): 72.

56. Packer, J. I. "Good Question: All Sins Are Not Equal." *Christianity Today* 49.1 (January 2005): 65.

57. Packer, J. I. "Good Question: Salvation Sans Jesus." *Christianity Today* 49.10 (October 2005): 88.

Conclusion: Packer, J. I. "Count Your Surprises: The High Spots of My Life Have Been Anything but Expected." *Christianity Today* 52.3 (March 2008): 66–67.

Epilogue: Noll, Mark A. "The Last Puritan." *Christianity Today* 40.10 (September 16, 1996): 51–53.

SCRIPTURE INDEX

Old Testament

New Testament